AMERICAN ECONOMIC THOUGHT IN THE SEVENTEENTH CENTURY

AMERICAN ECONOMIC THOUGHT IN THE SEVENTEENTH CENTURY

BY

E. A. J. JOHNSON, Ph.D.

Assistant Professor of Economics, Cornell University.

NEW YORK

RUSSELL & RUSSELL · INC

1961

To

CHARLES JESSE BULLOCK

SCHOLAR AND

TEACHER.

" If any tax me for wasting paper with recording these small matters, such may consider that little mothers bring forth little children, small commonwealths matters of small moment, the reading whereof yet is not to be dispised by the judicious, because small things in the beginning of natural or politic bodies are as remarkable as greater in bodies full grown."

THOMAS DUDLEY, *Letter to the*
Countess of Lincoln.

PREFACE

YEARS of painstaking scholarship have provided us with abundant knowledge of the beginnings of the American nation. The political and religious contributions of the colonial era have been carefully summarized and appraised. Yet with the political and religious purposes of the early Americans were mingled hopes of individual economic improvement, and aspirations that the whole pattern of economic life might be arranged in conformity with moral ideals. One object of this essay is to bring together the scattered colonial references to economic questions in the hope that, in assembled form, this economic philosophy will give us a more accurate understanding of the formative influences in American civilization.

Another object is to assemble the crude economic ideas of a century of pioneers in order to understand the subsequent differences between American and European economic thought. By the middle of the nineteenth century a wide gulf separated the two streams of ideas. Monographic studies of American economic thought do not go back farther than the writings of Franklin. Yet Franklin's economic ideas were, to a considerable degree, the outgrowth of previous philosophical and economic reasoning. Although the early period presents only fragmentary economic thought, it cannot be disregarded. History should try to begin at the beginning.

Lastly, the economic thought of the American seventeenth century is important in itself as one of the last outposts of medieval economic thought. The Reformation created renewed interest in the inter-relation between Christian ethics and economic conduct. Puritan leaders hoped that, in a new world, all economic activity could be made to conform with a moral pattern. Their resolute efforts to cleanse their miniature economic world by the rigid application of ethical tests for economic institutions, were not successful. The argument of this essay is that circumstance made impossible an arrangement of economic life which attempted conformity with a preconceived pattern. But although progress demanded compromise, the history of America has revealed the significance of ideals in economic life.

I should be remiss indeed if I did not acknowledge the assistance which I have received from two of my former teachers. Professor S. E. Morison, under whom I studied colonial history at Harvard, has given invaluable suggestions and criticism. Professor C. J. Bullock, who developed my interest in the history of economic thought, has given unsparingly of his time. Without his counsel, I could not have been able to interpret the maze of excerpts, within which lies the history of early American economic thought. My colleague, Professor P. T. Homan, kindly read and criticized the manuscript. I am his debtor as are all who receive his aid.

E. A. J. J.

Ithaca, New York.
February, 1932.

CONTENTS

CHAPTER I

HERITAGE AND CIRCUMSTANCE

" Yet let me hear make use of his [Peter Martyr's] conclusion, which in some sorte may be applied to this people : ' That with their miseries they opened a way to these new-lands ; and after these stormes, with what ease other men came to inhabite in them, in respecte of ye calamities these men suffered ; so as they seeme to goe to a bride feaste wher all things are provided for them.' "

William Bradford, *Of Plimoth Plantation.*

AMERICAN ECONOMIC THOUGHT
IN THE 17TH CENTURY

CHAPTER I

HERITAGE AND CIRCUMSTANCE

ENGLAND'S ambition for empire, the hope of English adventurers for fame and capitalists for profit, the deep religious longing of European men and women of varied origins, these persistent forces and others brought shipload after shipload of pioneers into America's first frontier. Spurred on by material or moral hopes, the early Americans established their homes along the water courses flowing into the Atlantic. They grew in knowledge, wealth, and numbers. With their children, grandchildren, servants and slaves, they comprised about a quarter-million souls by the close of the seventeenth century.

But the promised land flowed neither with milk nor with honey until human hands had transformed forests into fields, until economic institutions had been harmonized with environment, until the heritage of economic ideas had been modified and adjusted. By countless trials and countless errors the methods of making a living in pioneer communities were painfully and slowly discovered. Divergent interests both hampered and helped the evolution of economic policies ; the wishes of mother country and colony both collided and coalesced. Yet out of the ferment of economic purpose emerged a formative stream of ideas and a set of economic institutions whose immeasurable consequences have permeated American history.

The abundance of land in the new world had a profound

effect upon the seventeenth-century Americans. From the day when the English settled on the James river, the frontier began to condition habits and attitudes. Compact settlements were hard to maintain. Why should not each one be allowed to appropriate the land which nature gave so freely ? Yet the Virginia Massacre of 1622 was partly the result of reckless expansion ; while Bradford's sorrowful complaint that the richer lands of Duxbury had divided the Plymouth congregation attests again the influence of environment upon ideals. In the evolution of a land policy is found a record of the efforts and the failure of the early leaders to deal with land in traditional English fashion. In New England, the attempted compromise between commonage and severalty refused to be permanent. In fact, the common fields came to serve a new purpose. Instead of tying the mass of rural labour to the soil—*ascriptitii terræ*—as had been the case in feudal England, commonage economized on man-power until an adequate supply of social capital made land division possible. Neither were the manors which arose along the Chesapeake permanent in organization. The indented servant differed from the copy-holder, while the slave, in a later period, was even more dissimilar to the English agricultural labourer. Change and modification were hastened by new problems of agriculture, new methods of trade, new types of labour.

The three thousand and more miles of water which separated the English colonies from England were long miles indeed during the seventeenth century ! In consequence each colony had to make itself self-sufficient enough to cope with the irregularities of commerce. A lesser degree of specialization was economically permissible in the colonies than in England. Manufactures were partly born of necessity and the frontier household, as a result, became a most flexible factory. Due to its lack of a staple export commodity and because of the secessionist character of its population, New England tended to emphasize the trend toward self-sufficiency by legislation. As a guide for this programme, there existed an abundant supply of English precedents. Attempted encouragement of various industries by bounties, by tax remission, by colonial loans and by legislative mandate appear and reappear in the laws and records of New England.

Elizabethan England had hoped for fabulous profits from planting colonies in the new world. Yet history reveals that the world at large and the actual settlers gained while the promoters and shareholders usually lost. But the investors, like most unlucky investors, were exceedingly reluctant to submit to their losses. Their colonial representatives were charged with imposing a discipline upon the colonists which would produce profit. Plymouth groaned under the yoke of the English merchants and Governor Bradford resolutely commanded his labour battalions until the colony was able to buy itself free. In Virginia, the harshness of Dale's laws and the protests of people who lived under these laws, revealed the conflict of interest between capitalist and colonist. Yet the administration of a colony as a business venture demanded certain economic institutions. These institutions were first designed in England rather than in the colony, although it was left for the colony to test the applicability of the ready-made institutions. In general, the result was failure, but the very process elicited important discussion. Both Plymouth and Virginia temporarily experimented with a variety of common ownership and production for a common fund. Both fled from this type of economic organization as men are supposed to flee from evil. But in Plymouth and in Virginia, the respective experiments yielded important inquiries into the relative merits of communism and private property.

Inspired by the discovery of the new world, Sir Thomas More wrote his *Utopia* in 1515 or 1516. But More's imaginary island community living in honest felicity was not the only Utopia which the new world inspired. To thousands of Englishmen the Greek word meant not " nowhere," but America, and each person of the thousands who sought the

American Utopia defined it as his economic circumstance and as his mental horizon dictated. Whether the ends were virtuous or vainglorious, whether material or spiritual, the new world bred a buoyant optimism. Adventurers saw visions of endless fame, investors of prodigious wealth. Those who hungered after righteousness saw a new earth where they would be filled. The sobering influence of a wilderness which was neither a new heaven nor a new earth was painful. Yet the dream and the awakening had profound influence upon American thought and American institutions. Behind these varied Utopian hopes lay still and powerful forces. The right to do the very thing which Rousseau later signalized romantically as the cause of human sorrow : the right to enclose an area of the earth's crust and call it one's own had been denied in feudal society. The human energy which was unleashed by the hope of individual property in land is one of the imponderables of history. Add this powerful item to other ambitions of people in untoward circumstances ; couple with these the deep still stream of religious purpose of many of the first settlers and the sober yet buoyant optimism of the seventeenth-century colonists should be evident.

Extreme optimism, however, breeds anarchism. Witness the California gold rush or the opening of Indian Territory with its reckless stampede into America's last frontier. This very type of anarchism was not unknown in the seventeenth-century Atlantic frontier. But it was held in check by several forces. In the first place, complete freedom was limited by joint-stock company or proprietor. The London Company attempted strict control of Virginian economic activities under the first two charters. Even the enlightened policy of the Sandys administration necessarily insisted upon colonial economic surveillance. The English merchants who financed the Plymouth settlers showed little sympathy with Separatist hopes, but ruthlessly dictated the economic policy of the colony during its early years. Even William Penn did not wholly release the Pennsylvania settlers from economic discipline. Massachusetts Bay was unique, inasmuch as the members of the corporation were themselves colonists. The control was internal rather than external.

English legislation was a persistent force which tended to direct and regulate the pattern of American economic life. The dissolution of the London Company, in 1624, effected the substitution of one form of surveillance for another, although it must not be supposed that the influence of the Crown was negligible in the earlier period. The English Civil War and the Interregnum did not bring about a weakening of English control, but rather the reverse. As a result, colonial policy was partially codified in the Navigation Acts. New England, however, was able to evade English economic control to a larger extent than the other colonies. Geographical factors conditioned her relation to mercantilist England while the independent Puritans boldly refused to co-operate with the home country.

Important as were the disciplinary influences of joint-stock company, proprietor, or government, neither will compare with the restraint which was imposed by the colonial leaders upon the economic conduct of the community. The moral convictions of the Massachusetts Puritans, of Roger Williams, of Pastorius and of other leaders of religious groups were inflexible. With firmness which often approximated dogmatism, economic conduct was made to conform with a set of moral ideals. Those who dared to challenge the plans of New England's Bible Commonwealth discovered that the wrath of the clergy burst promptly into punitive form. The Maypole at Merry-mount was hewn down ; the New England common was provided with stocks and pillory ! Meantime the hope and belief that economic life could be harmonized with religious purpose led to constant and elaborate circumscription of wealth-getting. Economic discussion assumed a moral tone as the Scriptures were searched for the rules of business life. In consequence, much of the seventeenth-century economic discussion reveals a definite medieval flavour. The real purpose of life should be salvation, and to this all-important end every other interest ought to be subordinate. Yet material riches, although secondary, had an importance to individual and to community which could not be denied. But lest the pursuit of riches should overshadow man's real purpose, regulation, restraint and repression were believed necessary.

The architectonic qualities of colonial life did not emerge as easily as the religious leaders had expected. All sorts of difficulties beset the travellers into the promised land. Capitalists who had financed ventures for the sake of profit lacked the missionary zeal of the patriarchs. Officials of the Crown regarded silk, indigo or naval stores as more important than ethical perfection. Within the colony the abundance of land bred a rebellious attitude which gradually compelled recognition and ultimately forced the staunchest advocates of New Zion to compromise their religious idealism with economic reality.

American economic thought in the seventeenth century was therefore the outgrowth of heritage and circumstance. Strictly speaking, few ideas can be regarded as indigenous to American soil. In the settlement of new countries, the borrowings of tangibles and intangibles must perforce be extensive and that which can be called American in the economic philosophy of the seventeenth century is a matter of more or less. But new environment gives rise to novel economic problems for which the traditional solution or the premeditated solution may not suffice. Very gradually new surroundings and new problems modified the economic ideas which the American colonists had inherited. The failure of the Massachusetts expedition, sent out to take Quebec, created a desperate problem of public finance and thereby altered the trend of monetary discussion. The reluctance of skilled artisans to migrate to America coupled with the attractiveness of agricultural entrepreneurship led to a rise in wages. In the face of this persistent tendency the medieval doctrine of wages was scarcely applicable in its traditional form. John Cotton's effort to revive the doctrine of " just price " as a guide for business dealings was ineffectual and the medieval control of buying and selling ultimately went the way of all flesh.

With the theoretical or scientific problems of economics, the seventeenth-century Americans had little to do. Economics was regarded as an art, as a guide to conduct. It must be remembered that very little strictly scientific thinking had characterized economic inquiry elsewhere. That which was known about economic questions was inherited from ancient, medieval or mercantilist economic philosophy. Some of the better educated Americans, like Cotton Mather, knew the ancient literature at first hand. The medieval philosophy was received largely from English ecclesiastical sources. Mercantilist ideas were growing in importance during the whole of the seventeenth century and exerted a definite influence upon the American writers. But ancient, medieval or mercantilist writers were all concerned with economics as an art. Even Adam Smith, in the third quarter of the eighteenth century, was primarily interested in political economy as a guide to economic policy. To expect a scientific attitude toward economic problems by the seventeenth-century Americans would be rather unreasonable.

The very nature of establishing colonies further explains the American concern with what Adolf Wagner [1] designated as the practical problems of economics. The business of colonization requires decisions. Various institutions must be examined and appraised in order to ascertain their fitness and desirability. Some pronouncement must be made with regard to the goal or purpose which is sought. The means of attaining this goal must be decided upon. Moreover, the process of adaptation of economic institutions to a new physical environment gives prominence to practical problems. Theoretical speculation tends to be ancillary

---

[1] *Lehr und Handbuch der Politischen Oekonomie*, Leipzig, 1892. Whereas the " scientific " concern of economics is with structure, function and development, the " practical " interest lies in criticism, in setting up economic ideals and in devising a policy whereby the ideals may be realized.

to economic policy. The paper money pamphleteers, for example, were confronted with problems of public finance, with trade phenomena which tended to denude the colonies of specie. In their quest for solutions for these troublesome matters, these writers were compelled to make scientific inquiry into the nature of money, its origins, and functions. But their main interest lay in comparing the existing currency system with what they considered an ideal system and by this means to demonstrate the superiority of a projected paper circulation.

The frequency and magnitude of economic decisions in new communities further emphasized the colonial concern with the art of economics. Choice is, of course, characteristic of all living. But the settling of new countries increases the frequency and the importance of such decisions. Policies which succeed in the mother country may be quite unsuited to the colony. Often far reaching and important decisions must be made whereas no new questions of large import must suddenly be answered in older and more mature countries. " Muddling through " will not work as easily in new countries ; significant decisions must often be made at once. Communism may be pitted against private property, and the respective merits of either for accomplishing the social and economic ideals must be weighed.

Since the seventeenth century produced no great American philosophers, the economic thought of the century must be pieced together out of fragmentary sources. Casual and incidental considerations of economic matters must be carefully examined and evaluated in order to grasp the colonial conception of the economic order. Toward the close of the century, some tendencies toward broad philosophical inquiry did develop. But Cotton Mather's *Christian Philosopher* or Pastorius's *Bee-Hive* can scarcely be called systematic philosophy.

The diversity and fragmentary character of the sources makes the problem of ascertaining American colonial thought a very delicate one. Most of the literature was written either by men of affairs or theologians. Adventurers, colonizers, planters, agriculturalists, merchants, governors or soldiers as a rule are neither highly reflective nor philosophical in method. Yet the difficult business of planting new colonies did attract some serious and contemplative men of affairs. Bradford and Pastorius would certainly qualify as thinkers. As a rule, however, the writing of the men of affairs, although characterized by vigour and insight, lack a methodical and scientific approach to economic problems. The writings of the theologians contain a great deal of economic material. But the moral conservatism of the clergy tended to link their ideas closer to medieval than to contemporary thought. Moreover, the preacher is rarely scientific. The Christian concern with salvation compels him to be concerned with what should be rather than with what is. The American theologians were men of learning and intellectual energy. But they touched only incidentally on economic matters and when they did, it was to emphasize the moral implications and aspects of wealth-getting and wealth-using.

The histories not only recorded what occurred in the new communities, but reflected the convictions of their authors. The colonial laws and records presented a picture of the actual expedients which were employed in dealing with economic problems. Legislators consciously or intuitively take cognizance of some economic philosophy. The laws, therefore, represented an acquiescence in a set of prevailing economic ideas. On one point there is agreement. Preacher, planter, historian, diarist and law-maker insisted that government must regulate economic activity. This prevailing belief was partly a philosophical heritage from medieval times, partly a phase of contemporary mercantilist dogma and partly a necessary response to the immediate problems of circumstance.

CHAPTER II

THE CONTROL OF ECONOMIC ACTIVITY

" Where there is no honesty, nor equity, nor sanctitie, nor
veritie, nor pietie, nor good civilitie in such a Countrey, certainly
there can be no stabilitie."

John Smith, *The Generall Historie of Virginia,*
New England and the Sumer Isles.

CHAPTER II

THE CONTROL OF ECONOMIC ACTIVITY

I

'' T H E Welfare of a People depends much on what Laws they have," declared Increase Mather,[1] and thereby tersely epitomized the general belief of the seventeenth-century Americans. Economic regulation, whether engendered by deference toward England's colonial policy or designed to advance the separate interests of a colony, was regarded as indispensable. Control and surveillance were attempted over agriculture, industry, and trade in the hope that desired forms of economic activity could be fostered and the unwanted repressed.

In New England, the control of industry was partly ethical in purpose. The function of government, said Jonathan Mitchell, is to increase the welfare of the people.[2] But the preacher distinguished two phases of welfare : spiritual and temporal. Maintenance and furtherance of true religion, he regarded as " the chief and last end of Civil Policy." [3] Subordinate to religion, but nevertheless very important, lay material considerations : the duty of rulers to seek the " external, temporal welfare of the people." Mitchell defined " temporal welfare " as including public and personal safety, economic justice, material prosperity

---

[1] Mather, Increase. *Excellency of a Public Spirit*, Boston, 1702, pp. 17–18.
[2] Mitchell, Jonathan. *Nehemiah on the Wall in Troublesome Times, or a Serious and Seasonable Improvement of that Great Example of Magistratical Piety and Prudence*. (A Sermon preached at Boston, May 15th, 1667), p. 7.
[3] Mitchell, *op. cit.*, p. 3.

and public tranquillity.[1]   The economic function of government was therefore only one part of a larger obligation to
the community.   But within its sphere of influence, government was considered a positive force which could and should
assist the establishment and maintenance of economic well-
being.   Mitchell charged the colonial legislators with the
duty of assisting the " outward Estate and Livlyhood " of
the people " by such help as the care of Government may
contribute to that end." [2]   In characteristic medieval
fashion, wealth was signalized as secondary but necessary.
" Good rulers," concluded the Boston divine, " will gladly
be a furtherance thereunto." [3]   In this emphasis, Mitchell's
sermon is a typical example of the way in which a theological
attitude toward economic activity was blended with a belief
in the co-ordinating and regulating duties of government.

Colonial leaders very early discovered that the first
economic duty of government was to insure that colonists
had food.   Governor Bradford, of Plymouth Plantation,
understood that hunger is dangerous to the stability of any
government,[4] as did every other person who planted a
colony or a town.   The danger of famine and hardship gave
a primary reason for economic regulation and Mitchell's
principle that government must do its utmost in a " time of
distress and poverty or special scarcity " [5] was inescapable.
Moral and mercantilist purposes of economic control combined with the immediate necessity for communal regulation
and produced the maze of economic legislation with which
every student of colonial history is familiar.   As the century
advanced, however, moral forces became less dominant ;
the English mercantilist regulation was evaded ;   while the
growth of trade and industry, the accumulation of capital
and the development of individualism tended to reduce

[1] Mitchell, *op. cit.*, pp. 4–5.
[2] *Ibid.*, p. 4.
[3] *Ibid.*, p. 4.
[4] Bradford, William.   *Of Plimoth Plantation.*   Commonwealth Edition.
Boston, 1856, p. 200.   He quoted from Seneca : " That a great part of
libertie is a well governed belly, and to be patient in all things."
[5] Mitchell, *op. cit.*, p. 4.

economic insecurity. Yet, although the province of the state grew proportionately smaller, the mass of economic regulation increased. It can safely be said that the seventeenth century adhered quite definitely to the principle that the state could be a positive force, and should be an actively utilized agency in the production, exchange and even the consumption of wealth.

The colonial records are literally cluttered up with economic legislation. Least important were those regulations designed primarily for police purposes. The frontier hazard made it rather necessary to compel blacksmiths to repair firearms while men's ineradicable tendency toward dishonesty required the regulation of weights and measures. More important than these police measures were regulations governing quasi-public institutions. Inns, mills and ferries were subject to control. Charges were limited by law, and the obligations of such institutions were legislatively defined. From the control of quasi-public businesses, it was no far cry to regulation of general commercial practices. Efforts were made to determine fair prices, fair wages and reasonable profits. The quality of goods offered for sale was frequently the object of legislation while forestalling, regrating and engrossing were outlawed in characteristic medieval fashion.

The isolation of the new world demanded some legislation to insure a necessary degree of industrial diversification or to restrain the efflux of certain indispensable commodities. Exportation of foodstuffs was frequently forbidden, and the outflow of raw materials for necessary manufactures often restricted. Due to the unfavourable balance of trade which tended to denude the new world of specie, the export of gold and silver was repeatedly forbidden. Export prohibitions or restraints were partly compelled by the immediate economic problems confronting the colonists ; they were partly the result of an inescapable European tradition of economic control. But whatever the occasion or cause, the array of economic laws, the sheer abundance of legislation constitute *primâ facie* evidence of the persistent belief in the necessity of state interference in economic life.

It must not be supposed, however, that colonial economic legislation was wholly repressive. A great many laws were designed to promote desired forms of enterprise. Prohibitive legislation often had the double function of restraining exports in order to develop domestic industry. The export of leather, hides and skins was forbidden in order to develop the colonial leather industry. Even the meticulous regulation of consumption, of apparel, food and drink, was partly intended to restrict the misdirection of industry. Creation of capital was regarded as far more essential than the satisfaction of what plain Puritans regarded as luxury. Realization of the necessity of creating social capital was combined with a belief in the medieval doctrine of social classes, and thereby produced the curious colonial laws which attempted without great success to control the consumption of wealth.

Circumstance and heritage, both pointed the way for the law-maker. But one other force was also present : the ill-defined economic philosophy of mercantilism. As the economic side of nationalism, English mercantilism sought to develop a high degree of self-sufficiency by means of colonial expansion. But if colonies were to serve a useful purpose, they would have to be integrated into a consistent national economic programme. Throughout the seventeenth century, English mercantilism exerted a profound effect upon the colonial control of enterprise. The colonies were charged with the duty of encouraging the production of commodities which England lacked. If colonies could provide necessary raw materials, England would be relieved of dependence on " foreign " sources of supply. In response to the English programme, American colonial assemblies frequently attempted to develop and stimulate the production of raw materials such as silk, hemp, flax, naval stores and indigo. Meantime English mercantilism looked with disapproval upon the development of colonial manufacturing. Complete colonial acquiescence in England's mercantilism should presumably have produced legislation designed to restrict the growth of colonial industry.

But the mercantilism which influenced colonial economic life was not exclusively English mercantilism. In New England, there arose a colonial variety of the same economic philosophy. In more ways than one the planting of Massachusetts Bay Colony was an attempted secession from English jurisdiction. Moreover, the New England leaders attempted to make the separation economic as well as political.[1] In direct opposition to the wishes of the English government, a persistent effort was made in New England to develop a whole group of manufactures which would make the Bible Commonwealth economically independent. Attempts were made to foster the production of iron, stockings, cloth, rope, leather and other manufactures. Loans were made by the Massachusetts legislature to the glassmakers, bounties were offered for the manufacture of linen, tax exemption was granted to iron makers. Boldest of all were those laws which restrained the importation of English manufactured goods or forbade the export of raw materials to the mother country.

The colonial doctrine of the control of enterprise was therefore a consequence of at least three interacting causes : the medieval principle of economic surveillance, the compelling circumstance of new communities and the influence of English and colonial mercantilism. But in legislation causal forces cannot be segregated since laws usually represent the result of composite cause. Neither can the economic theory which lay behind government control very accurately be inferred from the laws. Fortunately the writings of the early Americans contain a few references to the necessity of economic control which throw some light upon the general relation of government to enterprise and

---

[1] For the legislative and documentary evidence of this hoped-for economic independence see Johnson, E. A. J., " Some Evidence of Mercantilism in the Massachusetts Bay." *New England Quarterly*, Vol. I., No. 3, pp. 371–395.

upon the particular duties of government toward agriculture
and industry.

II

A praise of self-sufficiency characterizes the opinions of
seventeenth-century Americans from Virginia to Massachusetts. Beverley, the Virginia historian, lamented the
indifference of the Virginia Assembly toward manufacturing.
Although abundant raw materials for industry were available, he alleged that the legislature gave " no manner of
encouragement." In characteristic mercantilist style,
Beverley decried the importation of foreign labour incorporated into goods and condemned the colonial " use of the
industry of England." [1] The author of *A Perfect Description
of Virginia* argued that it was an essential duty of a government to encourage those industries which would make a
colony self-sufficient.[2] In Pennsylvania, Thomas Budd [3]
strongly recommended a programme of agricultural diversification as a means of developing industries which would
make the colony economically independent. He proposed
that all farmers be required to produce a minimum quantity
of flax and that schools be established where children might
be " instructed in some Mystery or Trade." [4] In Massachusetts, the introspective Samuel Sewall advocated " the
raising of Hemp here, so as to make Sail-Cloth and Cordage." [5] The expected benefits of domestic production
have a colonial mercantilist flavour. Sewall argued that
colonial production of sail-cloth and rope would " hinder

---

[1] Beverley, Robert. *The History of Virginia*. London, 1705. 2nd
Edition, 1722, p. 283.
[2] " A Perfect Description of Virginia." London, 1649. Reprinted,
Peter Force Historical Tracts, Vol. II., Washington, 1837, p. 9.
[3] Budd, Thomas. *Good Order Established in Pennsylvania and New
Jersey in America*. Philadelphia, 1685. Reprinted, New York, 1865,
p. 47.
[4] *Ibid.*, p. 43.
[5] " Computation that the Importation of Negroes is not so possible as
that of White Servants." (Attributed to Samuel Sewall) Boston, 1706.
Reprinted, *Historical Magazine*, June, 1864, p. 199.

the Importing of it, and save a considerable sum in a year to make Returns."

Separate colonies meant separate spheres of jurisdiction. The disadvantages for purposes of control were soon evident. Beverley, like every Virginian, realized the futility of restraining tobacco cultivation in Virginia when Maryland could extend her tobacco fields.[1] He believed that it would have been infinitely better if Virginia and Maryland had been one colony because of the similarity of their economic interests. Beverley regarded the growth of tobacco plantations with disfavour, and suggested that the colonial legislature should restrain the agricultural dispersion of population, compel urbanization, and thereby develop industries.[2] Government was charged with the duty of designing the pattern of economic life. Among the multitude of proposals for economic control of enterprise, one rather unique suggestion is found in the writings of Pastorius,[3] the founder of Germantown. Government, said he, should refrain from giving an encouragement to the search for precious stones. These forms of wealth, said the jurist, have " been most shamefully abused by man, and have become the servants of human pride and ostentation." [4]

III

Control of agriculture and the formulation of land policies received more attention from the colonial writers than any other question of economic policy. The Scriptural commandment to subdue and replenish the earth, wrote the author of the *Essay on the Laying out of Towns*, gives jurisdiction over unused land.[5] But when land is appro-

---

[1] Beverley, *op. cit.*, pp. 59–60.
[2] *Ibid.*, p. 283.
[3] Pastorius, Francis. " A Particular Geographical Description of the Lately Discovered Province of Pennsylvania." Frankfort, 1700. Reprinted, *Old South Leaflets*, General Series, No. 95.
[4] *Ibid.*, p. 9.
[5] " Essay on the Laying out of Towns, &c." Winthrop Papers, Vol. III., *Coll. Mass. Hist. Soc.*, Vol. I., p. 476.

priated, it must be improved ; wherefore the essayist concluded :

"I canot yet se yt any man hath theological right unto any possession without a faithful practical care of ye performance of this principall condicion." [1]

It should therefore be the duty of governors to dispossess settlers who do not improve their land. Moreover, compulsion to improve land would prevent monopolizing of the soil by the first settlers. Edward Johnson repeatedly urged the Massachusetts government to forbid the engrossing of land.[2] John Winthrop argued that it was necessary for the General Court to limit the size of land grants for two reasons : "to prevent the neglect of trades," and to reserve "place to receive such as should come after." [3] One Puritan threatened land monopolists with God's wrath. Early settlers, said Edward Johnson, must not

"take up large accomodations for sale, to inrich themselves . . . for as soone as you shall seeke to engrosse the Lord's wast into your hands, he will ease you of your burden." [4]

Yet in spite of his prediction that the Lord would punish the engrosser, Johnson demanded legislation to curb land speculation.

A preference for agriculture was expressed by a number of the colonial writers. The author of the *Essay on the Laying out of Towns* cautioned governors to

"seek out faithful, skillful, honest husbandmen, & well to regard them, for they are ye tressells of ye tables of all ye kings of ye earth : as Solomon saith, the King also consisteth by the feild yt is tilled." [5]

Agriculture, wrote Thomas Ash, must of necessity precede

---

[1] *Essay on the Laying out of Towns*, p. 476.
[2] Johnson, Edward. "Wonder Working Providence of sions Savior in New England." London, 1653. Reprinted, *Original Narrative Series*, New York, 1910, p. 35.
[3] Winthrop, John. *The History of New England from 1630 to 1649.* Hartford, 1790. Reprinted, Boston, 1825, Vol. I., p. 152.
[4] Johnson, Edward, *op. cit.*, p. 35.
[5] *Essay on the Laying out of Towns*, p. 477.

manufacturing within a colony.[1] But Beverley believed that the type of agriculture which was practised in Virginia was economically hazardous. He felt that the production of tobacco had become so extensive that Virginia had not " even a necessary Provision against an incidental Scarcity." The Virginians were

" contenting themselves with a Supply of Food from Hand to Mouth, so that if it should please God to send them an unseasonable Year, there would not be found in the Country Provision sufficient to support the People for three Months extraordinairie." [2]

The settlers of Pennsylvania were advised by their famous proprietor to prefer agriculture to trade : " This occupation is industrious, healthy, honest and of good example." Moreover, Penn designated agriculture as pleasing to God, since it leads men

" to consider the works of God and nature of things that are good, and diverts the mind from being taken up with the vain arts and inventions of a luxurious world." [3]

But although this is a pious statement of the traditional moral superiority of agriculture over trade, Penn's correspondence with James Logan shows that Penn himself did not prefer agriculture to trade.[4]

Granted that agriculture is a fundamental occupation which ought to be encouraged, what should government do to stimulate it ? " Make your plantations so neere and great as you can," said John Smith, " for many hands make light worke." [5] Avoid minute terms for acquiring land and

[1] Ash, Thomas. "Carolina," London, 1682. Reprinted, *Hist. Coll. S. C.*, Vol. II., p. 67.

[2] Beverley, *op. cit.*, p. 283.

[3] Letter of William Penn, In Clarkson, Thomas, *A Portraiture of Quakerism*, New York, 1806, Vol. II., p. 44.

[4] Penn, William. "Correspondence between William Penn and James Logan." Philadelphia, 1870. *Publications of Hist. Soc. of Penna.*, Vols. IX. and X.

[5] Smith, John. *Advertisements for the Unexperienced Planters of New England, or Anywhere ; or The Pathway to Erect a Plantation.* London, 1631. Reprinted by William Veasie. Boston, 1865, p. 40.

hold commonage to a minimum.[1] " Let every man plant
freely without limitation so much as hee can." [2] The best
way to stimulate agriculture, in Smith's opinion, was to
reward the good husbandman with liberal amounts of land
in fee simple. The versatile Captain thus sounded the
keynote of the policy of the southern colonies with regard
to agriculture. Government should permit and encourage
private property in land.

Under the enforced communism at Plymouth, Governor
Bradford soon discovered the limitations of common
cultivation. Yearly allotments of land were first made in
1623,[3] but the next year Bradford made permanent allotments. It was unfair, he thought, that land " which ye
more industrious had brought into good culture (by much
pains) one year " should be turned over to another the next
year. Moreover, if land were reassigned, improvements
would not benefit the individual who made them and would
not be made.[4] For ethical and economic reasons, the
continuous use of land was believed necessary, and government should see to it that tenure was secure. Private
property in land, said the author of the *Essay on the Laying
out of Towns*, stimulates enterprise. For this reason, the
author advised all prospective towns to divide their land
" into portions by dooles as may be thought fitting." [5]
Private assignment of land, he said,

" will be such a goad in ye side of ye industrious to drawe in &
make ye spediest and best imployment of his knowne portion, yt
others will of necessity be drawne on by his good example, to
their much benefit & comffort." [6]

Temporarily, land might be allowed to " lye common " but

[1] Smith, *Advertisements for the Unexperienced Planters*, p. 40.
[2] *Ibid.* p. 41.
[3] Bradford alleged that in the yearly allotments, he followed the policy
of the early Romans. We know that Bradford had access to Bodin's
Republic, and this, no doubt, was the source of his knowledge, since Bodin
made frequent reference to the policies of Romulus.
[4] Bradford, *op. cit.*, p. 201.
[5] *Essay on the Laying out of Towns*, pp. 478–479.
[6] *Ibid.*, pp. 478–479.

"he yt knoweth ye benefit of inclosing, will omit noe dilligence to bring himselfe into an inclusive condicion."[1] For the benefits of enclosure were believed so evident, that "one acre inclosed is much more beneficiall than 5 falling to his share in common." Moreover, the partition of land would prevent waste of timber, since each person would have a direct inducement to conserve his supply. Private property in land, however, should not be allowed to breed economic isolation. Co-operation should be encouraged, because it would lead to a fuller utilization of draft animals, better supervision, and lower costs.[2]

New towns were compelled to lay down rules for the allotment of land and in many cases regulated its use. In order to insure a food supply, specific regulations were often made with regard to the cultivation of corn.[3] Rules concerning fencing were agreed upon,[4] and provision for the protection of crops and property.[5] In Plymouth, before 1632, damages were assessed against the owner of any livestock which had destroyed crops, even though the land was unenclosed. But these guarantees were withdrawn in 1632, and the Court provided that whosoever set corn upon open land did so at his own risk.[6]

Rules and laws illustrate the necessity of governmental interference in many minute details within new colonies or new communities. But with the expansion and development of agriculture, the character of state action was modified. Minute regulations could be given up entirely or delegated

---

[1] *Essay on the Laying out of Towns*, pp. 478–479.
[2] *Ibid.*, p. 478.
[3] The land company which settled Rehoboth, Massachusetts, for example, provided : "It is agreed that the ground that is most fit to be planted and hopefull for corne for the present be planted and fenced by such as possess it." See Bliss, Leonard. *The History of Rehoboth*, Boston, 1836, p. 24.
[4] In Rehoboth it was "ordered that those that have their lottes granted . . . should fence the one end of their lottes and their part in the common fence." *Ibid.*, pp. 24–25.
[5] "If any damages shale fale out by anny man's particular fence, the owner of the fence shale pay the dammage." Bliss, *op. cit.*, p. 24.
[6] *Records of Colony of New Plymouth.* Edited by Nathaniel B. Shurtleff. Boston, 1855, Vol. I., p. 6.

to local authority. The province of the state was the larger duty of holding agriculture in conformity with the ideals of the colony. In Plymouth, for example, Bradford did what he could to restrain the expansion of agriculture and the dispersion of population, because he feared these tendencies would weaken the influence of the church. But the expansion of the cattle industry demanded new land, and Bradford sorrowfully admitted that " ther was no longer any holding them together." [1] In Virginia the tobacco industry " made the Country fall into such an unhappy Settlement and Course of Trade." [2] It dispersed population and retarded, or virtually prevented, the growth of towns.[3] Beverley's opinion was like that of Bradford at Plymouth : that the government ought to restrain the agricultural dispersion. He proposed the establishment of staple towns and the " Confinement of all Shipping-Trade to them only." [4] In Pennsylvania, Thomas Budd urged that a land policy should be devised which would stimulate manufacturing and thereby decrease dependence on imported manufactured goods. For this reason he suggested that land be set aside by the assembly " the Rent or income of it to go toward the defraying of the charge of the School." [5] The purpose of the school should be to train artisans.

IV

In the Southern colonies the spread of extensive staple agriculture tended to eclipse the significance of manufacturing. But in spite of the pre-occupation of Southern colonists with tobacco cultivation, dissent was not unknown. Beverley, the Virginian historian, considered the neglect of industry an " Eternal Reproach " to Virginia.[6] In typical

---

[1] Bradford, *op. cit.*, p. 362.
[2] Beverley, *op. cit.*, p. 46.
[3] *Ibid.*, p. 47.
[4] *Ibid.*, p. 57.
[5] Budd, *op. cit.*, p. 44.
[6] Beverley, *op. cit.*, p. 255.

mercantilist fashion, he regarded the " use of the industry of England " as subversive to the interest of the colony.[1] He realized that manufacturing required some degree of urbanization and attributed the industrial lethargy to the "unfortunate method of the Settlement, and want of Cohabitation." [2] Agriculture restricted industry and the development of industry hinged on the control of agriculture.

Colonial economic circumstances during the seventeenth century, however, demanded concentration in the production of exportable staple commodities and thereby necessarily retarded the growth of manufactures. Edward Johnson, for example, pointed out that although New England possessed many raw materials, which might be converted into manufactured goods, trade would certainly be jeopardized if the supply of agricultural commodities became irregular or uncertain.[3] Maintenance of regular trade demanded concentration in agriculture and stock raising. Hubbard considered it the duty of a colony to provide manufactured goods when they could no longer be economically obtained by the sale of cattle or produce.[4] Other writers were more definitely inclined toward manufacturing, and demanded some positive form of governmental assistance.

Governor Berkeley, of Virginia, took the position that the state must assist in the development of industries where great cost is involved.[5] The reason why iron making and ship-building had not developed in Virginia, said he, was because " there was never yet any publick encouragement to assist the Planters in those most chargeable undertakings." Increase Mather believed that encouragement of some kind was necessary to quicken manufacturing. " Some Manu-

---

[1] Beverley, *op. cit.*, p. 283.
[2] An effort to build up staple towns in Virginia was made by the Act of Cohabitation of 1680.
[3] Johnson, Edward, *op. cit.*, p. 211.
[4] Hubbard, William. *A General History of New England from the Discoverie to 1680.* Boston, 1815. Reprinted, Boston, 1846, p. 238.
[5] Berkeley, Sir William. *A Discourse and View of Virginia.* London, 1663. Reprinted, Norwalk, Conn., 1914, p. 5.

factures there are amongst them," he wrote in 1689, " but
not a Twentieth part of what the Country hath need of, or
is consumed there." [1] Samuel Sewall recommended that
Massachusetts should grant a bounty upon all incoming
white servants as one means of supplying the colony with
artisans. [2]   Pastorius proposed that Germantown should
do its utmost to develop manufacturing : " We are also
endeavouring to introduce the cultivation of the vines, and
also the manufacture of wollen cloths and linens." [3]   Fairs,
he said, were established to " encourage our own industry."

Repeatedly, throughout the century, legislative assemblies
attempted to stimulate industrial diversification by requiring
the planting of a minimum number of mulberry trees, or
acres of hemp, flax, or indigo. Late in the century, Thomas
Budd appeared as an ardent apostle of this form of state
action. He recommended that the Pennsylvania Assembly
should require all persons to " sow one Acre of Flax, and
two acres of Hemp, which would be a means of supplying
us with Flax and Hemp, to carry on the Manufacturies of
Linnen-Cloth and Cordage." [4]   Massachusetts, in 1640,
had granted a bounty upon the production of cotton, linen
or woollen cloth. [5]   Five years later the towns were asked
to increase the number of sheep [6] while, in 1654, the towns
were instructed to assess each family for certain minimum
quantities of yarn to be spun. [7]   In Pennsylvania, Thomas
Budd proposed that agriculture should aid industry. Lands
should be set aside and the income therefrom should support
a set of trade schools. Domestic manufacturing, said Budd,
could thereby be expanded, since boys could be taught

[1] Mather, Increase. " A Brief Relation of the State of New England."
London, 1689. Reprinted, *Peter Force Hist. Tracts*, Vol. IV., Washington,
1838, p. 8.
[2] Sewall. *Computation that the Importation of Negroes, &c.*, p. 199.
[3] Pastorius. *Description of Pennsylvania*, p. 9.
[4] Budd, *op. cit.*, p. 47.
[5] *Records of the Governor and Company of the Massachusetts Bay in
New England.* Edited by Nathaniel Shurtleff. 5 vols. Boston, 1853–
1854, Vol. I., pp. 294 and 303.
[6] *Ibid.*, Vol. II., p. 105.
[7] *Ibid.*, Vol. IV., Part I., p. 256.

" Joynery, Twining, clock making, weaving, Shoemaking,"
while girls might be " instructed in Spinning of Flax or Wool,
and Knitting of Gloves and Stockings." [1]

Attempts to foster the growth of industry by bounties,
monopolies or subsidies were frequent. Massachusetts
granted a twenty-one year monopoly to the Braintree iron-
makers, together with " freedom from public charges,
trainings &c." [2] John Cotton included in his code of laws
a provision that

" Whosoever shall apply themselves to set forward the trade of
fishing, as fishermen, mariners, and shipwrights, shall be allowed,
man for man, or some or other of the labourers of the country,
to plant and reap for them, in the season of the year, *at a public
charge* of the Commonwealth." [3]

The Massachusetts Court, in 1639, made an order " that all
stocks employed in fishing should be free from public charges
for seven years." [4] Plymouth, in 1640, granted a monopoly
of " wood fitt for coopery growing upon Wood Island " to a
certain Wilton Maycumber " to be used by him so long as
he followed his trade." [5] Virginia, in 1661–62, exempted
tradesmen and artisans from the payment of tax levies. [6]
These few illustrations should indicate the varied colonial
efforts to stimulate and diversify industry. How far these
policies were successful is the concern of the economic
historian. That these policies were considered as legitimate
functions of government is sufficient evidence of the trend
of American economic ideas during the seventeenth century.

V

The colonial doctrine of economic surveillance went beyond
the control of enterprise. That the state must interfere in

[1] Budd, *op. cit.*, p. 43.
[2] Winthrop. *History of New England*, Vol. II., pp. 212–213.
[3] Cotton, John. *An Abstract of the Laws of New England as they are
now Established*. London, 1641. (In *I. Mass. Hist. Soc. Coll.* V.), p. 76.
[4] Winthrop. *History of New England*. Vol. I., p. 307.
[5] *Records of Colony of New Plymouth*. Vol. I., p. 159.
[6] Bruce, P. A. *Economic History of Virginia in the Seventeenth Century*.
New York, 1896. Vol. II., pp. 411–412.

the economic affairs of the individual was a belief that had been passed on to the seventeenth-century Americans from the teachings of the medieval period. The blissful hope that private pursuit of wealth would accomplish the greatest well-being of the group was yet unborn. Self-love was believed to have many anti-social consequences, and its evil effects demanded restraints upon the economic conduct of individuals.

The extent of colonial regulation of consumption will be considered later. It may be noted here, however, that this principle proceeded from the medieval theory of classes. "Excessive" consumption was relative to status rather than absolute excess. In New England, to be sure, the degree of Puritan asceticism did tend toward absolute restriction. But the chief concern was to keep each individual from transcending the bounds of his class. The colonial assemblies regulated individual dress and the character of expenditures.[1] The governing bodies attempted to classify persons according to their occupation, their amount of wealth, and their social position.[2] Persistent efforts were made in New England to regulate consumption, and the town records abound with accounts of trials.

The affairs of the market place were also subjected to governmental circumscription. Here again is the lingering influence of medieval paternalism. Price fixation or the determination of fair wages were designed to prevent the exploitation of buyers of commodities or services. The quality of goods brought to market was specified and failure to comply with qualitative regulations often led to prosecution. The assize of beer and ale was a characteristic colonial market place regulation. Craftsmen were warned to properly inspect the quality of wares offered for sale. *Caveat emptor* was seldom a rule of trade. Some of the market place control over the individual was a part of the

[1] Weeden, William. *Economic and Social History of New England.* 2 vols. 1891, pp. 106–107.
[2] *Ibid.*, pp. 226–227.

regulation of consumption. The demands for a limitation of wages often arose from a feeling that labourers were guilty of "excess of apparel" or other extravagant consumption.

The duty of the state to assist directly in the creation of individual well-being was never clearly accepted. Although regulation of the economic activity of the individual was highly paternalistic, it was essentially repressive rather than assisting. Laws were designed to restrain excessive expenditures, excessive prices or excessive wages. But the seventeenth century offered little in the direction of true constructive intervention. Mercantilists tend to look upon labourers as enemies, and the colonial labour laws in general have a distinct mercantilistic flavour. Maximum wage laws were far more frequently enacted than minimum wage laws ; the less fortunate members of society were more often legislated against than legislated for. This is illustrated in the matter of poor relief. It is true that the relief of the poor was not a serious problem during the seventeenth century. State action was therefore infrequent, but that which did emerge was ill devised. Workhouses were provided for [1] and commissioners were appointed to bind out the children of the poor.[2] The towns, to a considerable degree, followed the English precedent of attempting to shift the duty of poor relief.[3] In New England, the theological attitude was expressed by that self-appointed dispenser of God's vengeance, Cotton Mather. "As for your Common Beggars," said he,

" 'tis usually an Injury and a Dishonour unto the Country, for them to be Countenanced ; as for those who Indulge themselves in Idleness, the Express Command of God unto us, is, That we should let them Starve." [4]

[1] E.g., Plymouth, 1658. See Records, Vol. XI., p. 120.
[2] E.g., Plymouth, 1641. See Records, Vol. XI., p. 38.
[3] E.g., Plymouth, 1642. See Records, Vol. XI., p. 40. This was an attempt to make the individual responsible for the immigrant pauper personally chargeable.
[4] Mather. Durable Riches. Boston, 1695.

Only the unemployable, said Mather, should be the " objects
of your liberality." But the poor who " can work and won't,
the best liberality to them is to make them." [1] For mis-
applied charity, said Mather, leads to idleness, which is a
" reproach to any people." [2]

All of which shows that the American seventeenth-century
philosophy of economic control, whether of enterprise or
individual conduct, was profoundly influenced by the
medieval and mercantilist antecedents. It led to minute
interference for the maintenance of economic and social
classes, manifested itself both in encouragements and
restraints. Bounties, monopolies, and subsidies were means
of encouragement ; prohibitions and fines, the apparatus of
restraint. But it cannot be said that the mass of legislation
embodied an understanding of the principles of enlightened
intervention. Mercantilist influences were, for the time,
mingled and confused with medieval protection of the
individual. Enlightened intervention could not emerge
until most of the influences of mercantilism had been cast
off more than a century later.

[1] Mather. " The Boston Ebenezer." Lecture delivered April 7th, 1698.
Part II., p. 20. Reprinted, *Magnalia Christi Americana*. London, 1702.
 [2] *Ibid*.

CHAPTER III

ENGLISH THEORIES OF COLONIZATION

" Plantations are amongst ancient, primitive and heroical works. When the world was young it begat more children ; but now it is old, it begets fewer, for I may justly account new plantations to be the children of former kingdoms."

Francis Bacon, *Of Plantations*.

CHAPTER III

ENGLISH THEORIES OF COLONIZATION

I

T H E economic thought of the American colonies in the seventeenth century cannot be understood until English theories of colonization have been carefully examined. Plantation propaganda had a profound effect on colonial thought, since the colonies were the very fruition of colonization theory. The goals and motives for which settlements on the American continent were established were well understood both at home and in the colony. In the case of Massachusetts Bay, the promoters became the actual settlers and the motivating philosophy was infused into the minds of all the settlers. The influence of contemporary theories of colonization was inescapable.

Energetic and systematic discussion of colonization developed with the opening of the last quarter of the sixteenth century, the hey-day of Elizabethan maritime development. The inquiry continued to engage popular attention until it was submerged by the vital problems leading up to the crisis which culminated, in 1643, in Civil War. The dozen years which preceded the Civil War, however, witnessed a progressive decline in both the amount and the intensity of colonization propaganda. The most important agitation spans, therefore, a period of about fifty years, marked by the development of intense national feeling, of commercial rivalry, and by the growth of foreign trade. These years brought forward the arguments for colonization which bore fruit in the expansion of England, and paved the way for the Puritan emigration which

political events ultimately made expedient. The colonization
agitation and propaganda, because it is so inseparably connected with American settlement, must be examined in
detail to discover its main elements, its purposes, and its
ideals.   Many of the ideas put forth were to re-appear in the
writings of those who became the first Americans.

All the English writers on colonization were propagandists.
They were interested in colonies, though for different purposes. Some looked upon colonies as a means of attaining
wealth, many sought fame and distinction ; love of adventure attracted others, while some sought the greatness of
England and the overthrow of her enemies. Probably no
one, in fact, was influenced by only one motive. A complex
mixture of motives was rather present in each case. But
why writers on colonization were intrigued by the subject
is not of chief importance to the historian of economic
thought. These men wrote and published. Their views
became current. Whether they were preachers,[1] promoters,[2]
or philosophers,[3] matters not. They expressed ideas on
colonies, on their desirability, usefulness, and methods of
plantation. These views acquired wide circulation and
definitely affected all who were in any way connected with
the projects. Out of the writings emerged a great multi-
plicity of questions. What are colonies ? What sanctions
are there for their plantation ? Are they compatible with
Christian conduct ? What relation should they bear toward
the mother country from whence they issued ? What useful
purpose will they serve ? What net national advantage can
be provided by their agency ? To these questions Elizabethan Englishmen eagerly turned their attention.

II

The eminent desirability of colonies was a corollary of the
principle that foreign trade was a chief means of enriching a

---

[1] Like Hakluyt or White.
[2] Raleigh, Gilbert or Johnson.
[3] Hobbes and Bacon.

nation. " Domestic Marchandizing," wrote the author of *Nova Britannia*, " brings forth but poore effects in a Commonwealth " ; [1] and for proof thereof, he cited the case of England before " the golden daise of Queen Elizabeth." Industry coupled with foreign trade, it was urged, was the true means of attaining national wealth.   Thus Holland, with but little land, surpassed England in foodstuffs and in shipping, in spite of Britain's great natural resources.[2] Trade was believed to be a chief means of maintaining a kingdom,[3] and navigation the means of trade's expansion. How bountiful were the rewards of foreign trade, " experience hath lately taught us by some of our neighbours Provinces " (the Netherlands),[4] who thereby had been enabled not only to supply their own wants, but also commodities desired by other nations.   Together with the development of foreign trade would emerge maritime power and national greatness, as well as profit and honour for the individual colonizer.

But promotion or development of international trade demanded agencies of which the colony was among the most important.   Permanent trade relations could not be established by mere concessions from " doubtful friends," [5] nor were such arrangements consistent with national pride and the ideal of the self-sufficient nation.   On pure grounds of economy, also, the colony was regarded as a desirable means of commercial expansion.[6]   Foreign customs duties would

---

[1] Johnson, Robert. " Nova Britannia." London, 1609. Reprinted, *Peter Force Hist. Tracts*, Vol. I. Washington, 1836, pp. 17–18.

[2] *Ibid.*, p. 18.

[3] " Reasons for Raising a Fund for the Support of a Colony at Virginia," 1607. Printed in Alex. Brown, *Genesis of United States*. Boston, 1891, p. 37.

[4] *Nova Britannia*, p. 17.

[5] Hakluyt, Richard. "Notes given to certaine Gentlemen that went with M. Frobisher," 1578. Reprinted, *Hakluyt's Voyages*, Vol. 7.

[6] " No forren comoditie that comes into England comes without payment of custome once, twice or thrice, before it come into the realme, and so all forren comodities become derer to the subjects of this realme ; and by this course to Norumbega forren princes customes are avoided ; and the forren comodities cheaply purchased." Hakluyt, Richard. " Discourse on Western Planting." 1584. Printed *Coll. Maine Hist. Soc.*, 2nd Series, Vol. XI., Cambridge, 1877.

be avoided, and their avoidance would reduce the cost of imports. From another point of view, colonies were looked upon as the normal reproductive process of commonwealths.

"Plantations," said Francis Bacon, "are amongst ancient primitive and heroical works. When the world was young it begat more children; but now it is old, it begets fewer, for I may justly account new plantations to be the children of former kingdoms."[1] This was also the opinion of Hobbes, who discussed colonies under the subject of procreation of the commonwealth.[2] The offspring, he maintained, was therefore either a "commonwealth of themselves," or else an integral part of the "metropolis" which gave it birth.[3]

Suggestions as to the methods of establishing colonies were legion, and as varied as the personalities of those who propounded them. But some few general principles can be gathered out of the variety of plans which were commonly accepted. Thus plantations in unsettled countries were admittedly preferable to those in settled areas.[4] The wisdom of colonies in regions of rich natural resources was questioned by writers interested in promoting colonies in such regions as New England, lest "the overflowing of riches be enemies to labour, sobriety, justice, love and magnanimity: and the nurse of pride, wantonnesse, and contention."[5] As a general rule, however, the exploitation of bountiful natural resources was a chief argument for colonization and writers took pains to enumerate such possibilities. Development of staple products and the

[1] Bacon, Francis. "Of Plantations." London, 1625. Reprinted in Brown, *Genesis of United States*, pp. 799–802.
[2] Hobbes, Thomas. *Leviathan*. London, 1651. Dutton. Reprint, New York, p. 169.
[3] White's definition of a colony was "a society of men drawne out of one state of people, and transplanted into another Countrey," John White. "The Planters' Plea or the Grounds of Plantations Examined." London, 1630. Reprinted, *Peter Force Tracts*, Vol. II., Washington, 1838.
[4] "I like a plantation in a pure soil; that is where people are not displanted, to the end to plant in others, for else it is rather an extirpation than a plantation." Bacon, *op. cit.*, p. 799. See also Hobbes, *op. cit.*, p. 169.
[5] White, *op. cit.*, p. 18.

discovery of mines were accordingly emphasised. But Bacon was dubious of mining for "the hope of mines is very uncertain, and useth to make the planters lazy in other things." [1] Careful writers recognized that a plantation would not yield immediate profit,[2] and that failure to perceive this meant that profits would be drawn away prematurely and the success of the project jeopardized. That men require considerable inducement to tempt them to become colonists was clearly understood,[3] and consequently it was recognized that institutions of the new country must be attractive. The reluctance of people to colonize, further imposed upon promoters the necessity of economizing on labour. The successful colony, therefore, was one which could obtain the greatest benefits· with a minimum of labour.

III

More important than these matters of method, for they depend in the final analysis upon experiment, was the problem of sanction and justification. Was colonization, for example, consistent with natural law and compatible with Christian conduct ? "Natural commerce between nations" was held to be approved by the laws of God and man,[4] and the colonies designed to promote and further "natural commerce" were held to be sanctioned by the law of nations.[5] Theologians held that "colonies have their warrant from God's direction and command," [6] and that

[1] Bacon, op. cit., p. 800.
[2] Ibid., p. 799.
[3] Gray, Robert. A Good Speed to Virginia. London, 1609. Reprinted, J. P. Collier, Editor, London, 1864, p. 6. See also White, op. cit., p. 4 : " the love of ease and pleasure fixing men to the places and Countreys which they find ready furnished to their hand, by their predecessors labours and industry, takes from them a desire and will of undertaking such a laborious and unpleasant taske as the subdueing of unmanured countries."
[4] White, op. cit., p. 5.
[5] Peckham, Sir George. "A True report of the late discoveries, and possessions taken in the right of the Crowne of England of the Newfoundlands." 1583. Reprinted, Hakluyt's Voyages, Vol. 8, p. 97.
[6] White, op. cit., pp. 1–2.

till all vacant spaces of the earth have been replenished, Christians are bound by the Scriptural direction. The very gift of the earth to mankind imposes the duty of settling it, for God does nothing in vain and " how men should make benefit of the earth but by habitation and culture cannot be imagined."[1] Furthermore, the very nature of man justifies expansion to new countries for man's wants are " insatiable "[2] and " it cannot be denied but the life of every man is made more comfortable and afforded a more plentyful supply in a larger scope of ground." Domestic tranquillity would likewise be promoted by emigration and plantation as the history of Roman colonization had proved.[3] The probability of greater well-being as a result of greater land area was argued to be a general principle of nature, since trees prosper better in the large orchard than in the small nursery. So, in the civil state, would some individuals " over-top, and at last starve the weaker,"[4] whereas colonization would provide opportunities for all. To discover countries and leave them without plantation was condemned as ethically unjust and economically improvident,[5] for Christianity should be spread throughout the earth and temporal improvement should not be neglected. Christianity could not be preached without settling among " those poore people which have sitten so long in darkness."[6] Effectual promotion of the Gospel, therefore, demanded colonization.[7]

IV

The English literature of colonization was definitely influenced by the mercantilist notion of the desirability of

[1] White, *op. cit.*, p. 2.
[2] *Ibid.*
[3] Malynes, Gerard. *Consuetudo : vel Lex Mercatoria.* London, 1622. p. 164.
[4] White, *op. cit.*, p. 3.
[5] Malynes, *op. cit.*, p. 166.
[6] Hakluyt. *Discourse on Western Planting*, pp. 8-9.
[7] " Nowe the meanes to sende suche as shall labour effectually in this business ys by plantinge one or two colonies." Hakluyt, *op. cit.*, p. 9. See also White's discussion, *op. cit.*, p. 36.

economic self-sufficiency. For mercantilism had for its primary purpose the creation of a strong state,[1] and it was believed that this could best be accomplished if the nation and its colonies became a self-sufficient entity, largely independent of competing nations. In carrying out this programme, the colony was indispensable, since it became the means whereby the state could ramify throughout the various soils and climates and resources of the earth.

" The substances servinge," wrote Hakluyt, " wee may out of those partes receave the masse of wrought wares that now wee receave out of Fraunce, Flanders, Germayne, &c. ; and so wee may daunte the pride of some enemies of this realme." [2] Dependence upon foreign countries would accordingly be obviated by colonies,[3] and from such economic independence material economy would result. For the burden of " great Customs, and heavy impositions " [4] by foreign princes would be avoided and the costs of imports would therefore be reduced.[5] Moreover, risk would be minimized because immediate control over the source of supply would supersede dependence upon a " third market." [6] Well provided with colonial contacts, a kingdom would be " sufficient to serve itselfe," [7] and the trade between mother country and colony would be more comparable to a " home bread traffique than a forraigne exchange." [8]

Lastly, the colony could serve bullionist purposes in the mercantilist programme, by providing goods hitherto

---

[1] See Schmoller, Gustave. *The Mercantile System.*
[2] Hakluyt. *Discourse on Western Planting*, p. 158.
[3] " A True and Sincere Declaration of the purposes and ends of the Plantation begun in Virginia." London, 1610. Reprinted, Brown, *Genesis of United States.* Boston, 1891, p. 340.
[4] " A True and Sincere Declaration." Brown, *op. cit.*, p. 340.
[5] Hakluyt. *Discourse on Western Planting*, p. 157.
[6] Thus if wine culture were " brought to a just perfection " in the colonies, " no other nation could upon a quarrel betwixt us and Spain, and France, reap a benefit by selling us their wine at a third market." Williams, Edward. " Virginia, more especially the South part thereof, Richly and truely valued." London, 1650. Reprinted, *Peter Force Tracts*, Vol. 3. Washington, 1844, p. 18.
[7] *Reasons for Raising a Fund*, p. 39.
[8] *Ibid.*

imported from foreign nations ; it would eliminate the
export of specie which it was feared did " exceedingly enrich
our doubtfull friends." [1]   Exports previously required to
pay for imports could now be exchanged for treasure, to the
" enriching of the Commonwealth and the impoverishing of
our Enemies." [2]   Mercantilism was more than an exag-
geration of the importance of precious metals, but where
bullionist ideas predominated,[3] it must be admitted that
silver, gold and precious stones were indeed considered the
" three most precious darlings that lye and are cherished in
the Bosome of Nature." [4]

The relation of the colony to the mother country from
whence it issued was a matter of moment. On this score
Hobbes separated the offsprings of a nation into two great
classes. A newly settled plantation was either a new
commonwealth by itself, bound to its parent only by ties of
honour and friendship,[5] or else it remained united to the
mother country, a province rather than an emancipated
community. And indeed it was the latter definition of
colonial relationship that dominated. The fundamental
unity of colony and mother country was persistently maintained. The " state," said White, " must looke at the
mother and the daughter with an equal and indifferent eye ;
remembering that a Colony is a part and member of her own
body." [6] In the well-being of the offspring the parent
should have a peculiar interest, but on the same grounds the
plantation should be of advantage to the mother country
which gave it birth, because a " colony denying due respect
to the State from whose bowels it issued, is as great a
monster, as an unnatural child." [7]

[1] *Hakluyt Notes, &c.*, p. 248. Cf. also *Reasons for Raising a Fund*,
p. 39 : " our monies and wares that now run into the hands of our adver-
saries and cowld frendes shall pass into our frendes and natural kinsmen."
[2] Williams, Edward, *op. cit.*, p. 18.
[3] Hakluyt. *Discourse on Western Planting*, p. 157.
[4] Malynes, *op. cit.*, p. 166. Cf. also Misselden. *The Circle of Commerce.* London, 1623, p. 117.
[5] Hobbes, *op. cit.*, pp. 169–170.
[6] White, *op. cit.*, p. 19.
[7] *Ibid.*, p. 14.

Specific purposes of colonization grew essentially out of the encompassing philosophy of mercantilism. Thus the colony could serve as a source of supply of foods and materials, decreasing dependence on foreign countries ; it might provide a market for exports more constant and more certain than foreign markets ; and it could serve as a great school for mariners and so strengthen the parent country. Yet to explain all the hoped-for benefits of colonization in terms of mercantilist ambition alone would be inadequate. The hope that colonies would help England to deal with the troublesome problem of population was partly a phase of mercantilism and partly an independent problem.

In line with a fundamental mercantilist principle, all the colonization writers urged that the colony should serve as a source of supply of useful commodities. What the particular colony should provide was often limited only by the range of the imagination of some of the more optimistic advocates. But the very range of such imaginings is itself proof of the peculiar desirability of supplying the mother country with certain commodities. In general the articles desired fall into four groups. First came gold, silver, and precious minerals,[1] the forms of wealth most highly regarded by the bullionist school of mercantilists ; secondly, commodities incapable of being produced in the mother country, the supply of which must be had from foreigners ; thirdly, naval stores ; fourthly, those commodities for which there existed a fairly constant international demand and which therefore would provide excellent items of trade. Such commodities might in turn facilitate the inflow of specie and thereby accomplish the same result as the first group.

Since England possessed no mines, it was natural and logical that the influence of treasure as a goal of economic policy should pervade the colonization literature. Yet discussion of its direct acquisition takes a decidedly subordinate place when compared to its accumulation through adjustment of the items in the nations' merchandise balance.

[1] See Malynes. *The Center of the Circle of Commerce.* London, 1623.

Hakluyt pointed out that if colonies could provide fruits, wines, skins, flax, or naval stores, treasure could be saved.[1] The author of *Nova Britannia* urged colonization to provide " such needful things " which " can hardly be obtained from any other part of the world," [2] while Williams contended that the exports which have been used to pay for such goods as will thereafter be forthcoming from colonies would be paid for in bullion.[3] Special emphasis was laid also upon the principle that commodities which the colony would make available would be " substances unwroughte," [4] the manufacture of which would employ the people of the mother country and when sold abroad would ultimately bring home more treasure.

The supplying of readily saleable commodities for which the international demand was brisk, was scarcely less important, in the minds of the writers, than goods wanted by the parent country itself. In this classification came such articles as fish, salt, or timber.[5] These goods would command either goods or money elsewhere and " supplye the wantes of all our decayed trades." [6] With colonies adjacent to fishing banks, England, it was promised, could satisfy her own wants,[7] and moreover displace Holland in providing Europe with this important staple.[8] Given colonies supplying proper staple articles of trade, England could overcome her commercial rivals, " dryve them out of trade to idleness," [9] and further weaken them by " exhausting " them of their treasure.

Naval stores and shipping were sufficiently important in the writings of the colonization propagandists, to merit separate treatment. Since foreign trade was the means of

[1] *Hakluyt Notes, &c.*, p. 248.
[2] *Nova Britannia*, pp. 16–17.
[3] Williams, Edward, *op. cit.*, p. 18.
[4] Hakluyt. *Discourse on Western Planting*, pp. 42 and 43.
[5] *Ibid.*, p. 106.
[6] *Ibid.*, p. 19.
[7] Peckham, *op. cit.*, p. 110 ; also Williams, Edward, *op. cit.*, p. 22.
[8] Williams, Edward, *op. cit.*, p. 5.
[9] Hakluyt. *Discourse on Western Planting*, p. 158.

enriching a nation, the development of fleets and the training of seamen were the means of trade's development. For maritime supremacy meant power and national honour and

" the greatest jewell of this realme, and the chieftest strength and force of the same, for defense or offense in marshall matter and manner, is the multitude of ships, masters and mariners, ready to assist the most stately and royall navy." [1]

The development of colonies could stimulate shipping and increase the number of ships and men in three different ways. First, the very remoteness of the colony would give rise to a carrying trade,[2] since trans-oceanic colonies would demand " great shippes " and merchants would be induced to provide what was of inestimable value to the state.[3] A second manner in which the colony could give help in providing a merchant marine was the actual construction of ships. Thus Sir Humphrey Gilbert wrote of the northern colonies : " also here we shall increase both our ships and mariners without burdening of the state." [4] But by far the most important was the idea that colonies could supply commodities necessary for ship construction and especially those for which England was dependent upon foreign sources of supply. The availability of such necessary articles could not choose " but invite our men to the buildinge of greate shippinge." [5] Masts, tar, rosin, pitch, cordage—with these England was unprovided by nature, and " enjoyeth them only by the favor of forraigne potency." [6] But if colonial supplies of naval stores were extensive, the mother country could also, in addition to satisfying her own wants in ship-

---

[1] Peckham, *op. cit.*, p. 110.

[2] Hakluyt. *Discourse on Western Planting*, p. 90.

[3] *Ibid.* " No enterprise possibly can be devised more fitte to increase our greate shipping then this westerne fortifienge and plantinge . . . wee shall be constrayned of ourselves without chardginge of the Prince, to build greate shippes."

[4] Gilbert, Sir Humphrey. " A Discourse to Prove a Passage by the Northwest," 1576. Reprinted; *Hakluyt's Voyages*, Vol. 7. p. 187.

[5] Hakluyt. *Discourse on Western Planting*, p. 91.

[6] *Reasons for Raising a Fund*, p. 37.

ping, build ships for sale to other countries.[1] By these
several ways, therefore, the foreign plantations would
increase the maritime power of the nation.   Perhaps as
important a consideration as any was the promised emergence of a corps of skilful seamen, for " the life of shipping
resteth in the number of able mariners and worthy Chief-
tains." [2]   Increase of navigation would perforce increase
both the number and the skill [3] not only of sailors, but of
shipwrights [4] and builders.   For an abundance of ships and
the plentifulness of " skillful connynge, and stowte pilotts," [5]
was considered to provide " a brazen wall of this nation " [6]
against which no foe could prevail and within which the
economically self-sufficient state could prosper.

   To the argument that the colony should serve as a source
of supply was added the idea of the colony as a market for
the products of the home country.[7] This conception again
emphasised the importance of trade and stressed the policy
of exchanging exports either for imports or for bullion.
Hakluyt, for example, urged that by means of colonies,
England could " chaunge many cheape comodities of these
partes, for things of high valor there not esteemed ; and this
to the great inrichinge of the realme." [8]   But the general
argument went much further.   First of all, a colonial market
would be a controlled market unaffected by international
complications.[9]   It would increase the demand for suitable

   [1] *Nova Britannia*, pp. 16–17. This could apply as well to ships built
in the colonies.   Thus Hakluyt wrote, " also wee may there, withoute
payinge for the same, have tymber to builde greate navies, and may bringe
them into this realme, and have goodd sale of the same." Hakluyt,
Discourse, p. 105.
   [2] *Reasons for Raising a Fund*, p. 37.
   [3] *Nova Britannia*, p. 17. See also Peckham, *op. cit.*, p. 110.
   [4] Hakluyt, p. 91. This also would mean prosperity for the " supporta-
tion of all those occupations that depend upon the same."
   [5] Hakluyt. *Discourse on Western Planting*, pp. 89–91.
   [6] Williams, Edward, *op. cit.*, p. 5.
   [7] Beer in his *Origins of British Colonial System* has taken the position
that the expectation of new sources of supply was the most fundamental
motive for colonization.   True it appears perhaps most frequently, but
may not this have occurred because it was politic to stress this point ?
   [8] Hakluyt. *Discourse on Western Planting*, p. 157.
   [9] " Besides uttering of our countrey commodities, which the Indians

exports,[1] thereby benefitting the artisans of England, because such goods, would " passe out of this realme full wrought by our natural subjects in all degrees of labour." [2] Greatest emphasis was laid upon the development of a " mighty vent of English clothes " [3] which would restore the " ancient trade of clothing," [4] and insure labour and prosperity for all artisans therein engaged.[5]

The part the colony could play in increasing domestic employment assumed considerable importance in colonization discussions. Part of this emphasis was due to the immediate economic conditions in England, but the persistence of the argument shows that increased domestic employment was a part of the benefits ordinarily claimed for colonization. It was presumed that the natives of

&c. much esteem . . . whereby it plainly appeareth in what estimation they would have the clothes of this countrey, so that there would be found a far better vent for them by this meanes then yet this realme ever had : Portugall, Hamborow, Emden, or any other part of Europe." Gilbert, *op. cit.*, pp. 186–187.

[1] Hakluyt, p. 41. See also Carleil, Christopher. *A Briefe and Summary Discourse upon the Intended Voyage to the Hithermost Parts of America*, 1583, p. 140.

[2] Hakluyt. *Discourse on Western Planting*, p. 42. The idea of exporting only goods which had been " wroughte " or manufactured became a fundamental principle of mercantilism. As early as the writings of John Hales can the caution against exporting " unwroughte " merchandise be found. See Hales, John. *A Discourse of the Common Weal of This Realme of England.* Edited by Elizabeth Lamont, Cambridge, 1893, p. 126. As the mercantilist philosophy expanded, this principle assumed greater and greater importance. It proposed to facilitate domestic employment, to permit the growth of population, and to develop skilled artisans. From Hales onward, every thorough-going mercantilist made a place for this doctrine in his teachings. The highest development of this theory was at the hands of Sir James Steuart, who held that " in all trade two things are to be considered in the commodity sold. The first is the matter ; the second is the labour employed to render this matter useful. The matter exported from a country is what the country loses ; the price of the labour exported is what it gains." Steuart, Sir James. *An Inquiry into the Principles of Political Economy*, 1767. According to this philosophy the goal of economic policy was to " discourage the importation of work, and to encourage the exportation of it." A balance of labour supercedes the idea of a balance of trade.

[3] *Nova Britannia*, p. 22. Also Hakluyt, *Discourse*, pp. 41 and 153.

[4] *Ibid.* See also p. 107.

[5] Peckham, *op. cit.*, p. 111. " How great benefit to all such persons and artificers . . . clothiers, woolmen, carders, spinners, weavers, fullers, sheermen, diers, drapers, cappers, hatters."

colonized regions, together with the transported population in the new country, would consume considerable quantities of exported manufactured goods.[1] The net outcome would be abundant employment in the home country [2] leading to a minimum of social unrest among labourers,[3] and a minimum of poverty, idleness and oppression.[4] For next to the advancement of the Christian religion the " principall ende of the same [planting] is traficque, by which the metropolis is enriched and her subjects given employment." [5]

With more traffic, more industry, and more shipping, the state could in turn expect and obtain more revenue. " Whatsoever kind of commodities should be brought from thence," wrote Hakluyt, " or to be thither transported oute of the realme, cannot choose but enlarge the revenewes of the Crowne very mightely, and enrich all sorts of subjects in generally." [6] While Bacon advised that freedom from customs duties should be guaranteed to a new colony during its formative years,[7] the general theory of colonization regarded colonies as a means of increasing the income from both export and import duties.[8] One other means advanced

[1] Gilbert, *op. cit.*, p. 187. Also Hakluyt. *Discourse on Western Planting*, p. 38.
[2] Hakluyt. *Discourse*, p. 160.
[3] Malynes, *op. cit.*, p. 164.
[4] Hakluyt. *Discourse*, p. 39. The optimistic enthusiasm concerning the benefits of the colony are here well illustrated for " this enterprise will mynister matter for all sortes and states of men to worke upon ; namely, all severall kinds of artificers, husbandmen, seamen, marchauntes, soulders, capitaines, phisitions, lawyers, devines, cosmographers, hidrographers, astronomers, historiographers ; yea, olde folkes, lame persons, women, younge children, by many meanes which hereby shall still be mynistered unto them, shalbe kept from idleness." The solution of the problem of unemployment of cosmographers, hydrographers, astronomers and historiographers must have been a comforting promise !
[5] Hakluyt. *Notes, &c.*, pp. 247–248. The same view is expressed in his *Discourse*, p. 95.
[6] Hakluyt. *Discourse on Western Planting*, p. 88.
[7] Bacon, *op. cit.*, p. 801 : " Let there be freedom from custom, till the plantation be of strength : and not only freedom from custom, but freedom to carry their commodities where they make their best of them, except there be some special cause of caution."
[8] " The revenues and customes of her Majesty, both outwarde and inwarde, shall be mightely inlarged by the toll, excises and other dueties which without oppression may be raysed." Hakluyt, *Discourse*, p. 86 ; also p. 88.

to increase revenues was the collection of tonnage duties upon foreign vessels which might be compelled to repair to the English colonies from the Newfoundland fishing banks.[1]

V

Finally comes the extremely important matter of population and its relation to the theories of colonization. One prominent writer on English colonial policy[2] has undertaken to classify colonization motives primarily from the population point of view. The policy which the parent country takes toward the colony, according to Beer, depends upon the attitude of the mother country toward emigration. If it is believed that the home country is over-populated, the colony can provide a direct benefit by draining off the surplus. But if the state has no surplus population, but rather desired to increase its density, the colony becomes a source of weakness, and must provide generous reparation in the form of other benefits.[3] On the basis of this classification, Beer essays to test the English population situation and ascertain when these respective conditions prevailed. His conclusions are that the first condition (over-population) was believed to exist up to the time of the Restoration, and the second (under-population) in the period thereafter.[4]

But although the literature of the colonization period under discussion is replete with suggestion that colonies could be of value in ridding England of some of her population, plenty of evidence is available to show the general mercantilist predilection for a dense population. The interest in colonization during the period before 1660 cannot be explained in terms of a fetish of over-population.[5]

[1] Hakluyt. *Discourse on Western Planting*, p. 88.
[2] Beer, George L. *The Origins of the British Colonial System*, 1578–1660. New York, 1908.
[3] This classification is explained in Beer, *op. cit.*, p. 32, *et seq.*
[4] *Ibid.*, pp. 34–35.
[5] Beer holds that although there was no actual over-population, it was the erroneous belief that England did have a surplus population which influenced the writers of the period. Beer, *op. cit.*, pp. 44 and 45.

There are at least three significant reasons why the mercantilist argument for increasing the density of England's
population did not appear as frequently before the Restoration as it did thereafter.   In the first place, it must be
remembered that it was politic for promoters of colonies to
stress their immediate utility.   It is not surprising, therefore,
that the appeal of lower taxes, decreased poor rates, and
lower penal expenditures was emphasised.   In the second
place, the systematic development of the theory of mercantilism led progressively to greater emphasis upon population.   The economic philosophy of the period of Charles II.
was developed and mature compared with that of Elizabeth's
time.   In the third place, let it be recalled that supplying
people wherewith to colonize was one of the most difficult
problems of the early period.   Capital and adventurers were
readily available.[1]   The supply of dependable colonists was
the limiting factor.   Reference has already been made to the
reluctance with which settlers betook themselves to a new
country.[2]   It was clearly both expedient and necessary to
emphasize over-population in order to arouse state interest
in these several private projects.

The three foregoing reasons throw light on why the
colonization literature abounds with reference to " England's
over-population " problem.   But to attempt to classify
colonization motives from this point of view is misleading
and incorrect.   The population references in the writings of
the colonial advocates must be examined in the same way
that other arguments for colonies have been examined.
These references are fractions of the whole colonization ideal
rather than a keystone to the whole problem.   As far as the
writers of the period were mercantilists, they accepted the
principle of the desirability of a large population ; as far as

---

[1] The case of the Virginia Company illustrates this point.   The second
charter of 1609 was subscribed to by 56 companies of London and 659
persons, of whom 21 were peers, 96 knights, 11 doctors and ministers,
53 captains, 28 esquires, 58 gentlemen, 110 merchants, and 282 citizens
and others not classified.   Brown, *Genesis of United States*, p. 228 n.

[2] Baçon, *op. cit.*, p. 800, and White, *op. cit.*, p. 4.

they were promoters, they tempered their mercantilism with diplomacy.

The arguments for colonization as a means of draining population from the mother country centre around the expected decrease of domestic unemployment, the diminution of crime, lower cost of poor relief, and lower taxes. The writers of the period recognized symptoms of economic maladjustment. " What man so simple," wrote a pamphleteer [1] in 1612, " that doth not see the necessities of employment for our multitude of people." Population was considered redundant if a state had more people than it could nourish or employ.[2] The " disburthening of full states of unnecessary multitudes "[3] was approved by theologians and justified by the precedent of Rome.[4] A natural tendency toward over-population was premised by one writer unless " Wars, Famine, and Pestilence do purge that great Body."[5] The same view was expressed by the advocates of the Virginia Company[6] who recommended the " transplanting the ranckness and multitude of increase in our people " lest the " infiniteness " of them endanger the livelihood of all. Some writers who recognized that the honour of the king lay in the strength and multitude of his people, at the same time argued that population had a tendency to increase above a " due and proportionable number,"[7] and believed emigration must be the corrective.

More persistent were the statements that colonization would diminish crime by taking away its economic cause. Beer is correct in his emphasis on the fact that England was face to face with pauperism.[8] All contemporary evidence shows crime to have been a vexatious problem. Idle persons, it was said, lacking opportunity of employment " swarme

---

[1] Johnson, Robert. *New Life of Virginia*, pp. 218–219.
[2] White, *op. cit.*, p. 9.
[3] *Ibid.*, p. 6.
[4] Malynes, *op. cit.*, p. 164.
[5] *Ibid.*
[6] *A True and Sincere Declaration*, p. 340.
[7] Gray, *op. cit.*, p. 12.
[8] Beer, *op. cit.*, p. 45.

into lewde and naughtie practices, so that if we seeke not
some waise for their forreine employment, we must provide
shortly more prisons and corrections."[1] Mutiny, sedition,
commotion and rebellion, scarcity and poverty—all these
colonization would cure,[2] as well as theft and highway
robbery.[3] Moreover, disease and pestilence as well as crime
were results of " so great a bodie of many millions, which
yearly do increase amongst us."[4] These evils were, in
consequence, felt by everyone either by high taxes for maintenance of the afflicted,[5] or " in the taint of their vices and
bodily plagues."[6] Colonies could care for the poor and
thereby reduce the parish charges for poor relief.[7] With a
diminution in such taxes, it was urged, heavier levies could
be easily born, the proceeds of which might be used " to
maintaine, recruite, and incourage your Armies and Navies."[8]
The transported parish orphans and poor might in the colony
become useful subjects " advantageous to the place of their
nativity in particular, and their whole nation in generall,"[9]
whereas in their native parish they would become beggars or
day labourers at best. Thus would the plantation provide
economic opportunity for those who felt they had none in
the mother country. It would afford " a brave and ample
theatre to make their merits and abilities emergent, and a
large field to sow and reap the fruit of all their honest
industrious and public intentions."[10]

But while the idea that the colony could serve a useful
function in draining off population from the mother country
appears with considerable frequency in the colonization
literature before the Civil War, ideas on population are to
be found in the same period which are consistent with the

---

[1] *Nova Britannia*, p. 19. See also Hakluyt, *Discourse*, p. 37.
[2] Gray, *op. cit.*, p. 12.
[3] Williams, Edward, *op. cit.*, p. 4.
[4] *New Life of Virginia*, pp. 218–219.
[5] *Ibid.*, p. 219.
[6] *Ibid.*
[7] Williams, Edward, *op. cit.*, pp. 4–5.
[8] *Ibid.*
[9] Williams, Edward, *op. cit.*, p. 5.
[10] *Ibid.*

theory of mercantilism. In fact the very principle of emigration was sometimes held forth as a means whereby the mother country could ultimately support and maintain a denser population.[1] To thorough-going mercantilists the strength of the state lay in its population.[2] Some conceived of population as wealth, and consequently the husbanding of a nation's people was as important as the husbanding of her resources. Beer has failed to consider these mercantilist notions favourable to increased population in the pre-Restoration period.

As early as 1549, John Hales had decried any policy which might lead to depopulation, and preference for increased population appears repeatedly in his three dialogues.[3] Trade, in his opinion, should be so arranged that the greatest number of people could be set to work.[4] From this date onward, the mercantilist attitude toward population developed. To assume that it was entirely changed during the period of the colonization literature is absurd. Even Malynes, who feared a tendency toward over-population,[5] admitted that " the concourse of people causeth the greater consumption of all things, and the revenues are great by Impositions, and it giveth life to Traffique and Commerce." [6] Hakluyt, who saw in the tendency toward population increase the possibility of an increase in social unrest and crime,[7] and who was perhaps the warmest advocate of colonization, took the mercantilist position. He denied that England was over-populated, holding that the " honor

[1] Hakluyt. *Discourse on Western Planting*, p. 44.
[2] Fortrey, Davenant, Child and Petty.
[3] Hales, John, *op. cit.*, pp. 16, 93, and 126.
[4] *Ibid.*, p. 126.
[5] Cf. *supra*, p. 51, note 5.
[6] Malynes, *op. cit.*, p. 165.
[7] " Wee are growne more populous than ever heretofore : so that nowe there are of every arte and science so many, that they can hardly live one by another ; . . . many thousands of idle persons are within this realme, which having no way to be sett on work ; either be mutinous and seek alteration in the state, or at least very burdensome to the commonwealth and often fall to pilfering and theivinge and other lewdness whereby all the prisons of the lande are daily pestered and stuffed full of them." *Discourse on Western Planting*, p. 37.

and strengthe of a prince consisteth in the multitude of the people." [1] What was needed, in his opinion, was not a draining off of population, but employment for all. That colonies could provide this he was convinced, for even

" if the number of this realme were as great as all Spaine and Ffraunce have, the people being industrious, I say, there shoulde be found victualls enoughe at the full in all bounty to suffice them all. And takinge order to carry hence thither our clothes made in hose, coates, clokes, whoodes, &c., and to return thither hides of their owne beastes, tanned and turned into shoes and bootes, and other skynnes of goates, whereof they have store, into gloves, &c., no doubte but wee shall sett on worke in this realme, besides sailors and suche as shalbe seated there in those westerne discovered countries at the least C. M. subjectes to the great abatinge of the goodd estate of subjectes of forreine princes, enemies, or doubtful frendes." [2]

VI

Closely allied to the relation of the colony to the domestic population problem was the discussion of suitable colonizing material. Bacon held that no colony could be successful unless it obtained dependable artificers and trained agriculturists.[3] White urged that the equal regard with which the ruler should look at the mother country and colony should induce him to allow the colony " proportionable men as may bee sufficient to make the frame of that newly formed body," [4] while Gray maintained that " artificers and tradesmen must be nourished and cherished, for without artificers and tradesmen a commonwealth cannot flourish nor endure." [5] Malynes went into an elaborate discussion to show how artisans could be attracted to the colonies, the

[1] Hakluyt. *Discourse on Western Planting*, p. 43.
[2] *Ibid.*, p. 44.
[3] " The people wherewith you plant ought to be gardeners, ploughmen, laborers, smiths, carpenters, joiners, fishermen, fowlers, with some few apothecaries, surgeons, cooks and bakers." Bacon, *op. cit.*, p. 799.
[4] White, *op. cit.*, p. 19.
[5] Gray, *op. cit.*, p. 33.

general plan of which was to allow each to become a monopolist of his respective trade for a certain period.[1]

Opposed to the foregoing opinions was the idea that the
colony could be recruited from the poor and the criminal
classes. Sir Humphrey Gilbert advocated settlement with
" such needy people of our country, which now trouble the
commonwealth, and through want here at home are forced
to commit outrageous offences, whereby they are dayly
consumed with the gallowes." [2] If the poor and criminal
were drained off into colonies,[3] wrote the author of *Nova
Britannia*, deaths due to economic privation would be
prevented, and the cost of poor relief reduced. Hakluyt
recommended that petty thieves be condemned to labour in
the colonies supplying naval stores and timber.[4] But with
these plans Bacon had no sympathy. " It is a shameful and
unblessed thing," he wrote in his essay on plantations, " to
take the scum of people and wicked and condemned men, to
be the people with whom you plant." [5] They will spoil the
plantation, he warned, they will be lazy, mischievous, waste-
ful ; and they will discredit the plantation in the home
country. Even Robert Johnson admitted that a colony
could not be built out of criminals, but that men of all trades
and professions were needed, " honest wise and painefull
men." [6] White's views on this subject were most caustic.
This earnest, sincere preacher, who gave such stimulus to the
settlement of Massachusetts Bay, had no patience with the
views of men whose only interest in the colonies was commercial. " It seems to be a common and grosse error," he
wrote, " that Colonies ought to be Emunctories or sinckes of
States ; to drayne away their filth." [7] This fundamental
error, he conceived to have been the occasion of the " mis-
carriage of most of our colonies."

[1] Malynes, *op. cit.*, pp. 164–165.
[2] Gilbert, *op. cit.*, p. 186.
[3] Johnson, Robert, *op. cit.*, p. 19.
[4] Hakluyt. *Discourse on Western Planting*, p. 37.
[5] Bacon, *op. cit.*, p. 799.
[6] Johnson, Robert, *op. cit.*, p. 19.
[7] White, *op. cit.*, p. 19.

These specific purposes, then, could the colony serve : to supply various goods necessary for the economic prosperity of the mother country ; to provide a controlled market for her " wrought wares " ; to increase her public revenues ; to augment her shipping and her corps of seamen ; to help solve the population problem by either draining off people or providing domestic employment. To these main groups, a few more particularized anticipated results must yet be added, less obvious in emergence, and psychological rather than economic. Thus Hakluyt believed that colonies, by providing men with new opportunities, would salvage the degenerate. Here amid new surroundings they might be " raised againe, and doe their contrie goodd service." [1] The work of planting, White thought, would be a corrective to the moral decay which was evident, for it would reduce men to the " degrees of that frugality, industry and justice which hath been disused and forgotten." [2] The taking up of new land would foster not only frugality but invention,[3] because the very abundance of people in old countries represses invention since labourers are hostile to new machines.[4] But most optimistic of all was the belief that colonization would lead to virtue by removing the economic cause of sin and crime. For " the settling of new States," wrote White,

" requireth justice and affection to the common good : and the taking in of large countreys presents a natural remedy against covetousnesse, fraud and violence when every man may enjoy enough without wrong or injury to his neighbour." [5]

Only one great philosopher stood totally apart from this wave of optimism. Thomas Hobbes could project his vision far enough into the future to see that colonization was a palliative rather than a solution of the problem of population.

[1] Hakluyt. *Discourse on Western Planting*, p. 160.
[2] White, *op. cit.*, p. 5.
[3] *Ibid.*, p. 3.
[4] Williams, Edward, *op. cit.*, p. 6.
[5] White, *op. cit.*, p. 3.

To him colonization was a process in the peopling of the earth, but finally " when all the world is over-charged with inhabitants, then the last remedy of all is war, which provideth for every man, by victory or death." [1] Pessimism indeed, but who shall say that Hobbes was wrong ?

[1] Hobbes, *op. cit.*, p. 235.

Chapter IV

AMERICAN THEORIES OF COLONIZATION

" Not that we altogether, or principally, propound profit to be the main end of that we have undertaken, but the Glory of God, and the honor of our Country, in the enlarging of his Majesty's dominions. Yet wanting outward means to set things in that forwardness we desire, and to further the latter by the former, I thought meet to offer both to consideration, hoping that where religion and profit jump together (which is rare) in so honorable an action, it will encourage every honest man, either in person or purse, to set forward the same."

Edward Winslow, *Mourt's Relation.*

AMERICAN THEORIES OF COLONIZATION

I

T H E seventeenth-century American writers were no less European than the writers whose views on colonization have just been examined. With but few exceptions they were born in Europe, and many were of adult age when they migrated. But noticeable differences in ideas about colonization are to be found amid similarities, and these differences need careful analysis. Why did such dissimilarities emerge ? One can at once imagine possible explanations such as the segregating influence of emigration and the pressure of new economic surroundings. Will such hypotheses serve ?

American colonization ideas are differentiated from their English predecessors in two ways. In the first place, there is less emphasis upon the advantages of a colony to the mother country. Although most of the writers were essentially mercantilists, only a few dealt with colonization from the mercantilist point of view. In fact, John Smith, Governor Berkeley and John Hammond were the only writers who presented the home country arguments for colonization. Adrian Van der Donck, however, in his criticism of the Dutch West India Company, did point out that New Netherlands could be of distinct advantage to Holland if properly governed. In the second place, the American colonization literature reveals a pre-occupation with the justification of colonization and with theological and philosophical sanctions rather than economic considerations. With these two chief distinctions between English and American writers in mind, the colonization literature of the new world, pieced together from its fragmentary sources, must be examined in detail.

The English writers, it will be recalled, paid lip service to the diffusion of Christianity as a motive for colonization. In practically every case, however, the evangelical was subordinated to the economic. But this can by no means be said with the same confidence about the American writers. Colonization, to be sure, was motivated by an admixture of interests and both Christian and worldly considerations were combined. But the dissemination of Christianity and the creation of a Christian Commonwealth were integral parts of the New England philosophy of colonization.

" New England," wrote Cotton Mather,[1] " differs from other Foreign Plantations, in respect of the Grounds and Motives, inducing the First Planters to remove into that American Desert ; other Plantations were built upon Worldly Interests, New England upon that which is purely religious."

Whether the New England settlement was " purely religious " is a problem for the historian. The important thing is that Mather maintained that ideal colonization should be primarily ecclesiastical and in this he reiterated the belief of other New England writers. John Winthrop regarded a colony as a means to " improve our lives to doe more service to the Lord."[2] The Rev. Mr. Wilson conceived the purpose of a colony to " overcome Satan here and dispossess him of his Kingdom."[3] In the recital of the purposes of the Plymouth plantation the religious precede the non-religious.[4] Winthrop held that

[1] Mather, Cotton. " Some Considerations on the Bills of Credit now passing in New England." Boston, 1891. Reprinted, Prince Society, *Colonial Currency Reprints*, Vol. I., pp. 189–196. Boston, 1910.
[2] Winthrop, John. " A Modell of Christian Charity," 1630. Reprinted, 3 *Coll. Mass. Hist. Soc.*, VII., pp. 30–48.
[3] Winthrop, John. *The History of New England*, Vol. I., p. 81.
[4] *Records of the Colony of New Plymouth*, Vol. XI., p. 77. " For the better effecting the glory of God, The Inlargement of the dominions of our said Sov. Lord the Kinge, and the speciall good of his Subjects."

one of the " great and fundamental errors " in former plantations, was that " their maine end was carnall & not Religious." [1] Thomas Dudley, in his famous letter to the Countess of Lincoln wrote :

" That if any come hither to plant for worldly ends, that can live well at home, he commits an error, of which he will soon repent him ; but if for spiritual . . . he may find here what may well content him." [2]

In a similar manner Robert Cushman discouraged persons from colonizing at Plymouth who " look after great riches, ease, pleasures, dainties, and jollity in this world." [3] But those men who could be " content to lay out their estates, spend their time, labours and endeavors, for the benefit of them, that shall come after, and in a desire to further the Gospel " ; [4] such were ideal colonists ! Edward Winslow recognized that colonization was a matter of mixed motives ; that the Plymouth settlement had been undertaken for God's glory, for the expansion of England and for the profit of the adventurers. But " where religion and profit jump together (which is so rare)," he saw that it would be easy to appeal to men to become partakers in so great an adventure.[5] As late as 1679, the religious theory of colonization found expression in the Boston Synod of Churches. In that year the Elders of the Massachusetts churches declared, "we differ from other out-goings of our nation, in that it was not worldly considerations that brought our fathers into this wilderness, but religion, even that so they might build a sanctuary unto the Lord's name." [6]

[1] Winthrop, John. "Conclusions for the Plantation in New England." 1629. Reprinted, *Pro. Mass. Hist. Soc.*, 1865 ; also *Old South Leaflet*, No. 50, General Series, Boston, 1894.

[2] Young, Alexander. *Chronicles of Pilgrim Fathers*. Boston, 1841. p. 324.

[3] Cushman, Robert. Printed in Young's *Chronicles*, pp. 256–257.

[4] *Ibid.*

[5] Winslow, Edward. *Relation*. Printed in Young, *op. cit.*, p. 372.

[6] Mather, Increase. *Necessity of Reformation with the Expedients subservient thereunto ; agreed upon by the Elders and Messengers of the Churches assembled in the Synod at Boston*. Boston, 1679, p. 6.

The non-economic ideals were, however, largely confined to New England. The writers primarily interested in Virginia, New York, or Pennsylvania, for the most part, frankly admit the economic considerations. John Smith held that the history of all great nations was proof that " industrious, honest-hearted Publicans " who had a wholesome regard for " more provisions and necessaries for their people " alone could found new states.[1] Thomas Budd considered colonization to be a means of overcoming domestic unemployment, a cure for poverty, and a lucrative investment.[2] Adrian Van der Donck maintained that unrestricted individual gain was indispensable for colonial success.[3] Beverley, the Virginia historian, recorded that the chief design of the first colonists was to " fetch away the Treasure from thence." [4] These few illustrations have been offered merely to show the simultaneous existence of economic and non-economic motives for colonization.

II

The American discussion of the methods of colonization centre around three fundamental practical problems. Where should colonies be established ? By what means ? By what kind of colonists ? In these questions the American writers essentially parallel the English.

Bradford, like John White,[5] was dubious of plantations amid rich natural resources. For this reason, he opposed settlement in Guiana although he recognized that in warm climates " vigorous nature brought forth all things in abundance & plentie without any great labor or art of man." [6] The relative disadvantage of land in northern

---

[1] Smith, John. *Advertisements for the Unexperienced Planters*, pp. 22–23.
[2] Budd, *op. cit.*, p. 27.
[3] Donck, Adrian Van der. *The Representation of New Netherlands.* The Hague, 1650. Reprinted, New York, 1849, p. 39.
[4] Beverley, *op. cit.*, pp. 43–44.
[5] Cf. Chapter III., p. 38, note 5.
[6] Bradford, *op. cit.*, p. 36.

climates was considered by the Dutch writer, Adrian Van der Donck.[1] The French colonies in America he regarded as inferior to the Dutch, because of the greater cost of keeping domestic animals. On the same grounds, Thomas Ash urged that Carolina was to be preferred to any of the northern British colonies.[2] Bradford admitted the economy of labour in warmer climates, but held that the influences upon settlers would be too enervating to hazard.

All the American writers were in agreement that a permanent population was indispensable to colonial success. The failure of the first Virginia settlements, said Beverley, was due to its " aiming more at sudden Gain, than to form any regular colony." [3] The Dutch West India Company, according to Donck, had made the same mistake.[4] Nor did he believe that a colony could ever be successful when settled by employees of a joint-stock company. When such colonists return to their home country they will take with them nothing " except a little in their purses and a bad name for the country." [5] John Smith's rules for colonization were lucid : " Make your plantations so neere and great " as you can ; [6] avoid difficult terms for acquiring land ; hold commonage to a minimum, for it usually bears most heavily on the poor ; avoid harsh impositions for the sake of present gain. Smith believed that the colonial land policy must be a liberal one ; each person should have freedom to plant as much as feasible. Finally, he believed that the good husbandman who had shown his ability during a period of trial, should be rewarded by liberal amounts of land in fee simple.[7]

[1] Donck Adrian, Van der. "Description of the New Netherlands." Amsterdam, 1655. Reprinted, *Old South Leaflets*, General Series, No. 69. Boston, p. 2.

[2] " The [Carolina] Planter in winter takes no care for their Provision which is a great Advantage ; the Northern Plantations obliging the Planters to spend great part of their Summer to provide fodder and Provision for their cattle, to preserve them from starving in the Winter." Ash, *op. cit.*, pp. 71-72.

[3] Beverley, *op. cit.*, pp. 43-44.

[4] Donck. *Representation*, pp. 38-39.

[5] *Ibid.*, p. 38.

[6] Smith. *Advertisements for the Unexperienced Planters*, p. 40.

[7] *Ibid.*, p. 41.

But whereas the industrious should be rewarded, the indolent should be punished. Idleness, said Smith, is not permitted in insect communities. Nor should it be in human. "Little hony hath that hive, where there are more drones than Bees : and miserable is that Land, where more are idle then well employed." [1] Unlike Smith, John Winthrop feared that a liberal land policy would deter men from coming to the colony since land adjacent to the settlements would be taken up by the first settlers.[2] Colonization, in his opinion, must be a co-operative venture, based upon mutual regard and charity whereby the colonists " confederate together in civil and church estate." [3]

Only a few American writers considered the question of whether or not the mother country should assist a colony financially. Governor Berkeley believed that the parent country should assist the colony in developing industries where great cost was involved.[4] One obscure writer urged that the " transcribing of colonies is chargeable, fittest for princes or states to undertake." [5] Only then could plantations be successful, for colonies " must be well grounded, well followed, and managed with great stocks of money, by men of resolution, that will not be daunted by ordinary accidents." [6]

A third question of colonization method related to the kind of people desired. John Winthrop, like Bacon, insisted that skilled artisans must be provided if any colony were to be successful.[7] In John Smith's opinion, a colony had two

---

[1] Smith, John. "A Description of New England." London, 1616. Reprinted, *Travels and Works of Captain John Smith* (Edw. Arber Edit.) Edinburgh, 1910, p. 179.
[2] Winthrop. *History*, Vol. I., p. 152.
[3] *Ibid.*, Vol. II., p. 87.
[4] Berkeley, *op. cit.*, p. 5.
[5] Vincent, P. "A True Relation of the late Battell fought in New England." London, 1638. Reprinted, 3 *Mass. Hist. Soc. Coll.*, VI., p. 41.
[6] Vincent, *op. cit.*, p. 41.
[7] Winthrop, John. "Conclusions for the Plantation in New England." 1629. Printed, Boston. *Pro. Mass. Hist. Soc.* 1865. Reprinted, *Old South Leaflets*, No. 50. General Series, Boston, 1894, pp. 2–3. Winthrop's original scheme called for the migration of " Carpenters, Masons, Smithes,

avenues of acquiring wealth. It could either be a centre for plundering operations, or it could be a place where wealth was obtained by labour. But in British America, he pointed out, " there is no country to pillage as the Romans found : all you expect from thence must be by labor." [1] In such a colony idleness was intolerable.[2] This also was the opinion of Edward Winslow [3] and of Robert Cushman ; " idle drones are intolerable in a settled commonwealth, much more in a commonwealth which is but as it were in the bud." [4] To the American writers, therefore, the evidence was plain. A colony demanded artisans and husbandmen, skilful and industrious. " One hundred good laborers," wrote Smith, are " better than a thousand such Gallants as were sent me." [5] The necessity of husbandmen was early recognized,[6] and became a principle of town planting. " Skillfull, honest, husbandmen," said one writer, are " ye tressells of ye tables of all ye kings of ye earth." [7]

The ways and means of attracting desirable colonists necessarily engaged the attention of the American writers. The natural reluctance of men to abandon the known conditions in their native country to " seek out a new, hazardous and careful one in a Foreign wilderness " was readily admitted.[8] For it was clearly seen that skilful labourers, though most desired, were the most difficult to attract and " only such servants as have been brought up to no art or

Coopers, Turners, Brickburners, Potters, Husbandmen, Fowlers, Vignerons, Saltmakers, fishermen and other laborers."

[1] Smith, John. "The Generall Historie of Virginia, New England & the Summer Isles." London, 1624. Reprinted, *Travels and Works of Capt. John Smith* (Edw. Arber Edit.) Edinburgh, 1910, p. 619.

[2] Smith. *Description of New England*, p. 179.

[3] Young, *op. cit.*, p. 374.

[4] *Ibid.*, p. 26.

[5] Smith. *Advertisements for the Unexperienced Planter*, p. 15.

[6] Thus Archdale, in 1707, pointed out that natural advantages do not in themselves mean prosperity, but only when coupled with industrious people. Archdale, John. "A New Description of Carolina." London, 1707. Reprinted, *Hist. Coll. S. C.*, Vol. II., p. 118.

[7] *Essay on the Laying out of Towns*, p. 474.

[8] *Narratives of Early Pennsylvania, West New Jersey and Delaware.* 1630–1707 (Albert Cook Myers Edit.) New York, 1912, p. 326.

Trade, hunger and fear of prisons bring to us." [1] Berkeley
saw clearly that the mobility of skilled artisans is low, and
that very high wages were necessary to induce them to
migrate to the colonies.[2] But whereas the first two decades
of American settlement had been hampered by the want of
proper colonists, a definite change set in about 1630 which
was to alter the character of American colonization. " The
ill conditions of the tymes," wrote John Winthrop in 1629,
are " likely to furnish those plantations with better members
then usually have undertaken that worke in former tymes." [3]
Beverley recorded that a definite change in the character of
colonists took place in Virginia after the climate and the
nature of the soil was better known, and after the most
hazardous period was passed. " People of better Condition,"
he wrote, " retired thither with their Families, either to
increase the Estates they had before, or else to avoid being
persecuted for their Principles of Religion or Government." [4]
As regards the earliest period of the Virginia colony, however,
he agreed with what Sir Josiah Child had said of the character
of the colonists.[5] New colonies, said Beverley, by their very
nature at first appeal to " Persons of low circumstances."
For men " of plentiful Estate " do not quickly " abandon a
happy certainty, to roam after imaginary advantages in a
new world." [6]

The theory that criminals would serve as colonists had its
adherents in the American colonies. Sir Thomas Dale wrote
from Virginia, in 1611, that the exportation of English felons
to that colony " would be a readie way to furnish us with
men, and not allwayse with the worst kinde of men either
for birth, spiritts or Bodie." [7] Governor Berkeley held that

---

[1] Berkeley, *op. cit.*, p. 4.
[2] *Ibid.*
[3] Winthrop. *Conclusions*, p. 1.
[4] Beverley, *op. cit.*, p. 249.
[5] Child, Sir Josiah. *New Discourse on Trade*, 1690. 5th Edition,
Glasgow, 1751, p. 138. " Virginia and Barbadoes were first peopled by a
sort of loose vagrant people, vicious and destitute of means," etc.
[6] Beverley, *op. cit.*, pp. 247–248.
[7] Letter of Sir Thomas Dale to Salisbury, 1611. Brown, *op. cit.*,
Vol. I., p. 506.

criminals and " those of the meanest quality and corruptest
lives " [1] make good colonizing material. " Rome," he
urged, was thus " begun and composed." Such men, in his
opinion, could endure the severity of colonization. Moreover they would guard the territory well. But like Bacon
and White in England, John Winthrop expressed his un-
qualified dissent. He purposed to avoid the causes of
failure of previous plantations one of which he conceived to
be the use of " unfitt instruments a multitude of rude &
misgoverned persons, the very scumme of the people." [2]

What, then, were the qualities of the good colonist ?

" The Utopian fancy of any projector," wrote Hubbard
in his *History of New England,* " may easily in imagination
frame a flourishing Plantation, in such a country as was
New England ; but to the actual accomplishing thereof there
is required a good number of resolving people, qualified with
industry, experience, prudence and estate." [3]

That which disqualified a colonist, in Edward Winslow's
opinion, was " a proud heart, a dainty tooth, a beggar's
purse, and an idle hand." [4] The desirable colonists, wrote
Pastorius from Pennsylvania, " must not only bring over
money, but a firm determination to labor and make themselves useful to our infant colony." [5] Among the American
writers there was no disagreement. The good colonist must
combine good sense, ability to labour and the possession of
capital.

III

With meticulous detail the American writers presented
the evidence to prove that colonization was theologically and
philosophically justifiable. In the case of John Winthrop,
the arguments were so prolix that one is prone to believe
he was in the process of convincing himself. In developing

[1] Berkeley, *op. cit.,* p. 3.
[2] Winthrop. *Conclusions,* p. 8.
[3] Hubbard, *op. cit.,* p. 87.
[4] Young, *op. cit.,* p. 374.
[5] Pastorius. *Description of Pennsylvania,* p. 16.

their arguments, the American writers necessarily drew
extensively upon similar English discussions and little new
material is discoverable.[1] The first scriptural warrant for
colonization was God's commandment that man should
increase, multiply, and replenish the earth.[2] Winthrop held
that this was the condition on which the gift of the earth to
man was made.[3] Even John Smith reiterated the familiar
theory that God made the world to be inhabited and that
the taking up of new land was necessarily warranted
thereby.[4] From this position it was a simple transition to
the thesis that unused land was scripturally seizable. " If
any sonne of Adam come and find a place empty," wrote
John Cotton, " he hath liberty to come and fill and subdue
the earth there." [5] Moreover, Cotton conceived this to be a

[1] The most laboured argument to prove the justice of American coloni-
zation was written by George Scot, in 1685, in his *Model of the Government
of the Province of East New Jersey.* Edinburgh, 1685. Reprinted, *Coll.
N. J. Hist. Soc.,* Vol. I., pp. 229–333, (1846). Scot added example to
precept, embarked for America but died before he reached the country.
He has accordingly been excluded from the American writers. Scot's
Model contains little original material. It repeats practically all of
White's *Planters Plea* as well as John Cotton's arguments. The gist of
Scot's argument may be summarized thus : Colonization is justified by
divine scripture and by nature ; the commandment to replenish and subdue
the earth makes expansion mandatory, for this was a universal not a
temporary precept. It binds mankind while any void places on earth
continue to exist. Wherever vacant land exists, therefore, colonies may
be established without the consent of the inhabitants. Since the earth is
God's gift to man, it would be an injury to God's majesty not to use it, and
only by habitation and culture can it be used. The institution of marriage
is a prototype of colonization and a further scriptural warrant. Colonization redounds to God's honour for it reveals the extent of his munificence
to the Sons of Men. God has sanctioned colonies for the " disburthening "
of excess population and for replenishing waste areas. How much more
readily does God sanction colonization for the spreading of Christianity !
Colonization is compatible with natural law, for Nature teaches bees to
swarm. When the hive of the kingdom is full, tradesmen should do likewise. Colonization is theologically lawful when it is a means of permitting
the individual to better employ his talents. It is lawful for men to go to
colonies to seek knowledge. Finally, since colonization is theologically
and philosophically warranted, the state should proclaim liberty to migrate
for those who may wish to do so. Scot, *op. cit.,* pp. 250–258.
[2] Hubbard, *op. cit.,* p. 26 ; Winthrop. *Conclusions,* p. 5 ; Cotton,
John. *God's Promise to His Plantation.* London, 1630, p. 5.
[3] Winthrop. *Conclusions,* p. 5.
[4] Smith. *Advertisements for Unexperienced Planters,* p. 22.
[5] Cotton. *God's Promise to His Plantation,* p. 5.

" principle in Nature " ;[1] and in this opinion he was supported by Winthrop, Cushman, and John Smith.

Winthrop, in his *Conclusions*, argued that men have a double right to the earth ; a natural and a civil right. The natural right to the earth existed when men held all land in common. To this was added a special or civil right to specific areas of land " by enclosing, and peculiar manurance, and this in time gave them a Civill right."[2] This enunciation of a labour theory of property[3] was therefore sufficient justification for the taking up of land in New England, " for the Natives . . . inclose noe land neither have any setled habitation nor any tame cattle to improve their land by."[4] The establishment of the early Christian churches in Asia Minor was colonization approved by God.[5] Nature teaches bees to swarm and " seeke abroad for new dwellings."[6] It is sinful to allow land to be unoccupied when scarcity of land elsewhere means distress.[7] If it was lawful for the patriarchs to migrate to less crowded areas,[8] so was it as lawful to appropriate the land of the American aborigines who had neither " art, science, skill, faculty to use either the land or the commodities of it."[9] Colonization, therefore, was an honourable work,[10] warranted by God's direction, consonant with the principle of Nature, and economically advantageous. In England, said Winthrop, men may spend

" as much labour & cost to recover or keep somtymes a Acre or two of land as would procure them many hundred as good or better in another country and in ye mean tyme suffer a whole Continent as fruitful and convenient for the use of man to lie waste."[11]

[1] Cotton. *God's Promise to His Plantation*, p. 5.
[2] Winthrop. *Conclusions*, p. 6.
[3] The same theory is to be found in Grotius, *De Belli et Pacis*, I., 3, 8, 6.
[4] Winthrop. *Conclusions*, p. 7.
[5] Cotton. *God's Promise to His Plantation*, p. 9.
[6] *Ibid.*
[7] Smith. *Advertisements for the Unexperienced Planters*, p. 22.
[8] Mourt, G. *A Relation or Journal of the Beginnings and Proceedings of the English Plantation settled at Plimouth*. London, 1622. Dexter Edit., Boston, 1865, p. 243.
[9] Cushman, Robert. In Young, *op. cit.*, p. 244.
[10] *Ibid.*, p. 263.
[11] Winthrop. *Conclusions*, p. 5.

IV

Whereas the English writers on colonization were zealous in enumerating the economic benefits which the mother country would derive from colonies, only a few of the Americans stated the home country arguments. John Smith incorporated into his writings a passage from Strachey's *Virginia* in which it was argued that Virginia could supply those commodities which England had previously imported from " Muscovia and Polonia." This would eliminate the loss of specie necessary to pay for Baltic imports, and make England self-sufficient.[1] Berkeley explained, that from England's point of view, Virginia was economically superior to Barbadoes, because whereas the former could provide her own food, Barbadoes would be " forced to expend one-fifth part of their [exportable] Merchandise to provide Victuals." [2] A good colony, said Ash, must be self-sufficient in food and livestock [3] if it is to be of advantage to the mother country. The benefit of a colony to the mother country, said John Archdale, should consist of consuming commodities of the mother country and by " bringing great Duties to the Crown, by importing Goods or Commodities thence." [4] John Hammond was caught up with the mercantilist dream of economic self-sufficiency when he wrote :

" It is the glory of every Nation to enlarge themselves, to encourage their own forraign attempts, and to be able to have of their own, within their territories, as many several commodities as they can attain to that so others may rather be beholding to them, than they to others." [5]

---

[1] Smith, John. " A Map of Virginia." Oxford, 1612. Reprinted, *Travels and Works of Captain John Smith* (Edw. Arber Edit.) Edinburgh, 1910, p. 64. Cf. Strachey, William. *The Historie of Travaile into Virginia Britannia*. Printed by the Hakluyt Society, London, 1849.

[2] Berkeley, *op. cit.*, p. 12.

[3] Ash, *op. cit.*, p. 67.

[4] Archdale, *op. cit.*, p. 97.

[5] Hammond, John. " Leah and Rachel or the Two Fruitful Sisters Virginia and Maryland." London, 1656. Reprinted, *Peter Force Hist. Tracts*. Vol. III., Washington, 1844, p. 6.

But writers who presented the home country argument were the exception rather than the rule. In fact, even those who did take the mother country point of view often tempered it with a colonial point of view. Berkeley, for example, accepted the principle that colonial trade should be confined to the mother country only on the condition that it "be found either beneficial to the Crown or our Mother Country." [1] But unless the benefits were evident, "we cannot but resent, that forty thousand people should be impoverish'd to enrich little more than forty Merchants." However, if colonial interests were guarded, colonies could supply the mother country with goods previously bought from foreigners and thereby eliminate the efflux of specie.[2] He estimated that colonial provision of sugar and cotton would save "yearly a Million of pounds sterling." [3] Donck presented the home country argument in essentially the same vein. In his criticism of the Dutch West India Company, he alleged that the administration of the colony by the Company retarded the growth of population in the colony. Yet, if New Netherlands were properly administered and governed, he predicted that it could become the means whereby Holland might become economically independent of other countries.[4] But " good privileges and exemptions," he conceived to be the " mother of population " [5] and these the Company did not provide. It is clear, then, that few American writers took the home country point of view regarding the colonies, and some of those who did take this position were really seeking a politic way of furthering the ends of the colonists.

V

What economic benefits did the American writers expect colonies to provide ? In the order of their relative importance, four functions seem clear : first, refuge from economic

[1] Berkeley, *op. cit.*, pp. 6–7.
[2] *Ibid.*, p. 10.
[3] *Ibid.*
[4] Donck. *Representation of New Netherlands*, p. 36.
[5] *Ibid.*, pp. 69–70.

oppression and the provision of economic opportunity ;
secondly, opportunity to regulate economic matters in
accordance with religious or moral ideals ; thirdly, a solution
of the English population problem ; and lastly, provision
of goods desired by the mother country. This programme
was similar to that of the English writers and at the same
time strangely dissimilar in its emphasis.

In new colonies, wrote John Smith, there are " no hard
Landlords to racke us with high rents," nor " tedious pleas
in law to consume us with their many years disputation for
Justice." [1] If men are overburdened with debts, said John
Cotton, a colony will provide a place to which they may
retire, " not to defraud their creditors (for God is an avenger
of such things) but to gaine further opportunity to discharge
their debts." [2] Abraham and Lot, said Robert Cushman,
parted because of " the straitness of the land." [3] In
England, a similar " straitness " demanded colonization as
a remedy. Emigration would result in a double advantage :
mitigation of England's economic distress, and the improvement of the condition of the colonist. [4] Winthrop believed
moral decay in England had brought about the economic
oppression which colonization could overcome. [5] Even if
the colony could not provide abundance, life could be
simplified and at least the rank inequality of old countries
could be alleviated. [6] Self interest, therefore, coupled with
a feeling of charity, should impell emigration. [7] Moreover,
in the colony, " nature and liberty affords us that freely,
which in England we want, or it costeth us dear." [8] The

---

[1] Smith. *Description of New England*, pp. 195–196.
[2] Cotton. *God's Promise to His Plantation*, p. 10.
[3] Young, *op. cit.*, pp. 246–247.
[4] *Ibid.*, p. 249. " The present consumption which grows upon us here
[England or Holland ?], whilst the land groaneth under so many closefisted and unmerciful men, being compared with the easiness, plainness and
plentyfulness in living in these remote parts, may quickly persuade any
man to a liking of this course and to practice a removal."
[5] Winthrop. *Conclusions*, p. 5.
[6] Cushman, Robert. In Young, *op. cit.*, p. 248.
[7] Winthrop. *Conclusions*, p. 2.
[8] Smith. *Description of New England*, pp. 212–213.

American colonies, wrote Gabriel Thomas, would provide genuine opportunities, " for Poor People (both men and women) of all kinds, can here get three times the wages for their Labour they can in England or Wales." [1] Thomas saw that this differential was largely caused by the possibility which labourers had of becoming agricultural entrepreneurs in a country where land was abundant. [2]

A second economic advantage which colonies could provide was the opportunity to regulate economic matters in accordance with religious or moral ideals. This goal of colonization was an important consideration in American colonial theory which found chief expression in New England. The belief that a group of colonists should have unrestricted right to create what they believed to be a correct or ethical economic system was a corner-stone of American Puritanism. [3] Winthrop complained that in England " all arts & trades are carried on in that deceiptfull & unrighteous course, as it is almost impossible for a good & upright man to maintaine his charge and live comfortable in them." [4] Only in a new colony could economic reconstruction in the economic sphere be effected. The whole history of early New England is the proof of this belief. Those who were considered a menace to the religious ideals of the colony were summarily dealt with. The very actions of the Puritan leaders revealed their colonial philosophy. In Plymouth, Governor Bradford tried to control the situation by the distribution of economic privilege. Colonization for the purposes of trade was indeed considered lawful, but the pursuit of trade must in no way

[1] Thomas, Gabriel. " An Historical and Geographical Account of Pennsilvania and of West New Jersey." London, 1698. Reprinted, *Narratives of Early Pennsylvania, West New Jersey and Delaware.* New York, 1912, p. 326.
[2] *Ibid.*, p. 328.
[3] No satisfactory exposition of this doctrine as a factor in the character of New England's economic development is available. Roland Usher saw clearly its importance in the history of Plymouth and has shown how the power of withholding economic privilege was the means whereby the Plymouth colony attempted to mould its economic development in conformity with a preconceived ideal. Cf. Usher, Roland G. *The Pilgrims and their History.* New York, 1918. Chapter XVI.
[4] Winthrop. *Conclusions*, p. 5.

obstruct the more laudable purposes for which colonies were to be founded.[1] With militant earnestness, Edward Johnson declared, " let not any Merchants Inkeepers, Taverners and men of Trade in hope of gaine, fling open the gates so wide, as that by letting in all sorts you mar the worke of Christ intended." [2]

A third function, which the American writers believed a colony could perform, was to help solve the English population problem. It is unfortunate, said Higginson, that there should exist simultaneously unoccupied land and economic distress.[3] He believed that England's economic distress was caused by the " populousnesse thereof," and that colonization was the remedy. Cushman held the same view : " Let us not thus oppress, straiten and afflict one another, but seeing there is a spacious land, the way to which is through the sea, we will end this difference in a day." [4] Winthrop likewise considered depopulation of England as one function of a colony. The density of population, he believed, necessitated emigration since " this land growes weary of her Inhabitants." [5] Efflux of people to colonies, he urged, would decrease the burden of poor relief, and would render unnecessary all legislation about cottages designed to restrict the increase of population, for " if things were right," an increase of people instead of being a burden, " would be the chieftest earthly blessinge." [6] John Smith argued that colonies could serve as an outlet for the poor artificers and labourers of England and showed that their exodus would lower the parish charges for poor relief.[7]

Last in the category of economic benefits came provision of goods desired by the mother country. Neglect of this subject differentiates the American from the English writers.

---

[1] Cotton. *God's Promise to His Plantation*, pp. 8–9.
[2] Johnson, *op. cit.*, p. 35.
[3] Higginson, Rev. Francis. *New England's Plantation.* London, 1630. Facsimile Edition, Salem, 1908, p. 34.
[4] Young, *op. cit.*, p. 247.
[5] Winthrop. *Conclusions*, p. 5.
[6] *Ibid.*
[7] Smith. *Advertisements for the Unexperienced Planters*, p. 19.

As has been already shown, there were only a few of the American writers who advanced the home country argument for colonies, among whom John Smith was the ablest exponent. The real usefulness of the colonies, he held, lay in their capacity to provide commodities which the mother country could not produce. Such goods would tend to make the mother country self-sufficient and if there were commodities for which there was a brisk international demand, these could be sold to foreigners by the mother country and become " the means whereby they raise that mighty charge of drawing out their gold and silver to the great and clear revenue of their King." [1] Gold and silver, he went on to say, are not the greatest wealth that a plantation can afford,[2] in fact, the economic position of Holland, Smith held, was rather due to her fisheries ; " This contemptible trade of fish . . . is their myne ; and the Sea the source of those silvered streames of all their virtues ; which hath made them now the very miracle of industrie." [3] Smith even disparaged the much heralded advantage of Spain. The rich gains of that nation, he explained, were due to the pillage of a relatively advanced civilization.[4] Such gains are of doubtful benefit in the long run, he argued, because the sources of treasure are soon exhausted and the " charge of getting those Metals is grown excessive." [5]

In brief, only John Smith and a few others developed the principle that the colony could serve mercantilist purposes of the mother country. Other writers, like Winthrop [6] and Higginson,[7] enumerated the goods which an American colony could produce. But they failed to develop the argument that this was a *raison d'être* of a colony. Berkeley made a passing remark that probably the English plantations would make England independent of Turkey, Persia, Germany,

[1] Smith. *Generall Historie*, p. 582.
[2] *Ibid.*, p. 581.
[3] Smith. *Description of New England*, p. 194.
[4] Smith. *Generall Historie*, p. 464.
[5] *Ibid.*, p. 587.
[6] Winthrop. *Conclusions*, p. 2.
[7] Higginson, *op. cit.*, p. 34.

Poland, Russia, France and Spain,[1] while Budd pointed out that the abundance of timber would make possible the development of shipbuilding.[2] John Smith believed that the colonies could be a

" nurse for soldiers, a practice for mariners, a trade for merchants, a reward for the good, and that which is most of all, a businesse (most acceptible to God) to bring such poore infidels to the true knowledge of God and his holy Gospell." [3]

The optimistic belief of the English writers that colonization would effect a moral regeneration found an echo in the colonies as well. An improvement in economic conditions, said Berkeley, will alter and improve human nature ; men of " ungoverned manners and affections " will " change them there for sober and thrifty passions." [4] The hope and possibility of acquiring an economic competence, he believed, quickens industry and bridles intemperance while the " manifest knowledge of this makes men industrious and vigilant." So confident was John Smith of the regenerating force of colonies that he naïvely remarked that a colony could be literally founded with idlers, because

" could they but once taste the sweet fruites of their owne labours, doubtlesse many thousands would be advised by good discipline, to take more pleasure in honest industrie, then in their humors of dissolute idlenesse." [5]

The elaborate mercantilist justification of colonies, which the English writers had advanced, finds but a feeble echo among the American pioneers who sought to make the colonial dream a reality. The colonist naturally looked upon the colony as a place which should provide greater personal economic opportunity ; religious groups hoped for freedom

[1] Berkeley, *op. cit.*, p. 7.
[2] Budd, *op. cit.*, p. 42.
[3] Smith. *Map of Virginia*, p. 64.
[4] Berkeley, *op. cit.*, pp. 3–4.
[5] Smith. *Description of New England*, p. 202. Only one reference has been found to the idea that colonization would decrease crime. Miller, John. *New York Considered and Improved*, 1695. Printed, Cleveland, 1903, p. 63.

to devise economic institutions which would harmonize with their ethical ideals. Men with genuine humanitarian instincts considered the colony as a place of refuge for England's poor. Only a few writers proposed that the colony should serve the mercantilist purposes which England sought. Perhaps these writers were more diplomatic than sincere.

ETHICS AND ECONOMICS: THE VINDICATION OF WEALTH

" All we have, is but a Loan from the Great God unto us. Now, if we be so Unthankful, that we will not particularly and Affectionately Recognize the Kindness of God unto us in such a Loan, is it not very Reasonable that we should come to have a Loss instead of a Loan ? "

Cotton Mather, *Durable Riches*.

CHAPTER V

ETHICS AND ECONOMICS:
THE VINDICATION OF WEALTH

I

PREMISES for speculations which were as incidental and as subordinate to economic policy as were those of the seventeenth century cannot be expected to be accurately expressed or even clearly conceived. Colonial ideas of the nature of man as an economic being, and of man's wealth-obtaining and wealth-using activities, are fragmentary, poorly expressed and scarce. But in the literature of the period a considerable number of pertinent suggestions are to be found. A worthy effort was made to appraise wealth and to assign a place to wealth-getting in a general scale of values.

The discussion of economic matters by the seventeenth-century Americans, in comparison with modern economic literature, is distinctly theological. But it must not be supposed that the limitation of economic matters by moral considerations was peculiar to the seventeenth-century Americans or that it was anything new in the history of ideas. The ideal that a moral principle should guide men in their economic relations is as old as antiquity. The Greek writers made this a fundamental part of their social theory. With the rise of the Christian religion the moral principle in the economic sphere was further emphasized, and the exact moral considerations which should obtain in economic relations were set forth with care by the Church Fathers and the Schoolmen. Lest, however, the ideals of the founders of the American colonies should appear novel, it may be well to summarize, in briefest form, some economic aspects of medieval philosophy.

Wealth, said the medieval theologians, is a necessary means whereby man accomplishes his destiny ! [1] A certain amount of wealth is necessary for the practice of virtue. Thus a man must support his family, and it is justifiable to accumulate for that purpose. Moreover, men are appointed, by God's providence, for certain tasks ; each has a function to perform. For the accomplishment of these respective missions, more or less wealth is necessary. Acquisition is necessary and reasonable if directed to a meritorious end. But the means whereby this end is accomplished must not be allowed to obscure the end itself. God endowed the earth with wealth and intended man should use it, but man must make good use of the divine gift. If wealth is properly used, the result will be the accomplishment of social peace. The Christian theory of duty gave the key to the ways of using wealth. Man's duty to God made the good use of wealth mandatory, while man's duty to his fellow man demanded that wealth should be administered with temperance, prudence and charity. The proper use of wealth is discoverable from Scripture and by reason. Liberality must be balanced against prodigality, temperance must prevent excess and luxury, charity demands relief of the poor and oppressed. The state must have wealth, because the ruler must maintain social well-being. But wealth must always be a means to attaining the Christian's ideal : a life in conformity with God's commandments.

The American writers dealt with man's acquisitive activities ; with wealth, its purposes, use, and desirability, in a method essentially similar to that of their ecclesiastical predecessors. But the details are significant and must be examined with care.

[1] What moralists have said about wealth and man's relation to wealth is co-extensive with the history of philosophy. The medieval theories represent, however, a high development of these theories and suffice as an introduction to the American discussion. The most concise statement of medieval economic philosophy is in Brant's, Victor, *Èsquisse Des Théories Économiques Des XIIIe et XIVe Siècles.* Louvain, 1895.

II

The persistence of man's acquisitive propensities was explained by Winthrop on theological grounds ; by Mitchell on the rationality of accumulation. Adam, said Winthrop, was originally a " perfect modell of mankind." [1] But Adam " rent himselfe from his Creator, rent all his posterity allsoe one from another." [2] In consequence of this original sin, man is " borne with this principle in him to love and seeke himselfe only." [3] The results of this innate tendency were held to be both beneficial and undesirable ; were both condoned and condemned. One important duty of a ruler, said Jonathan Mitchell, in an election sermon, is to seek the wealth and welfare of the people. If this be the duty of the ruler, " then surely people themselves are not to prejudice or neglect their own welfare." [4]

The American writers understood that human wants are capable of indefinite expansion. Every philosopher who had plumbed deeply enough into the nature of man has understood this tendency. William Hughes, in the preface to his *American Physician*, showed that he was acquainted with what philosophers said on the subject when he wrote :

"As for Riches no philosopher ever yet, either Ancient or Modern, could give a sufficient or satisfactory definition of it, there being no bounds to be set to a covetous man's desire." [5]

If man's wants are insatiable, man was evidently " made for some more notable end " than the mere accumulation of wealth. " Riches," wrote the author of *Good News from Virginia*, " have no limits, but still crie, plus ultra, still more." [6] Wealth is a relative matter. No person is " absolutely rich," but only " in comparison of a poorer man . . .

---

[1] Winthrop. *Modell of Christian Charity*, p. 41.
[2] *Ibid.*
[3] " And thus," continued Winthrop, " a man continueth until Christ comes and takes possession of the soule and infuseth another principle."
[4] Mitchell, Jonathan. *Nehemiah on the Wall*, p. 24.
[5] Hughes, William. *The American Physician*. London, 1672, Preface.
[6] " Good News from Virginia," Brown, *op. cit.*, p. 580.

that hath lesse than he." [1]   If wealth were in reality as important as men are prone to believe, why did Christ disregard it ?   Indeed this writer concluded that wealth is a " heavy burthen to some, an Idoll to others, and profitable to few."

The pursuit of wealth was recognized to be an engrossing one,[2] and the Christian was cautioned that the striving after wealth might become so dominant as to become the equivalent of worship.[3]   To Bradford, riches were " mutable things of this unstable world." [4]   Yet as a faithful recorder of human nature, he added that " men set their harts upon them, though they dayly see ye vanity therof." [5]   But whereas Bradford condemned the pursuit of wealth as " vanity ", it by no means follows that there was no place in his philosophy or actual practice for the acquisition of wealth.   His stern criticism of communism, for its failure to produce a sufficiency of goods, is proof enough that he approved of wealth and its acquisition.   Bradford was rather concerned with the subordination of economic to spiritual activity.   His co-worker, Edward Winslow, gave more definite expression to this ideal.   The end which man should seek should be God's glory " as a principal, and all outward good things but as accessories." [6]   Those enterprises, therefore, in which religion and profit were combined were the particular province for the Christian.[7]

The belief of the seventeenth-century American writers that wealth was a necessary incentive to industry and progress can be inferred from two sources : from the few positive statements that are to be found, and from the criticisms of communistic experiments.   The hope of economic competence, said Berkeley, quickens industry and

[1] " Good News from Virginia," Brown, *op. cit.*, p. 580.
[2] Mitchell, *op. cit.*, pp. 5–6.
[3] Williams, Roger. " Letters." *Publications of the Narragansett Club.* Vol. VI. Providence, 1874, p. 319.
[4] Bradford, *op. cit.*, p. 160.
[5] *Ibid.*
[6] Young, *op. cit.*, p. 374.
[7] *Ibid.*, p. 372.

bridles intemperance.[1] Adrian Van der Donck held that
the economic welfare of New Netherlands was dependent
upon freedom and that any restriction of " individual gain or
private trade " would lead to economic decay.[2] Bradford
recognized that only if individuals were permitted to have
the continuous use of land would the greatest production be
forthcoming.[3] This principle was subsequently recognized
in the laying out of new towns.[4] John Smith took pains to
point out that all great migrations in history had been
caused by men's attempts to better themselves economically,[5] and Beverley demonstrated that a profit motive had
overshadowed other motives in the settlement of new
plantations.[6] Donck held that heavy taxation tends to
repress enterprise.[7]

Further evidence of the necessity of economic motives is
found in the colonial criticism of communism. Most of this
discussion is not concerned with communism in the abstract
but with the actual experiences with communistic attempts
in the early colonies. Whatever generalizations are available
proceed from these experiences. Bradford said that the
Plymouth experiment " was found to breed much confusion
& discontent, and retard much employment that would have
been to their benefite and comforte." [8] The individual use
of land, on the other hand, " made all hands very industrious," [9] because it made labour much less irksome. In
modern phraseology, it eliminated the subjective conditions,
which, under communism, had increased the real costs of
production. The author of the *Essay on the Laying out of
Towns* condemned communism of land because it would
tend to repress enterprise. But under private property, he

---

[1] Berkeley, *op. cit.*, pp. 3–4.
[2] Donck. *Representation of New Netherlands*, p. 39.
[3] Bradford, *op. cit.*, p. 201.
[4] *Essay on the Laying out of Towns*, pp. 478–479.
[5] Smith. *Advertisements for the Unexperienced Planters*, pp. 22–23.
[6] Beverley, *op. cit.*, pp. 43–44.
[7] Donck. *Description of New Netherlands*, p. 64.
[8] Bradford. *op. cit.*, p. 163.
[9] *Ibid.*, p. 162.

urged, each land holder would strive to emulate his neighbour.[1] Winslow maintained that self-love, "wherewith every man in a measure more or less, loveth and prefereth his own good before his neighbours,"[2] made communism inexpedient. Bradford echoed the venerable theological argument that communism was an ideal economy for ideal men, but added that " seeing all men have this corruption in them, God in his wisdome saw another course fiter for them."[3]

From the colonial writers' remarks on economic motives, we may therefore conclude that man's acquisitive activity, except in an ideal society, proceeds from self-love. Self-love is the consequence of ethical imperfections which were brought about by man's fall from grace. But given these imperfections, economic striving for private gain emerges. This striving is worthy of cultivation only because of the superior social consequences which result as compared with economic productivity of a form of socialism whereof the social constituents are imperfect ethical beings.

III

But this interesting rationalization of the basis of economic society by no means gave " carte blanche " to unrestrained private acquisitive activity. Mere avaricious self-seeking was consistently condemned. Self-seeking was relegated to a strictly utilitarian position, rather than exalted as a cardinal principle of social structure. With the great colonizers of history, said John Smith, wealth was a servant, not a master.[4] Edward Johnson gave warning that the gates must not be opened too wide for merchants and inkeepers,[5]

---

[1] *Essay on the Laying out of Towns*, pp. 478–479.
[2] Young, *op. cit.*, p. 347.
[3] Bradford, *op. cit.*, p. 164.   Similarly in England, Bishop Hugh Latimer adduced as proof that communism was not in the divine intention the argument that the Mosaic commandment, " Thou shalt not steal," would have been unnecessary had God intended a state of communism. Latimer, Bishop Hugh. "Remains," Vol. I., p. 406 ff. *Publications of Parker Society.*
[4] Smith.   *Advertisements for the Unexperienced Planters*, pp. 22–23.
[5] Johnson, *op. cit.*, p. 254.

because unrestricted seeking of profit might jeopardize the attaining of the more fundamental ideals for which the Massachusetts Bay Colony had been established. Pure self-seeking can never bring success, declared Robert Cushman.[1] Beverley pointed out that the pursuit of private gain did not necessarily bring about social well-being,[2] and maintained that the quest for profits in Virginia had prevented the diversification of industry and true economic prosperity.[3] " Whilst men are all for their private profit," wrote Vincent, " the public good is neglected and languisheth."[4] Increase Mather preached that search for profit does not bring social welfare. As proof thereof, he pointed to the export of money whereby an individual might grow rich, while the country as a whole suffered from lack of currency.[5] Indeed, said this famous divine, " sometimes one man by seeking to advance himself has brought great misery on whole nations."[6] The wise man, said Thomas Morton, desires "neither riches nor poverty . . . but a meane between both."[7]

Neither did the seventeenth-century Americans countenance the unrestrained consumption of wealth. Intemperance in consumption, said Winthrop, degenerates public morals.[8] The colonial records abound with condemnation of excessive consumption and a long series of laws attempted to repress this social evil. Literally thousands of criticisms of intemperate consumption are to be found, but a few illustrations will suffice. Edward Johnson lamented that " the plenty of cloathing hath caused much excess of late."[9] Winthrop took Thomas Dudley to task for constructing an unnecessarily elaborate house for himself and thereby setting

[1] Young, *op. cit.*, p. 265.
[2] Beverley, *op. cit.*, p. 46.
[3] *Ibid.*, p. 281.
[4] Vincent. *True Relation*, p. 41.
[5] Mather, Increase. *The Excellency of a Public Spirit*, p. 26.
[6] *Ibid.*
[7] Morton, Thomas. *New English Canaan*. Amsterdam, 1637, p. 12.
[8] Winthrop. *Conclusions*, p. 5.
[9] Johnson, *op. cit.*, p. 211.

a bad example for the community.[1] Winthrop also recorded,
in his history, that in 1638 the General Court

" taking into consideration the great disorder through the
country in costliness of apparel, and following new fashions, sent
for the elders of the churches and conferred with them about it,
and laid it upon them, as belonging to them to redress it." [2]

Through the century the clergy were eloquent in condemning
excessive consumption while at the very close of the century
Cotton Mather upbraided prodigals who " squander away a
vast deal of their Estates in Profane, Wicked, Wretched
uses ; and in the pleasing of some Lust or other." [3] The
legislative records give further evidence of the prevailing
colonial belief that positive prohibitions could regulate consumption.   Hubbard believed undesirable consumption
could be deterred by taxation.[4]

IV

The author of *Good News from Virginia* classified human
wants as Aristotle had classified them in the *Politics*.[5]
" The wants of man bee divers," wrote the Virginian ;
" some are of the minde, some of the bodie, and some be of
the outward goods." [6] Among the American writers, both
the Christian doctrine of stewardship and the Aristotelian
classification of the nature of human wants pointed to the
necessity of wealth.   Aristotle and the medieval theologians
wrestled with the problem of how much wealth men should
seek.   The American patriarchs did likewise.

The requisite amount of wealth, however, is both an

---

[1] Winthrop. *History of New England.*   Vol. I., pp. 73-74.
[2] *Ibid.*, Vol. I., p. 275.
[3] Mather. *Durable Riches*, Part 2, p. 33.
[4] Hubbard, *op. cit.*, p. 520.
[5] " Certainly no one will dispute the propriety of that partition of goods
which separates them into three classes, viz., external goods, goods of the
body and goods of the soul, or deny that the happy man must have all
three." Aristotle. *Politics.* (Translated by Benjamin Jowett) Oxford
University Press Edition.   Oxford, 1920, p. 257.
[6] " Good News from Virginia," Brown, *op. cit.*, p. 581.

economic problem and an ethical question. Bradford understood that more wealth was necessary in temperate climates than in the tropical.[1] Donck pointed out that less was needed in New Netherlands than in New France,[2] while Ash held that less was needed in Carolina than in the northern British colonies.[3] William Wood pointed out that, in America, what might appear to be poverty might actually be well-being due to the abundance and cheapness of necessaries.[4] Morton, in his curious polemic, idealized the Indian economy in which men " live by the light of nature." [5] John Miller implied that men are better off where wealth is limited. In the early history of New York, he said, the " mean accomodations or at best the no great riches," explained the minimum of thieving and robbing.[6]

By wealth, said the learned Cotton Mather, " we are furnished against the Natural Inconveniences of Humane Life." It is obtained neither by skill nor chance but through God's bounty. Men are rich or poor according to God's election.[7] Winthrop had voiced the same opinion in his *Conclusions* [8] and in his *Modell of Christian Charity*,[9] and to this thesis Judge Sewall lent his assent.[10] Wealth is a part of the welfare of a people, said Jonathan Mitchell, " though not the greatest part, as the world is apt to esteem it." [11] But that the state must have wealth was clearly recognized, and John Cotton when he drew up his ideal code of laws for Massachusetts Bay, provided for legislation

---

[1] Bradford, *op. cit.*, p. 36.
[2] Donck. *Description of New Netherlands*, p. 2.
[3] Ash, *op. cit.*, pp. 71-72.
[4] Wood, William. *New England's Prospect*. London, 1634. Reprinted, Boston, 1764. Boynton Edition, 1898, p. 51. " And howsoever they are accounted poore, they are well contented, and look not so much at abundance, as a competence." *Ibid.*
[5] Morton, *op. cit.*, p. 57.
[6] Miller, *op. cit.*, p. 63.
[7] Mather. *Durable Riches*, Part II., p. 2.
[8] Winthrop. *Conclusions*, p. 6.
[9] Winthrop. *Modell of Christian Charity*, p. 34.
[10] Sewall, Samuel. " The Selling of Joseph." Boston, 1700. Reprinted *Historical Magazine*, June, 1864, p. 195.
[11] Mitchell, Jonathan. *Nehemiah on the Wall*, p. 4.

which would create and maintain a treasury, " because no commonwealth can maintain either their authority at home or their honor and power abroad, without a sufficient treasury." [1]   Increase Mather held that to seek the wealth of the community is " in a singular manner the duty of Rulers." [2]   Jonathan Mitchell, in his election sermon of 1667, laid the same obligation upon the good ruler.   To further the wealth of the commonwealth was an essential province of government " especially in reference to necessary livelyhood." [3]

Much has been written recently about the Calvinistic explanation of the rise of capitalism.[4]   There is little significant evidence to support this thesis in the writings of the American Puritans.   To be sure one finds the familiar doctrine of stewardship as a part of the American philosophy of wealth, but this is not peculiar to Calvinism.   There is no more idealization of wealth accumulation than there is in the Catholic economic literature.   Winthrop, in his *Modell of Christian Charity*, does say that the Gospel law not only sanctions but expects the accumulation of wealth, but this is not a blanket justification, since Winthrop qualifies the statement.   " It is not only lawfull but necessary to *lay upp as Joseph did* to have ready upon such occasions, as the Lord (whose stewards wee are of them) shall call for them from us." [5]   But to " lay up as Joseph did " and to accumulate indefinitely are two quite different ideas.   The American Puritans admitted the necessity of wealth, for the state and for the individual, but they did not glorify wealth accumulation.   Rather the pursuit of wealth took its place among other activities all subordinate to the spiritual.   The temporal welfare of a people, said Jonathan Mitchell, consists in safety (public and personal) ;   the maintenance of civil honesty ;   " Prosperity in matters of outward Estate and

---

[1] Cotton, John. *An Abstract of the Laws of New England.*
[2] Mather. *Excellency of Public Spirit*, p. 11.
[3] Mitchell, Jonathan. *Nehemiah on the Wall*, p. 4.
[4] Cf. the writings of Werner Sombart, Max Weber, and R. H. Tawney
[5] Winthrop. *Modell of Christian Charity*, p. 57.

Liveleyhood " ; [1] tranquillity for the enjoyment of all religious and civil good things. In this classification wealth is but one among many desired things of life.

V

That wealth was a loan to man from a benevolent God was a cornerstone of the American economic thought of the seventeenth century. " Free men," said Roger Williams, " are not free Lords of their owne estates, but are onely stewards under God." [2] In accordance with this celestial origin, therefore, must wealth be administered and disposed. It must not be wasted or mis-spent, for a strict account will be required of each legatee at the day of judgment.[3] Indeed the temporary use of God-given wealth should result in human gratitude. Cotton Mather tersely epitomized the doctrine when he said :

" All that we have is but a Loan from the Great God unto us. Now, if we be so Unthankful, that we will not particularly and affectionately Recognize the Kindness of God unto us in such a Loan, is it not very Reasonable that we should come to have a Loss instead of a Loan ? " [4]

The wealth given to man must be improved for God's glory ; it is the " Means of Cultivation Employ'd by the Great God upon us." [5] Economic reverses, according to Mather, were manifestations of God's displeasure. Nor should this be the occasion for surprise or wonder because " if we are Unfruitful

---

[1] Mitchell, Jonathan. *Nehemiah on the Wall*, pp. 3–5.

[2] Williams, Roger. "The Bloody Tenant of Persecution." 1664. Reprinted, *Publications of the Narragansett Club*, Vol. III., Providence, 1867, p. 254.

[3] Neill, Edward D. *History of the Virginia Company of London*, Albany, 1869, p. 81. " How shamefully do the most of you either miserably detaine or wickedly mispend God's goods whereof he made you his stewards. The Prodigal men of our land make hast to fling away God's treasure. . . . How much better were it for those men to remember the affliction of Joseph, to extend the bowels of their compassion to the poore, the fatherless, the afflicted and the like than to mispend that which they must give a strict account of at the day of Judgment."

[4] Mather. *Durable Riches*, p. 13.

[5] *Ibid.*, p. 14.

after all 'tis but Reasonable that we should be deprived of those Means." [1] The ownership of wealth is never man's to enjoy ; only the use of wealth is his privilege. God " has not parted with His own Right in it all. No, He still is the Lord Proprietor of all." [2]

It was the doctrine of stewardship of wealth which formed the logical understructure of the colonial theory of the use of wealth. Reference has already been made to man's obligation to husband carefully his economic resources. But the discussion went much farther. What constitutes proper use of wealth ? This was a nice theological problem which Roger Williams and Cotton Mather sought respectively to solve. Inquiries such as these exhibit in detail the character of American economic thought of the seventeenth century. The primary concern was not to observe, classify or explain a series of economic facts, but rather to construct and defend a set of ideals.

Material goods, said Roger Williams, are only incidental and ancillary to the achievement of spiritual grace. These " earthly comforts " must accordingly be used only " as a stool or ladder to help us upward to heavenly comforts." [3] With the full vigour of Christian idealism, he declared, that God's children " must use this world, and all the comforts of it, with dead and weaned, and mortified affections." [4] But this was no special condemnation of wealth as such. If wealth interferes with the Christian life it must be despised but so must all else that interferes with godly pursuits. " Gold, silver, yea house, land, yea wives children, yea life itselfe, as they allure and drawe us from God in Christ, are to be abominated and hated." [5]

It was Cotton Mather who examined the problem of the use of wealth with greatest care in his tract on *Durable*

---

[1] Mather. *Durable Riches*, p. 14.
[2] *Ibid.*, Part II., p. 3.
[3] Williams, Roger. *Experiments of Spiritual Life and Health.* London, 1652. Reprinted, Providence, 1862, p. 49.
[4] *Ibid.*, p. 48.
[5] Williams. *Bloody Tenant*, p. 319.

Riches.[1] This essay represents the most complete attempt of the seventeenth century at an ecclesiastical pronouncement upon economic matters. The problem of the disposition and use of wealth by the individual is analyzed from the scriptural and theological positions with extraordinary clarity.

The purpose of wealth, said Mather, is twofold : first, to provide for one's family and even to lay up riches for one's children ;[2] secondly, consecration of wealth for pious uses.[3] These pious uses of wealth consist of " paying, lending, giving and forgiving." [4]

Under the pious use of wealth designated as " paying," Mather included the disposition of wealth for the support of the government and the ministry. Necessary " public servants of the place, must by our Estates be made capable to Discharge what obligations we have laid upon them." [5] " Paying " included the maintenance of the " Administration of Justice " and the guaranteeing " that Schoolmasters and Souldiers & other such Officers, do not want their Salaries." [6] Wealth should accordingly be devoted to these civil payments by the " cheerful Payment of the Taxes needful in order hereunto." [7] But more important than " civil payments " were " sacred payments " for the services of " Laborious and Religious Ministers." These indispensable persons must be handsomely provided for, that they may become " neither Discouraged nor Contemptible in their work." [8]

The second pious use of wealth which Mather recognized was " lending." Following the medieval precedent, Mather held that whereas " the Ready Lending of what may Assist

[1] Mather, Cotton. *Durable Riches*, Boston, 1695.
[2] " We May even Lay up for our children a part thereof, if that may be done without Defrauding of such other Objects, as God has required us, as long as we live, to be helpful unto." *Durable Riches*, Part II., pp. 3–4.
[3] *Durable Riches*, Part II., p. 4.
[4] *Ibid.*, Part II., p. 5.
[5] *Ibid.*
[6] *Ibid.*, Part II., p. 6.
[7] *Ibid.*
[8] *Ibid.*, Part II., p. 6.

those that want Means and Helps for their Trades " [1] is one of the " Pious Uses which our estates are to be placed in," the lending to spendthrifts and idlers is one of the " indiscreet abuses of our Estates." [2] Lending, therefore, comprised the extension of productive loans, while loans for consumption were disposed of under the next category of " giving." The " Giving of what may supply the necessities, and Relive the Calamities of the indigent " was a pious use sanctioned repeatedly by Scripture.[3] " Giving " should also include " contributions for the Propagation of the Gospel," education of the poor, dispersion of " Devout and useful Books," [4] relief of distress, care of the sick and of widows and orphans, redemption of captives and prisoners. " And unto this File," added the great American divine, " belongs that Hospitality, in which Christians must be Exemplary." [5]

The last pious use of wealth which Mather enumerated was " forgiving." This category he separated distinctly from the previous one of " giving." " Forgiving " was wholly contingent upon circumstance. If a debt has been incurred and " the Hand of God has made the Borrower unable to Discharge it," [6] then it is a pious use of wealth to forgive this obligation. " This," said Mather," is that which the Word of God recommends unto us in Ezek. xviii. 7. and elsewhere, under that Expression of Restoring the Pledge." [7] But where insolvency is caused by " Bad Courses," there should be no forgiving. Only when the " pure Frowns of God, have brought the Debtor Low," [8]

---

[1] Mather. *Durable Riches*, p. 7.

[2] *Ibid.*, p. 8. " A lending to idle Vagrants and Varlets, or those whom we may suppose to borrow with the mind of the wicked man, which the Scripture tells us, is, Never to Pay again ; this is not among the Pious Uses, but the indiscreet Abuses of our Estates ; our Lending should be to such, as are likely thereby to come into a way of what they may call their own."

[3] *Ibid.*

[4] *Ibid.*, Part II., p. 9.

[5] *Ibid.*

[6] *Ibid.*

[7] *Ibid.*

[8] *Ibid.*, Part II., p. 10.

should the scriptural maxim, " we will Require Nothing of them," be followed. Exactly how the good citizen should distinguish between " bad courses " and " the pure Frowns of God," the learned Mather did not expound! But the Christian precept of " Lend, hoping for nothing again "[1] he took pains to explain. The Christian should lend " with the Disposition to call for Nothing again, in case the Hand of God should Impoverish the Borrower."[2] The Greek version of Luke vi. 35, he further argued, means to despair. The Christian should, therefore, lend with the supposition " that the Debt may become Desperate ; and be ready to Release Principal as well as Interest."[3] Finally, that part of men's wealth consecrated to pious uses, must be devoted willingly, helpfully and prudently.[4] Disposition of wealth must not aim at honour, nor must all be given away, for charity must begin at home. Wealth under no circumstances should be dispersed with such a free hand as to encourage begging, drunkenness or vice.[5] Indeed, what is now expended at taverns, said Mather, would support churches, schools and commonwealth.[6]

Consistent with the ancient and medieval philosophy, gold and silver were singled out for special condemnation. Roger Williams in his enumeration of all that is to be despised by the Christian begins with gold and silver.[7] Precious stones, said Pastorius, are not desirable forms of wealth because they have been abused by man and have become servants to pride and ostentation.[8] John Smith declared that the general belief that gold and silver were the highest forms of wealth is erroneous.[9] Holland, he urged, owed her economic position to her fisheries which were

[1] *Luke* vi. 35.
[2] Mather. *Durable Riches*, Part II., p. 10.
[3] *Ibid.*
[4] *Ibid.*, Part II., pp. 11–18.
[5] *Ibid.*, Part II., p. 20.
[6] *Ibid.*, Part II., p. 33.
[7] Williams. *Bloody Tenant*, p. 319.
[8] Pastorius. *Description of Pennsylvania*, p. 9.
[9] Smith. *Generall Historie*, p. 581.

veritable mines that made possible the abundance of her
wealth.[1]   Fish, said Thomas Morton, " is a commodity
better than the golden mines of the Spanish Indies." [2]

VI

Two aspects of riches remain to be considered : the
ultimate importance of wealth to man, and the consequences
of its accumulation.   As far as wealth is concerned, wrote
William Hughes,

" no philosopher ever yet, either Ancient or Modern, could give
a sufficient or satisfactory definition of it, there being no bounds
to be set to a covetous man's desire and therefore doubtless man
was made for some more notable end than this." [3]

Bradford alluded to the inability of wealth to give real
satisfaction by sagely noting that wealth is falsely prized
by man though " mutable." [4]   Reference has already been
made to the argument of the author of *Good News from
Virginia*, who urged that if riches had real satisfying power,
Christ would not have disregarded them.[5]   " Worldly Goods
and Comforts," said Roger Williams in his melancholy
style, " are the common portion of the men of this perishable [world], who must perish together with them.   Let
us muse upon their insufficiency to content." [6]

Is wealth after all a good thing ?   What are the consequences of its accumulation ?   To these questions the seventeenth-century Americans gave several answers.   Bradford
noted sorrowfully that in Plymouth " as their stocks
increased, and ye increse vendible," [7] that population soon
was dispersed over a wide area and that " no man thought
he could live, except he had catle and a great deale of

[1] Smith. *Description of New England*, p. 194.
[2] Morton, *op. cit.*, pp. 86–87.
[3] Hughes, *op. cit.*, Preface.
[4] Bradford, *op. cit.*, p. 160.
[5] *Good News from Virginia*, Brown, *op. cit.*, p. 580.
[6] Williams. *Experiments of Spiritual Life*, p. 48.
[7] Bradford, *op. cit.*, p. 362.

ground." [1] But this was but a particular phenomenon. From a point of view of national security, Woodbridge, who was an advocate of paper money, noted that the accumulation of wealth, especially treasure, allures enemies. [2] This danger William Wood had considered before and dismissed with the bold remark that " it is hoped that when Bees have Honie in their Hives, they will have stings in their tailes." [3]

Different in character was the complaint of that group of persons who feared that wealth accumulation might endanger the moral welfare of a people. Thus the Boston Synod of Churches declared it their belief, in 1679, that " inordinate affection unto the world " was one of the greatest evils of the time. [4] The Synod lamented that the " insatiable desire after land and worldly accommodations " had led men to forsake churches and " live like heathen." The accumulation of wealth, in the minds of this body, had dimmed the spiritual ardour of the New England congregations and " Farms and Merchandisings have been preferred before the things of God." [5] Roger Williams feared that land would become the people's God, " as great a God with us English as God Gold was with the Spainiards." [6] Prosperity, said Cotton Mather in the *Magnalia*, brings about a decline in religion : " Relegio peperit Divitias, et filia devoravit matrem." [7] If wealth were properly used, the growth of wealth should lead to an increase in the " quit-rents unto the God " who gives men power to get wealth. [8] Robert Cushman discussed the mutations of fortunes, and noted that prosperity often quickly changes to a degree of poverty from which men " cannot get out again for seven genera-

[1] Bradford, *op. cit.*, p. 362.
[2] Woodbridge, John. "Severals Relating to the Fund." Boston, 1682. Reprinted, Prince Society, *Colonial Currency Reprints*, Vol. I., Boston, 1910, p. 115.
[3] Wood, *op. cit.*, p. 57.
[4] *Necessity of Reformation*, p. 6.
[5] *Ibid.*
[6] Williams. *Letters*, p. 319.
[7] Mather, Cotton. *Magnalia Christi Americana*. London, 1702. Reprinted, Hartford, 1853. 2 vols. Vol. I., p. 63.
[8] *Ibid.*

tions." [1] Perhaps the most interesting commentary upon the consequences of wealth accumulation was that of Pastorius in his curious " *Beehive* " in which he recorded his thoughts.[2] The manuscript has inscribed on it a circle divided into seven segments and labelled respectively : Poverty, Lowliness, Peace, Traffic, Wealth, Pride, and War. The diagram is followed by a verse to explain the consequence of wealth :

> " War begets Poverty, Poverty Peace
> Then people will traffic & Riches increase.
> Riches produceth Pride, Pride is War's ground,
> War begets Poverty, So we go round." [3]

[1] Young, *op. cit.*, pp. 248–249.

[2] Pastorius' *Beehive* has never been published. Only a few extracts of this curious diary, which was written in seven languages, in prose and in poetry, have been printed.

[3] Pastorius, Francis Daniel. "Extracts from Beehive," *Americana Germanica*. Vol. I., No. 4, 1897, pp. 97–98.

THE WAY OF WEALTH'S INCREASE

" What soever wee stand in need of is treasured in the earth,
by the Creato^r & is to be fetched thence by the sweat of o^r
Browes."

John Winthrop, *Conclusions for the Plantation
in New England.*

CHAPTER VI

THE WAY OF WEALTH'S INCREASE

I

T H E quest for economic competence necessarily turned the attention of early Americans to means whereby wealth might be increased. Most of the discussion reflects the theological pre-conceptions concerning wealth, although man's *rôle* received increasing attention. That the ultimate source of wealth was a manifestation of the benevolence of a gracious God or a generous Nature was a heritage of the past. The ancient Greek philosophy of natural bounty found continuation and elaboration in the medieval writings. Puritan New England repeatedly expressed a theological doctrine of wealth's origin as did also many of the writers in the southern and middle colonies. But man's function was recognized as something more than passive acceptance of divine or natural gifts. Moral duty and economic motive combined to develop a philosophy of man's active and purposeful participation in the generation of a stream of wealth.

"The original grant of divine bounty," said William Hubbard, "is the grand tenure whereby mankind do hold in capite, of the supreme Head and Governor of the world." [1] This bounty, he explained, is manifest in the capacity of the earth to provide food for man and animals, so that men's "granaries may be full, their oxen strong to labor and other creatures bring forth thousands in their streets." [2] The original source of wealth, said John Smith, is God's bounty,[3] "gotte from the rude earth, by God's blessing and

[1] Hubbard, *op. cit.*, p. 239.
[2] *Ibid.*
[3] Smith, John. *A Description of New England*, p. 208.

his [man's] owne industrie." Indeed, said Beverley, men may " depend altogether upon the Liberality of Nature " ; [1] slothful individuals may " spunge upon the Blessings of a warm Sun," and, where nature's gifts are abundant, " almost grutch the Pains of gathering in the Bounties of the Earth." [2] God gives men the power to obtain wealth, said Cotton Mather,[3] and can also prevent men from acquiring it. But God's attitude toward man is one of benevolence ; he has endowed the earth with substances in accordance to man's needs. Thus the " metals of most necessary Uses are the most plentiful," while others " that may be better spared, there is a rarity of them." [4] Yet God, said Edward Johnson, has done more than extend his bounty to man. This he has done for all his creatures ; but man " hath he taught to Sow Reape, carry into Barnes and Spin, and indeed herein the Lord hath answered his people abundantly." [5] The beasts and fowls, he pointed out, get a living from the earth's bounty. But men obtain more, for they appropriate this same bounty under divine guidance. Even this militant churchman, then, was compelled to admit another factor, in addition to God's bounty, to explain the production of wealth. For labour after all, even if under divine guidance is labour, and, as such, a means of producing wealth. The *rôle* of labour was clearly recognized in Winthrop's terse and cogent statement that " what soever wee stand in need of is treasured in the earth, by the Creato^r & is to be fetched thence by the sweat of o^r Browes." [6]

II

Second only to a natural bounty, and almost inseparable from the idea of a bounty, was the concept of labour as a

---

[1] Beverley, *op. cit.*, pp. 283–284.
[2] *Ibid.*
[3] Mather. *Durable Riches*, p. 5.
[4] Mather, Cotton. *Christian Philosopher*. London, 1721, p. 120.
[5] Johnson, *op. cit.*, p. 154.
[6] Winthrop. *Conclusions*, p. 9.

factor of production. Winthrop and other writers, it will be recalled, had advanced a labour theory of property,[1] while the statement just quoted shows Winthrop's acceptance of the idea that human labour was equivalent to appropriation. Thomas Budd argued that Pennsylvania would be able to build ships cheaper than England, " the Timber costing us nothing but Labour." [2] Johnson saw labour as appropriation except that in the appropriation process, " the Lord hath taught them to labour with more ease." [3] John Smith declared that, in the long run, wealth can only be obtained by means of labour [4] and protested that the rich gains of Spain in her colonies were no exception, because this acquisition was in reality the spoliation of the labour of the aborigines.[5] Labour and land, he urged, are the ultimate causes of wealth.[6] Blackwell said that " art and industry " are the means whereby goods are produced.[7] Roger Williams recognized the significance of labour as an agent of production in his criticism of the Indian economy. The Indians were poor, he said, because they " endure not that life of labour and indeavor, wherein that plenty and better state is found." [8] More illustrations need not be cited. Labour was a means of producing wealth because by means of labour was the natural " bounty " appropriated and " plenty " was the result of labour.

Little was said by the seventeenth-century Americans of the principle of the division of labour. Richard Frame, in doggerel verse, referred to the simple division of labour,[9]

---

[1] Winthrop, *Conclusions*, pp. 6–7.   Compare Chapter IV., p. 71, note 3.
[2] Budd, *op. cit.*, p. 42.
[3] Johnson, *op. cit.*, p. 154.
[4] Smith. *Generall Historie*, p. 619.
[5] *Ibid.*, p. 464.
[6] Smith. *Description of New England*, pp. 195–196.
[7] Blackwell, John. " A Discourse in Explanation of the Bank of Credit." MSS. Winthrop Papers, *Mass. Hist. Soc.* Printed, Prince Society, *Colonial Currency Reprints*, Vol. I., pp. 124–125.
[8] Williams. *Experiments of Spiritual Life*, p. 15.
[9] Frame, Richard. *A Short Description of Pennsilvania*, Philadelphia, 1692. Reprinted, 1867, pp. 7–8 :

" There [Germantown] grows the flax, as also you may know
That from the same they do divide the Low ;

but Beverley was the only writer who saw the advantage of
the complex division of labour. He pointed out that the
dispersion of the Virginia population hindered division of
labour which is indispensable for most effective production.
" It is thought too much for the same Man, to make the
wheat, and grind it, bolt it, and bake it himself." [1]   To
overcome this, mills and equipment are necessary where
division of labour can be facilitated. But " these things,"
Beverley continued, " can never be expected from a single
Family : But if they had Cohabitations, it might be thought
worth attempting." [2]

The influence of the quality of labour upon production
was considered by William Wood : " It is not the multi-
plicity of many bad servants but the industry of the faithful
and diligent labourer that enricheth the carefull Master." [3]
While " dronish servants " may make a man poor, " an industrious family " is certain to bring wealth.   Nor did he think
that the payment of high wages was to be feared, since high
wages stimulate labourers.   Contented labourers are efficient.
By the payment of wages, money is merely exchanged for
wealth of another kind and masters in the payment of wages
" have lesse monie by reason of them, but never the lesse
riches." [4]   If only labour be correctly directed, wealth is
certain to emerge.   To be sure, " if any men be so improvident as to set men about building of Castles in the Aire, or
other unnecessary employments, they may grow poore." [5]
But those who employ labour in the " planting of Corne,
building of houses, fencing in of ground, fishing and divers

> Their Trade fits well within their Habitation
> We find convenience for their occupation
> One Trade brings in imployment for another
> So that we may suppose each Trade a Brother ;
> From Linnin Rags good paper doth derive
> The first Trade keeps the second Trade alive."

[1] Beverley, *op. cit.*, pp. 280–281.
[2] *Ibid.*
[3] Wood, *op. cit.*, p. 54.
[4] *Ibid.*, p. 57.
[5] *Ibid.*

other necessary occasions," need have no fear. Well-directed labour creates wealth.

Since labour, in the minds of the colonial writers, was the primary means whereby the bounty of nature was made useful, it is not difficult to understand their stern attitude toward the matter of idleness. To countenance idleness was to permit the very arresting of wealth's production. Add to this the moral danger of idleness and the colonial policy becomes quite a plausible one. Men cannot " live in plenty and idleness, both at a time," said William Wood,[1] and it is a pity that " he that can worke and will not, should eate." Beverley was reluctant, he said, to " publish this slothful Indolence " [2] of his countrymen, but he hoped that thereby he might " excite them to make the most of all those happy advantages which Nature has given them." John Smith urged that idleness was not permitted in insect communities, and that mankind should follow this wise example. For idleness, said he, can only lead to misery.[3] Cotton Mather feared that charity might lead to idleness " which is a reproach to any people." [4] Like all those fortunate persons who can find the one cause for historical changes, the learned Mather related how he had read that a citizen of Pisa had admitted that the decay of that city was largely caused because there were no laws to punish idleness.[5]

The American colonies certainly did not suffer from want of legislation. Laws for repressing idleness were legion. The Plymouth law of 1654 may be cited as an illustration. The grandjurymen of each town were instructed

" to take a speciall view and notice of all manor of persons married or single dwelling within theire severall townshipes that have smale means to maintain themselves and are suspected to live Idley and loosely and to require an account of them how

---

[1] Wood, *op. cit.*, p. 50.
[2] Beverley, *op. cit.*, pp. 283–284.
[3] Smith. *Description of New England*, p. 179.
[4] Mather, Cotton. *The Boston Ebenezer.* Lecture delivered April 7th, 1698. Reprinted, *Magnalia Christi Americana ;* also, *Old South Leaflets*, No. 67, p. 16.
[5] *Ibid.*

they live and such as they find delinquent and cannot give a good account thereof unto them that they cause the Constable to bring them before the Magistrate in theire towne." [1]

This law was followed four years later by legislation providing for a " worke house " for the disciplining of " all such vagrants as wander up and downe without any lawfull calling and allsoe all Idle persons." [2]   It was this type of legislation that Cotton Mather was still advocating at the close of the century.   Charity, he urged, should be confined to the unemployable ; " But the poor who can work and won't, the best liberality to them is to make them.   I beseech you, sirs, to find out a method quickly, that the idle persons in the town may earn their bread." [3]   This, he declared, would be the best charity of all, because it would being " equity unto us all."   Nor must one forget the moral danger which the seventeenth century saw in idleness. When man lacks " some honest exercise " in which to employ his time, then are " the allurements of the world " [4] most difficult to resist.   Indeed, said Cotton Mather, idleness is the " most Concealed and yet the most violent, of our Passions," because it corrupts most certainly and " layes Adamantine chains of Death and Darkness upon us." [5]

With labour clearly recognized as a means of producing wealth, the matter of population could not escape attention. An increase of people was equivalent to increasing the supply of the agents whereby wealth is produced.   A thickening of population, said Archdale, strengthens a colony, increases trade, and raises land values. [6]   Where natural resources are abundant, wrote Miller from New York, wealth depends upon industry and the growth of population. [7]   Since population is eminently desirable,

---

[1] *Records of the Colony of New Plymouth*, Vol. XI., pp. 90–91.
[2] *Ibid.*, Vol. XI., p. 120.
[3] Mather. *Boston Ebenezer*, p. 17.
[4] Hughes, *op. cit.*, Preface.
[5] Mather, Cotton. *Bonifacius, An Essay upon the Good*, Boston, 1710, p. 10.
[6] Archdale, *op. cit.*, p. 117.
[7] Miller, *op. cit.*, p. 45.

everything should be done which will foster its growth, and the extension of good privileges and exemptions by the mother country, said Adrian Van der Donck, is the mother of population in a colony.[1] But the vast natural resources of the new world deflected the thoughts of the colonial writers from any consideration of the ultimate consequences of continued population increase. It was only those writers who had grown to adult age in the old world who understood anything of the nature of this problem. Higginson, for example, pointed out that the density of population increased the difficulty of obtaining a comfortable existence.[2] Cotton compared the need for colonization by mankind to the swarming of bees,[3] and Winthrop, speaking of the want of economic opportunity in England, said that there the " earth grows weary of her inhabitants." [4] But these writers, it will be observed, were referring to English conditions. No further reference to an economic limit to population is to be found among the American writers. The constant presence of a frontier of free land deflected their thoughts from this problem.

Several colonial writers discussed the subject of slavery. Beverley explained the customs of slavery and servitude in Virginia ; [5] John Wise, of Ipswich, discoursed on the philosophic unsoundness of the institution of slavery ; [6] and Pastorius was the author of the " Germantown Friends Protest against Slavery " which essayed to prove that slavery was unjust and incompatible with Christianity.[7] But Judge Sewall was the only writer who examined the economic considerations involved in slavery and servitude.[8]

---

[1] Donck. *Representation of New Netherlands*, pp. 69–71.
[2] Higginson, *op. cit.*, p. 34.
[3] Cotton. *God's Promise to His Plantation*, p. 9.
[4] Winthrop. *Conclusions*, p. 5.
[5] Beverley, *op. cit.*, p. 235.
[6] Wise, John. *A Vindication of the Government of New England Churches.* Boston, 1717, pp. 32–43.
[7] Learned, M. D. *Pastorius' Bee Hive*, p. 261.
[8] Sewall, Samuel. *The Selling of Joseph.* Boston, 1700 ; also *Computation that the Importation of Negroes is not so profitable as that of White*

Slavery, said Sewall, in the first place, has no ethical foundation ; all men are sons of Adam to whom, as co-heirs, " God
hath given the Earth (with all its commodities)." [1] The
famous thesis of Aristotle that some men are by nature
slaves, Judge Sewall flatly denied : " Originally and
Naturally, there is no such thing as Slavery." [2] Nay, rather
slavery is forbidden by divine law.[3] With these statements
as an introduction, Sewall turned to the economic considerations involved.

White servants, said the famous Boston justice, are
economically superior to slaves. Negroes are constantly
longing for liberty, " and this continual aspíring after their
forbidden Liberty, renders them unwilling Servants." [4]
Moreover, differences in colour prevent the negroes from
being assimilated and, as a consequence, they are not suited
for peopling of the country. Rather they " remain in our
Body Politick as a kind of extravasat Blood." [5] From the
political point of view, negro slaves are undesirable, because
they are not useful for defence ; they are undependable
servants ; [6] and they are not useful to people the country.
From the test of cost and return, Sewall concluded that
white servants were to be preferred to black. The risk, in
the first place, is much less, so that " three years Interest of
the price of the Negro, will near upon if not altogether
purchase a white man Servant." [7] Sewall propounded a
detailed computation to demonstrate the monetary advantage of importing white servants rather than negroes, and

Servants. Boston, 1706. Both tracts reprinted, *Historical Magazine,*
June, 1864.
    [1] Sewall. *Selling of Joseph,* p. 195.
    [2] *Ibid.* " Joseph was rightfully no more a slave to his Brethren, than
they were to him ; and they had no more Authority to Sell him, than they
had to slay him."
    [3] *Ibid.* " He that Stealeth a Man, and Selleth him, or if he be found
in his Hand, he shall surely be put to Death."
    [4] *Ibid.,* pp. 195–196.
    [5] *Ibid.,* p. 196.
    [6] " Negroes are generally Eye-Servants, great thieves much addicted
to Stealing, Lying and Purloining." *Ibid.,* p. 198.
    [7] Sewall, Samuel. *Computation that the Importation of Negroes is not so
profitable as that of White Servants,* p. 198.

he urged that the government should pay a bounty upon the importation of white servants. As an ardent advocate of an enlarged population, he pointed out that if the usual period of servitude were four years, then after the first four years, there would be a constant stream of liberated servants who would settle the frontier.[1] In Boston, in one year, concluded Sewall, a loss of £1,320 was occasioned by the death of forty-four negroes, " and for a less loss (if it may unproperly be so called) for a 1000*l*. the country may have 500 men in 5 years' time for the 44 negroes dead in one year."

III

The abundance of natural resources in the new world apparently eliminated any analysis of the necessity of diversified natural resources as a requisite for economic prosperity. Only a limited number of writers make any mention of the dependence of well-being upon varied resources. Abundant land, if cheap, said William Wood, is more important than scarce and dear land.[2] Miller realized that the very abundance of resources may retard industry, although if " Industrious Art seconds natures bounty," great wealth is produced.[3] John Smith[4] and Donck[5] both emphasized the necessity of careful exploitation of natural resources if great wealth were to be produced. Smith took pains to point out that the sea was as important an agent of production as the mines of the earth : " let not the word fish distaste you," he wrote, " for it will afford as good gold as the mines of Guiana or Potossie."[6] William Hubbard called attention to the fact that land had more than one use in producing wealth. " That which the land produceth upon the surface thereof," said he, " is that upon which the

---

[1] Sewall. *Computation*, p. 199.
[2] Wood, *op. cit.*, p. 14.
[3] Miller, *op. cit.*, p. 45.
[4] Smith. *Description of New England*, pp. 195–196.
[5] Donck. *Description of New Netherlands*, p. 19.
[6] Smith. *Generall Historie*, p. 784.

inhabitants have their dependence for the most certain part of their wealth." [1] A new community, he pointed out, must first develop agriculture, because that occupation, as opposed to mining, promises an immediate return. The mineral content of the earth, on the other hand, is only available if " leisure or ability to ransack so deep underground is provided." [2]

The contemporary English economic literature made continual references to " art " as one means of increasing wealth. The American writers also made frequent reference to " art " as a productive agent. Not until the latter part of the seventeenth century was any deliberate effort made in England to define the term,[3] when Sir William Petty, by his illustrative method gave a proximate degree of precision to the term. If by simple labour, said Petty,

" I could dig and prepare for seed a hundred Acres in a thousand days ; suppose then I spent a hundred days in studying a more compendious way, and in contriving Tools for the same purpose ; but in all that hundred days dig nothing, but in the remaining 900 days I dig two hundred acres of Ground, then I say, that the said *Art* which cost but 100 days Invention is worth one man's labour for ever ; because the New Art and one man performed as much as two men could have done without it." [4]

A detailed examination of English economic literature of the seventeenth century has revealed several ideas which were implied by the word " art ".[5] As a productive force distinct from Nature, " art " gave rise to " artificial " as opposed to " natural " wealth. As a means of abridging

---

[1] Hubbard, *op. cit.*, pp. 23–24.

[2] *Ibid.*

[3] The English writers on colonization used the term frequently, although its meaning was consistently vague : *e.g.*, " If bare nature be so amiable in its naked kind, what may we hope, when *Arte* and Nature both shall joyne and strive together." Johnson, Robert. *Nova Britannia*, p. 12 ; *cf.* also Gray, Robert. *A Good Speed to Virginia*, p. 29 ; and Hakluyt, Richard. *Notes Given to Certain Gentlemen, &c.*, p. 249.

[4] Petty, Sir William. *Economic Writings*. Edited by C. H. Hull, Cambridge, 1899, p. 182.

[5] Johnson, Edgar, A. J. " The Mercantilist Concept of ' Art ' and ' Ingenious Labour.' " *Economic History*, Vol. II., No. 6, January, 1931, pp. 234–253.

labour, it produced wealth by more skilful methods. The skill which was implied by " art " might be crystallized into machines, formulæ or devices, and thereby provide a technological means of producing more wealth. Petty conceived of " art " as a separate factor of production whose value might be determined by capitalizing its annual productive power.

The American references to " art " as a means of producing wealth are even more nebulous than the contemporary English references. But although lacking precise definition, there was none the less a belief that human skill was indispensable to furthering the increase of wealth. There is, however, this difference between the English and American discussion of " art " : England's mercantilist programme demanded the expansion of manufactures as a vehicle for national greatness ; the American colonists realized that their economy by its very location would tend to be predominately agricultural. They could scarcely hope to attain as highly differentiated an economic society. The technological aspect of " art " was accordingly less emphasized.

Frequent references to " art " are scattered through the early American writings. Bradford recorded that some members of the Leyden congregation favoured colonization in Guiana where " vigorous nature brought forth all things in abundance & plentie without any great labor or art of man." [1] Cushman referred to " art " as a means of producing wealth, as did Blackwell, much later in the century.[2] Beverley conceived production to consist of improving the gifts of Nature by " art or industry," [3] although he recognized that where natural resources are abundant, men may find a sufficiency of food without " art." [4] Miller's usage of the term illustrated the vagueness of its meaning, for to him, the greatest production was

[1] Bradford, *op. cit.*, p. 36.
[2] Young, *op. cit.*, pp. 243–244 ; Blackwell, *op. cit.*, pp. 124–125.
[3] Beverley, *op. cit.*, pp. 283–284.
[4] *Ibid.*, p. 259.

forthcoming where " Industrious Art seconds Nature's bounty." [1]

The evolution of the term " capital " was not without its counterpart in America.[2] The term " estate " was employed to designate an accumulation of economic goods consisting of consumption goods, capital goods or both.[3] It was the *sine qua non* of the good colonist. William Wood said :

" A man of estate must first scatter before he gathers, he must lay out monies for transporting of servants, and cattle and goods, for houses and fences and gardens &c. This may make his purse seem light, and to the eye of others seeme a leaking in his estate, whereas these disbursements are for his future enrichments." [4]

Like their English contemporaries, the American writers often confused the word " estate " and " stock." The iron-works at Braintree, said Johnson, " profited the owners little, but rather wasted their *stock*." [5] Thomas Budd defined " stock " as consisting of " Oxen, Horses, Cows, Sows, Sheep and Servants, by which they [settlers in Pennsylvania] will be enabled to carry on their Husbandry." [6] John Winthrop, speaking of the manufacture of iron,[7] said, " the business was well approved by the court, as a thing much conducing to the good of the country, but we had no *stock* in the treasury to give furtherance to it." The term " stock," therefore, in seventeenth-century parlance, although it seemed sometimes to designate capital goods, was so often used synonymously with " estate," that one cannot say that a differentiation had taken place

---

[1] Miller, *op. cit.*, p. 45.

[2] See Cannan, Edwin. " Early History of the term Capital." *Quarterly ournal of Economics*, Vol. 35, pp. 469–481.

[3] Thus Edward Johnson recorded that " divers persons of good rank and quality were stirred up by the provident hand of the Lord to *venture* their *estates* upon an iron work." Johnson, *op. cit.*, p. 246. William Wood explained that there were no very rich persons in New England (1634) " because none of such great estate went over yet." Wood, *op. cit.*, p. 51.

[4] Wood, *op. cit.*, p. 51.

[5] Johnson, *op. cit.*, p. 246.

[6] Budd, *op. cit.*, p. 50.

[7] Winthrop. *History of New England*, Vol. II., pp. 212–213.

between the terms. Edward Johnson, for example, wrote that the "provident hand of the Lord" induced certain persons " to venture their *estates* " upon an iron work. But the enterprise " profited the owners little, but rather wasted their *stock.*" [1]

That production requires time, and that a portion of men's " estates " must be temporarily tied up in a mass of intermediate goods, not available for consumption purposes, was clearly understood by William Wood : a " man of estate " (capitalist entrepreneur) must first " scatter before he gathers." [2] This investment may cause him to appear poor, but these expenditures lead to his " future enrichment." Here, in fact, is an elementary capital theory recognizing that production requires time, that wealth must be committed to an assisting form, and that the final outcome of this temporary direction of wealth is a product larger than would be available otherwise. To this must be added the risk element. Sewall recognized the factor of risk in his computation of the economic advantages of white servitude over slavery.[3] Hire, declared an ecclesiastical pronouncement of 1699, should be carefully distinguished from usury,[4] because in the receipt of usury the owners of the " estate " involved are " not running the risque of the principal," [5] although money was held to be " as really improveable a thing as any other commodity." [6] Such was the status of the capital concept in the American discussion. The colonization writers, as previously mentioned, had insisted that the colonists must be provided with money or pro-

---

[1] Johnson, *op. cit.*, p. 246. The several uses of the word " stock " are in accord with Professor Cannon's findings. Often the term denoted the actual things owned rather than their money value. This was the sense in which Budd used the term (*cf.* note 6, p. 114), whereas Winthrop and Johnson evidently referred to a money equivalent. See Cannon, *op. cit.*, p. 475.

[2] Wood, *op. cit.*, p. 51.

[3] *Cf. supra*, p. 110, note 7.

[4] *Thirty Important Cases Resolved with Evidence of Scripture and Reason.* By Several Pastors of Adjacent Churches meeting in Cambridge, New England. (Published by Cotton Mather.) Boston, 1699, p. 260.

[5] *Ibid.*, p. 259.

[6] *Ibid.*

perty.[1] Wood and Johnson perceived the essential nature
of capital as a productive agent ; Sewall, Johnson, and the
Massachusetts ministers, recognized the element of risk. The
necessity of a return upon capital will be discussed in a
subsequent chapter.

Beginning with the theological concept of God's bounty
as the original source of wealth, the colonial writers analysed
the various means whereby these natural gifts could be
appropriated for man's use. Human labour was the means
of improving God-given resources. Slavery was considered
an undesirable form of labour organization by the New
England and Middle-colony moralists. " Art " was recognized as a productive force, since it made labour more
effective ; " stock " was an indispensable item in the
organization of a productive economy. If efficient labour
were combined with bountiful natural resources, wealth
must certainly be forthcoming.[2]   Spreading production
over time increased the ultimate product, although this
procedure required a money investment.[3] " Spirit, Purse
and Hand," said John Woodbridge, are " the ingredients
that must center as in one, for any considerable undertaking." [4]   Yet even though the necessary factors were
combined, uncertainty was recognized as a peculiar characteristic of wealth-getting. " Riches," said Hubbard, do not
always come to " men of understanding, but time and chance
happens to them all." [5]

IV

Did the American writers realize that there were limits
or restraints to the increase of wealth ? The answer is
uncertain. Some writers seemed to imply that wealth would
increase as population increased. Others apparently per-

---

[1] For representative illustrations *cf.* Hubbard, *op. cit.*, p. 87; or
Pastorius. *Description of Pennsylvania*, p. 16.
[2] *E.g.*, Smith. *Description of New England*, p. 197.
[3] Wood, *op. cit.*, p. 57.
[4] Woodbridge, *op. cit.*, p. 115.
[5] Hubbard, *op. cit.*, p. 334.

ceived that in agriculture and mining, more wealth involved a proportionately greater expenditure of labour. A few writers recognized that the American colonies had a distinct advantage in producing certain commodities and only relative advantage in others.

Advocates of an enlarged population appear to have assumed that, in America, production would increase in proportion to an increase in labour. Miller, in 1695, lamented that the inhabitants of New York were not sufficiently industrious. He delighted in visualizing " how plentifull & beneficiall a Country it would be did but Industrious Art second Nature's bounty & were but the Inhabitants more in number." [1] Quite the opposite point of view was stated by Winthrop and Higginson. But it must be remembered that they were referring to English, not American economic conditions. Winthrop called attention to the limited economic opportunity in England, and implied that a limited land area can support only a limited population : " England," he wrote, " growes weary of her Inhabitants." [2] Higginson's opinion was essentially the same. The increase in England's population, said he, makes it a " very hard shift to live one by the other." [3]

John Smith apparently believed that the production of precious metals involved increasing costs. The first rewards of the Spaniards, he pointed out, were very large, because they plundered a "mighty store of treasure from the Natives," and secondly, because " the Indians shewed them entire and rich Mines." [4] But because of continued operation of the Spanish mines, they " are exceedingly wasted, so that now the charge of getting those metals is growne excessive."[5] The profitableness of mining, he believed, was reduced while the human expense had increased.[6]

[1] Miller, *op. cit.*, p. 45.
[2] Winthrop. *Conclusions*, p. 5.
[3] Higginson, *op. cit.*, p. 34.
[4] Smith. *Generall Historie*, p. 581.
[5] *Ibid*.
[6] " Besides the consuming the lives of many by their pestilent smoke

The effect of diversity of natural resources upon production was considered by the colonial writers. Bradford referred to the different amounts of product resulting from similar expenditures of labour in warm as opposed to cold climates.[1] But the disadvantage of cold climates, he believed, was offset by an increase in human industry. Ash urged that Carolina was preferable to the northern colonies, since no labour need be spent there to accumulate winter provisions for cattle.[2] Donck used the same argument to show the superiority of the Dutch colony over the French colonies.[3] In America, said Smith, "nature and liberty affords us that freely, which in England we want, or it costeth us dearly."[4] Wood likewise held that less labour was needed in America than in England to produce the same amount of foodstuffs[5] while John Winthrop wrote that the necessary "labor & cost to recover or keep somtymes a Acre or two of land" would, in America, "procure them many hundred as good or better."[6] Donck argued that New Netherlands could produce a great variety of products "and with less trouble and tilling than in Netherlands."[7]

That labour spent in the production of certain commodities was particularly effective seems also to have been understood. Tobacco was exclusively produced in Virginia, according to Smith, because in tobacco "they value a man's labour a yeere worth fifty or threescore pound, but in Corne not worth ten pound,"[8] and in the second place, because "tobacco will furnish them with all things."[9] Beverley demonstrated that it was this relative advantage in tobacco

and vapours in digging and refining them [metals], so that all things considered, the cleere gaines of those metals, the Kings part defraid, to the Adventures is but small." Smith. *Generall Historie*, p. 581.

[1] Bradford, *op. cit.*, p. 36.
[2] Ash, *op. cit.*, pp. 71–72.
[3] Donck, *op. cit.*, p. 2.
[4] Smith. *Description of New England*, pp. 212–213.
[5] Wood, *op. cit.*, p. 57.
[6] Winthrop. *Conclusions*, p. 5.
[7] Donck. *Representation of New Netherlands*, p. 13.
[8] Smith. *Generall Historie*, pp. 615–616.
[9] *Ibid.*

which prevented the development of the linen and silk industry. " Such Manufactures are always neglected," he said, "when Tobacco bears anything of a Price." [1] The distinct advantage in tobacco production " puts out all endeavors from the attempting of other more Staple, and Sollid, and rich Commodities, out of the heads of the Common people," wrote the author of *A Perfect Description of Virginia*.[2] The relative disadvantage of other occupations, he believed, could be overcome if the wealthier planters would set an example by developing neglected industries. Present loss, it was promised, would be compensated by ultimate gain.[3]

The colonial belief in the necessity of controlling wealth-getting institutions has already been briefly considered.[4] There was little or no confidence in the liberal doctrine that spontaneous self-seeking would provide a self-adjusting mechanism for the increase of wealth. Government was charged with the duty of overseeing and sanctioning various types of economic pursuits. Winthrop's *History* gives abundant illustration of this governmental theory during the first twenty years of Massachusetts Bay, while the various colonial records are veritable mines from which similar evidence can be extracted. Wealth-getting, according to colonial opinion, must be harmonized with social and religious ideals. Government must lay down economic policies consistent with these ideals.

A few institutions were considered from the point of view of economic merit. Diffusion of population was challenged in Virginia [5] and in New England.[6] Enclosure of land was signalized as a means of increasing agricultural production. The author of the *Essay on the Laying out of Towns* prophesied that " one acre inclosed is much more beneficial than

---

[1] Beverley, *op. cit.*, p. 281.
[2] *A Perfect Description of Virginia*.
[3] *Ibid.*
[4] Chapter II.
[5] Beverley, *op. cit.*, pp. 280–281
[6] Bradford, *op. cit.*, p. 362.

5 falling to his share in comon."[1]   Private property in land was generally recognized as a means of stimulating enterprise, eliciting emulation, and obviating waste of natural resources.   Yet the history of colonial America is in many ways a chapter in the history of co-operation.   Since capital was scarce, co-operation was recognized as a means of utilizing draft animals to the fullest extent.   The institutional metamorphosis of early American economic life is itself a manifestation of the quest for better means of wealth's increase.

[1] *Essay on the Laying out of Towns*, pp. 478–479.

THE MORALITY OF THE MARKET-PLACE

"A remarkable instance was that year [1639] given in one E. P. [Edward Palmer] who, for asking an excessive price for a pair of stocks which he was hired to frame, had the honor to sit an hour in them first himself, to warn others not to offend in a like manner."

William Hubbard, *A General History o New England from the Discoverie to* 1680.

THE MORALITY OF THE MARKET-PLACE

I

No community, however youthful, can disregard the processes whereby economic goods derive their value. The American colonial sources contain considerable reference to price phenomena, to competition, to demand and supply, and to markets. But the bulk of the early value discussion centres around an economic ideal inherited from medieval economic philosophy : the idea of a " just price." This concept stands as the root and stem of the value discussion, while from it proceed, as first exfoliations, the complaints about " oppression " in prices and the demands for legislative control of markets. But the colonial discussion, lacking the uniformity of the medieval thought from which it borrowed its seed, could not retain the harmony and completeness of the medieval economic doctrine. The thoughts of practical colonists are never those of monastic theologians, and as a consequence, the medieval value legacy at the hands of the seventeenth-century Americans was modified and amplified rather than crystallized around the concept of " just price."

John Cotton's " rules for trading " which he set forth to his Boston audience in 1639, represents the most concise statement of the doctrine of " just price," and Winthrop has given us a faithful record, in his *History*, of the events which called forth this pronouncement.[1] A certain Robert Keaine, a merchant of Boston, was haled before the Great

---

[1] Winthrop. *History of New England*, Vol. I., pp. 313–317.

and General Court charged with " notoriously " oppressing the buyers of his goods. He was found guilty and fined £200. The " corrupt practice of this man " was particularly detestable, since he was " an ancient professor of the gospel "; he was wealthy, and had only one child ; he had come to Massachusetts Bay " for conscience sake." Moreover, he had been previously admonished by his friends and also by " some of the magistrates and elders." The House of Deputies set his fine at £200, but the magistrates were disposed to be more lenient for several reasons. They urged that there was no law in force which limited profits, that it was common practice in other countries " for men to make use of advantages for raising the prices of their commodities," that Keaine was not the sole offender, that the law of God appoints no other punishment but double restitution.[1] Most important, however, for the history of American economic thought, was their objection that perfectly equitable prices can neither be determined or prescribed. According to Winthrop, the magistrates alleged that

" a certain rule could not be found out for an equal rate between buyer and seller, though much labour had been bestowed in it and divers laws had been made, which, upon experience, were repealed, as being neither safe nor equal." [2]

But the deputies would not consent to a diminution of the fine, although they did agree that only £100 must be paid at once while " the other should be respited to the further consideration of the next general court." [3]

Encouraged by the doubt thrown upon the existence of a " just price " by these arguments adduced in his behalf by the magistrates, Keaine sought to make excuses for his conduct when he was summoned before the church of Boston. He argued that the cause of his oppressive trading was twofold : " ignorance of the true price of some wares," and

---

[1] Winthrop.   *History of New England*, p. 316.
[2] *Ibid.*
[3] *Ibid.*, p. 315.

secondly and more important, that he had been misled by some " false principles of trade." [1] These principles were :

" 1. That, if a man lost in one commoditie, he might help himself in the price of another. 2. That if, through want of skill or other occasion, his commodity cost him more than the price of the market in England, he might then sell it for more than the price of the market in New England."

Here was a situation which the Boston clergy could not disregard : oppression of the public by a merchant, doubts as to the existence of such a thing as a " just price " by the magistrates ; and admission by the defendant and sinner that he had been misled by " false principles." John Cotton " in his publick exercise the next lecture day " set forth the ecclesiastical position on value and price. Following the method of Thomas Aquinas he enumerated the reasons which induced men to sell their goods at oppressive prices. Then against each of these arguments he set the " rules for trading " which were consistent with the Christian life.

The first false principle, which Cotton sought to refute, was " that a man might sell as dear as he can, and buy as cheap as he can." [2] He set over against this his first " rule for trading," in which the old doctrine of " just price " was summarized :

" A man may not sell above the current price, i.e., such a price as is *usual in the time and place, and as another (who knows the worth of the commodity) would give for it*, if he had occasion to use it ; as that is called current money, which every man will take." [3]

A " just price " was defined, therefore, as the price which would be paid by a buyer who " knows the worth of the

---

[1] Winthrop. *History of New England*, p. 316.
[2] *Ibid.*
[3] *Ibid.*, pp. 316–317 (italics mine). For comparison with the medieval philosophy, *cf.* Thomas Aquinas. *Summa Theologica*. Literally translated by Fathers of English Dominican Province. New York, 1918. Part II., Second Number, Question LXXVII., pp. 317–328.

commodity " and whose demand for the commodity was such, that he had use for it but was under no economic compulsion to buy. The seller of goods must therefore determine a " just price " by means of the fiction of an intelligent, uncoerced buyer !

The second false principle : " If a man lose by casualty of sea, &c. in some of his commodities, he may raise the price of the rest," Cotton refuted on Calvinistic grounds. "Where a man loseth by casualty of sea," declared this famous law-giver,

" it is a loss cast upon himself by providence, and he may not ease himself of it by casting it upon another ; for so a man should seem to provide against all providences, &c. that he should never lose ; but where there is a scarcity of the commodity, there men may raise their price ; for now it is the hand of God upon the commodity, and not the person."

The modern reader of these " rules for trading " can scarcely avoid wondering why a shipwreck was the " hand of God " raised against a particular merchant, whereas, a hail storm was the " hand of God " upon wheat or barley !

A third reason, said Cotton, why merchants were led astray, was the belief that a man " may sell as he bought, though he paid too dear, &c. and though the commodity be fallen, &c." Cotton's answer to this was brief : " A man may not ask any more for his commodity than his selling price, as Ephron to Abraham, *the land is worth thus much.*" From this statement and from the preceding rule, one must imply that, given the hand of God for or against any commodity, there is a price which is the " just price " ; it is " worth thus much."

The answer to the third false principle was also a partial answer to the fourth : " that, as a man may take advantage of his own skill or ability, so may he of another's ignorance or necessity." The learned Mr. Cotton would yield no quarter to this worldly argument. Commodities have a value which the seller can determine by the fiction of the intelligent buyer and " when a man loseth in his commodity for want of skill, &c. he must look at it as his own fault or cross, and therefore must not lay it upon another."

The details of Keaine's misdemeanour have been explained to show the early divergence between the attitude of the clergy and the men of affairs. The doctrine of " just price " becomes, as has already been suggested, the root and stem from which the colonial value theory emerged, and it is now necessary to examine the process whereby modification took place. Regulations for the fixation of wages had been made at the first assembly of the Massachusetts Court of Assistants because, as Hubbard put it, men are " apt to run wild and grow unruly without good laws." [1] This theory continued to be held by the clergy although the growth of industry and commerce rapidly altered the general belief in the efficacy of such legislation. " Those good orders," wrote Hubbard, " were not of long continuance, but did expire with the first and golden age in this new world." [2] It is interesting to note that this " golden age " of New England, which Hubbard considers to have ended in 1641, was the period in which John Cotton was in the zenith of his power. This extraordinary minister, as Tyler has well said,[3] " acquired a marvelous ascendency, personal and professional,—an ascendency more sovereign, probably, than any other American clergyman has ever reached." In 1636, Cotton prepared for the General Court a body of fundamental law based upon the Old Testament and which he entitled, " *Moses his judicials.*" [4] This model was rejected by the General Court and the code prepared by Nathaniel Ward became instead the " Body of Liberties " of Massachusetts Bay. The rejection of Cotton's stern code, in 1639, and the dissenting opinion of the magistrates in the same year con-

[1] Hubbard, *op. cit.*, pp. 146–147.
[2] *Ibid.*, p. 158.
[3] Tyler, Moses, Coit. *A History of American Literature during the Colonial Time.* New York, 1878. 2nd Edit., 1897, p. 211.
[4] Winthrop. *History of New England*, Vol. I., p. 202. See also Gray, F. C. " Remarks on the Early Laws of Massachusetts Bay." 3 *Mass. Hist. Soc. Coll.*, VIII., pp. 191–194. Also Ford, Worthington C. 2 *Mass. Hist. Soc. Proceeding*, XVI., pp. 279–280.

cerning the magnitude of Keaine's misdemeanour, represents a considerable growth of more liberal opinions and an undermining of the dominant position of the New England clergy.

Cotton's proposed code of law for Massachusetts had accepted the doctrine of " just price " and the necessity of fixation of prices. The section on Commerce provided that

" to the intent that all oppression in buying and selling may be avoided, it shall be lawful for the judges in every town, with the consent of the free burgesses, to appoint certain selectmen, to set reasonable rates upon all commodities, and proportionably to limit the wages of workmen and labourers, and the rates agreed upon by them and ratified by the judges, to bind all the inhabitants of the town." [1]

In the discussion of the rights to sell land, Cotton's code again defined " just price " as " due price, answerable to what others offer without fraud." [2]

By 1640, however, the trend in thought was away from fixation of prices. Trade was developing and merchants were pitting their ideas against those of the church. Hubbard referred to the period from 1630 to 1641 as the " golden age of New England, when vice was crushed . . . especially oppression and extortion in prices and wages." [3]   With approval, he cites the case of Edward Palmer who had charged an excessive price for a pair of stocks and who " had the honor to sit an hour in them first himself, to warn others not to offend in a like manner." [4]   But whereas in 1639, " seeking above 33£ per cent " had led to exemplary punishment, " since that time the common practice of the country hath made double that advance no sin." [5]   The clergy continued to protest, however, and as late as 1679, the Boston Synod of churches declared, " There are some Traders who sell their goods at excessive Rates." [6]   But the

---

[1] Cotton. *Abstract of the Laws of New England*, p. 180.
[2] *Ibid.*, p. 179.
[3] Hubbard, *op. cit.*, p. 248.
[4] *Ibid.*
[5] *Ibid.*
[6] *Necessity of Reformation*, p. 7.

men of affairs had long been doubtful of the wisdom of regulating prices and wages. Even Winthrop had admitted as early as 1640 that the General Court had

" found by experience that it would not avail by any law to redress the excessive rates of labourers' and workmens' wages, &c. (for being restrained, they would either remove to other places where they might have more, or else being able to live by planting and other employments of their own, they would not be hired at all)." [1]

The colonial value discussion, therefore, never crystallized around the doctrine of just price. Cotton's " Rules for Trading " and the colonial records represent the extent to which the doctrine was accepted. Before passing on to the subsequent value discussion, however, it is worth while to examine a few legislative records to ascertain what the legislators understood by " just price." Plymouth plantation allowed the " Milner at Scituate to charge no more than one sixteenth of bushel for grinding," and this was considered " competent toule." [2] The modern reader is curious to know just what " competent " meant—competent to cover cost ? In 1639, at Plymouth, Thomas Clark was fined thirty shillings " for extortion, in buy. a paire of bootes & spurs for Xs. and selling them againe for XVs." [3] A fifty per cent. mark-up was evidently extortion. More significant was the case of John Barnes who bought rye at four shillings a bushel and sold it again at five, " without adventure or long forbeareance in one and the same place." [4] Here is evidence that at Plymouth, a " just price " depended upon cost, for Barnes' case implies that a legitimate charge could be made for risk, transportation, and for the interest involved in carrying an inventory of goods. A twenty-five per cent. mark-up was extortion, *not per se*, but because it was charged when there had been no " *adventure or long forbeareance* " and

[1] Winthrop. *History of New England*, Vol. II., pp. 25–26.
[2] *Records of the Colony of New Plymouth*, Vol. XI., p. 30.
[3] *Ibid.*, Vol. I., p. 137.
[4] *Ibid.*, Vol. II., p. 5.

the goods were bought and sold "*in one and the same place.*" This definition of just price is exactly similar to that of Thomas Aquinas who had sanctioned an increase in price if the good had meantime been "changed for the better," because such increase would then be but the just reward for the labour involved.[1]

II

The influence of demand and supply was understood even during the years when the doctrine of "just price" was still the dominant note. Bradford noted that corn and cattle rose to high prices "by reason of ye flowing of many people into ye cuntrie, espetially into ye Bay of ye Massachusets."[2] He recognized the influence of the growth of a market, while his understanding of the principle of demand is evident. Similarly, Hubbard recorded a change in the conditions of demand, "for whereas before, all sorts of great cattle were usually sold for £25 the head, by reason of the continual coming of new families every year to plant the wilderness, now that fountain began to be dried."[3] The consequence of this diminution of demand was that New England would be forced "to seek of a way to provide themselves of clothing which they could not obtain by selling their cattle as before." Adrian Van der Donck recognized that where demand is inelastic a monopolist can charge very high prices. Under such circumstances, goods can be sold "at a hundred per cent advance, and higher or lower according as it suits them" (the monopolists), because the "common man cannot do without them."[4] The phenomenon of inelastic demand was also understood in the framing of a Plymouth law of 1638. This law forbade "regrating," and "engrossing" or the "oppressing" of buyers "when their necessyties do constraine them to buy [such goods] at any

---

[1] Thomas Aquinas. *Summa Theologica.* Edition cited, Part II., Second Number, p. 328.
[2] Bradford, *op. cit.*, p. 361.
[3] Hubbard, *op. cit.*, p. 238.
[4] Donck. *Representation of New Netherlands*, p. 40.

price." [1] Much later in the century, Blackwell displayed a clear understanding of the influences of demand and supply in the determination of value. In a barter economy, said he, exchange could be facilitated by " a frequent setting a just and equal value of the Price of all commodities, by public authority, *according as the plenty or scarcity of them shall require*, and the market had ruled." [2] But this action requires a measure of value. In barter, he pointed out, that

" unlesse both the parties dealing had like occasion reciprocally of each othcrs, the lesse necessitous over-reached the greater, by imposing ye Price of both ; to his owne advantage, and the others detriment." [3]

The significance of supply in price determination was as well recognized as the influence of demand. Bradford recorded that when wampum " grew to be a commoditye," the Indians began to increase the supply. Although " it hath now continued a current commoditie aboute this 20 years," continued Bradford, " it may prove a drugg in time." [4] Edward Johnson likewise saw that if the supply is greater than the amount demanded, prices must fall.[5] Winthrop recorded that prices fell when supply was excessive : " Corn being plenty divers years before," he wrote in 1643, " it was so undervalued as it would not pass for any commodity." [6] But when the conditions of supply were altered in the other direction, labourers and artificers " would have done any work, or parted with any commodity, for corn." [7] The Plymouth law of 1638, already cited, made it unlawful for merchants to " buy any goods or comodyties . . . to engrosse them into their hands to the end the price may be enhaunced." [8]

[1] *Records of the Colony of New Plymouth*, Vol. XI., p. 29.
[2] Blackwell, *op. cit.*, pp. 122–123.
[3] *Ibid.*, p. 122.
[4] Bradford, *op. cit.*, pp. 282–283.
[5] " Insomuch that Marchandizing being stopped at present [1637] they begin question what to do with their Corne." Johnson, Edward, *op. cit.*, p. 154.
[6] Winthrop. *History of New England*, Vol. II., p. 94.
[7] *Ibid.*
[8] *Records of the Colony of New Plymouth*, Vol. XI., p. 29.

Winthrop related that the scarcity of labourers led to such a rise in wages, in 1633, that the General Court attempted to prevent it by fixation of wage rates.[1] Moreover, "those who had commodities to sell, advanced their prices." Future costs of production evidently had their influence. In Virginia, Beverley said, that the large immigration, in 1621, "was the Occasion of making so much Tobacco, as to overstock the Market."[2] This situation, the Crown attempted to remedy by restricting each planter to producing but one hundred pounds. Likewise, in 1663, Beverley recorded, that in retaliation against the Navigation Act, "their assembly could think of no Remedy, but to be even with the Merchants, and make their Tobacco scarce."[3] But since Maryland would not agree to this restriction of supply, the Assembly was compelled to repeal this law, and the planters returned "to their old Drudgery of planting Tobacco without profiting by it."[4] Beverley saw that Virginia and Maryland must co-operate if any useful control over supply could be effected. Under separate governments he thought this impossible, because

"when one Colony goes about to prohibit the Trash or mend the Staple of that Commodity, to help the Market ; then the other to take Advantage of that Market, pours into England all they can make, both good and bad without distinction."[5]

Price control, he recognized, was dependent upon control of supply. Cotton Mather in his discussion, "Of Minerals," in the *Christian Philosopher*, recognized that the value of metals depends upon their relative abundance, but believed that their abundance was decided upon by God.[6] While the value of other minerals fluctuates, "There is a surprizing Providence of God in keeping up the value of Gold and Silver, nothwithstanding the vast Quantities dug out of the

[1] Winthrop. *History of New England*, Vol. I., p. 116.
[2] Beverley, *op. cit.*, p. 37.
[3] *Ibid.*, pp. 59–60.
[4] *Ibid.*
[5] *Ibid.*, p. 47.
[6] Mather. *Christian Philosopher*, p. 120.

Earth in all Ages." [1] Mather's point here is obscure. He may have meant that the demand for gold and silver had, through the ages, bolstered up their value, or he may have believed, as Xenophon did, about silver, that the precious metals had a constant value in spite of the quantities produced. One can only say that had this been true, it were a " surprizing Providence " indeed !

III

The influence of competition was often referred to in the colonial value discussion. Thus Beverley recognized that where buyers' competition is eliminated, the sellers suffer. The Navigation Act he branded as a

" Misfortune that cut with a double Edge : For, First, it reduced their Staple Tobacco to a very low Price ; and, Secondly, it raised the Value of European Goods, to what the Merchants pleased to put upon them." [2]

Such also was the opinion of Donck. " Plenty of shipping makes good markets," he wrote as a marginal summary. He realized the advantage of a wide market and " if shipping were abundant," said he, " everything could be better sold." [3] Where competition was to a person's advantage, it was welcomed and praised ; where it interfered with profits, it was decried and lamented. The town of Springfield, said Edward Johnson, was well located for the beaver trade " till the merchants encreased so many, that it became worth little by reason of their out-buying one another." [4] Neither was Bradford kindly disposed toward those who " wente and fild ye Indians with corne, and beat down ye prise, giving them twise as much as they [the Pilgrim Fathers] had done, and undertraded them in other commodities allso." [5] Richard Bellingham wrote to Bradford,

---

[1] Mather. *Christian Philosopher*, p. 120.
[2] Beverley, *op. cit.*, p. 59.
[3] Donck. *Representation of New Netherlands*, p. 63.
[4] Johnson, *op. cit.*, p. 237.
[5] Bradford, *op. cit.*, p. 252.

from Boston, that for the success of the beaver trade there would have to be " a company to order it in every jurisdiction among ye English." If such companies be not established and " agree in generall of their way of trade," said he, " the trade will be overthrowne." [1] Bellingham assured Bradford that the Boston people in trade had held " an orderly course, & have been sory to see ye spoyle thereof by others." [2] To Beverley also, competition was most undesirable, when it reduced profits. The expansion of tobacco planting in Virginia, he related, " exasperated the People, because now they found themselves under a Necessity of exchanging their commodities with the Merchants of England at their own terms." [3] Thomas Budd was of the same opinion. The consequence of the low price of producing pork, in Pennsylvania, he wrote, would be that " Inhabitants will seldom have their market spoiled by any that come from England." [4]

The importance of the cost of production in influencing the value of goods was referred to by a few of the American writers, especially Thomas Budd. The price of goods, wrote this Pennsylvania propagandist, must be enough to cover the cost of manufacture, freight, customs and mercantile profits. [5] Because of the costs of transportation, said Budd, " doubtless materials made of Hemp, must be sold in America by the Retailer, at double price as it cost where it grew." [6] If hemp-growing were carried on in America, he went on to say, labour would be very well paid. For " if we do get such Prices [foreign cost plus cost of transportation] for the cloth that we make, then we shall have double for our labour to what they have." [7] It is not clear whether he believed that prices would be governed by the cost of the most expensive part of the supply but only under such

[1] Letter of Richard Bellingham. Bradford, *op. cit.*, p. 462.
[2] *Ibid., op. cit.*, p. 462.
[3] Beverley, *op. cit.*, p. 60.
[4] Budd, *op. cit.*, p. 37.
[5] *Ibid.*, pp. 46–47.
[6] *Ibid.*, p. 42.
[7] *Ibid.*, p. 47.

circumstances could the Pennsylvania producers have obtained " double for [their] Labour." Budd also pointed out that if manufacturing were developed in Pennsylvania, cargoes would be available in either direction. Merchants would then have " Goods to freight their ships, which would tend to the benefit of all the inhabitants in general." [1] Just how it would benefit all, he does not explain, and one can only surmise that he may have meant a reduction in costs of transportation by a utilization of shipping to its capacity. Hartwell, Blair and Chilton, in Virginia, referred to the same problem. They clearly recognized interest as a cost of production. The slowness with which ships could be loaded in Virginia, and the necessity of ships lying idle for months awaiting cargo, " inflames the freight to almost double the price of what it needed to be, if the ships had a quick dispatch." [2]

Lastly, a few statements are to be found regarding the influences of a money economy upon value and price. Where money is available in adequate amounts, said John Woodbridge, " no buyer will be bound to one Person, or Market." [3] Prices will be promptly determined and there need be no " higling to suit ends." [4] Exchange and price determination will be facilitated because " money is but a measure of the value of other things." [5] In a barter economy, a means of fair exchange could be provided by the fixation of just value ratios for commodities by public authority. But to equate values, requires a " common standard," and for this " Money hath obteyned & been admitted as the best balance of Trade." [6] The paper money writers were eloquent in their attempts to prove that an increase in the volume of

---

[1] Budd, *op. cit.*, p. 33.
[2] Hartwell, Henry ; Blair, James ; and Chilton, Edward. "An Account of the Present State and Government of Virginia." Written, 1696–1698. Printed, London, 1727. Reprinted, 1 *Mass. Hist. Soc. Coll.*, Vol. 5, pp. 128–129.
[3] Woodbridge, *op. cit.*, p. 112.
[4] *Ibid.*, p. 111.
[5] Blackwell, *op. cit.*, p. 122.
[6] *Ibid.*, pp. 122–123.

money was the solution of all problems of value and price. Detailed analysis of what the seventeenth-century Americans understood about the relations between the quantity of money and the level of prices must be reserved for a subsequent chapter. For the present, it is only necessary to note that the colonial writers did recognize that the determination of the value of commodities was not only dependent upon their relative abundance or scarcity; it also hinged upon the mechanism whereby such commodities could be equated in the market.

TRADE, FETTERED AND FREE

" Since Trade hath flourished, she has made as many and considerable changes in the world as ever Empire did : How often has not she made a poor People rich, a little People Great, and an Ignorant People Wise."

The Humble Address of the Publicans of New England.

TRADE, FETTERED AND FREE

I

WHEREAS the seventeenth century in America mirrored a good deal of the medieval doctrine of " just price," very little of the scholastic criticism of men's "chrematistic" activities was reproduced. One does find a preference for agriculture often expressed, as well as a distrust of merchants. But the attitude of the American writers toward trade is conspicuously less medieval than their attitude toward most economic problems. It must be recalled, however, that the American colonies were offsprings of the mercantile expansion of England and Holland, and it would be quite remarkable if the philosophy of the American colonists had not been affected by the significant commercial changes which had transpired in Europe since the Summæ of the Schoolmen. Indeed, in their ideas on trade, on money and banking, and on the balance of trade, the seventeenth-century Americans were most nearly in harmony with their English contemporaries.

The realization of the importance of trade and the necessity of encouraging its growth pervades the literature of the century. " There is nothing more enricheth a commonwealth than much trade," wrote John Smith,[1] in 1631. He advised new colonies to impose low duties on shipping and to " use all commers with that respect, courtesie, and liberty [which] is fitting." [2] The Virginia Assembly in their protests against the restoration of any trade monopoly over that colony, asserted that trade is " the blood and life of a

[1] Smith. *Advertisements for the Unexperienced Planters*, p. 60.
[2] *Ibid.*

commonwealth." [1]   The Dutch, wrote Adrian Van der
Donck, " hold their place with the first " of the people of the
world " who have in any wise saluted the threshold of
history," because they have been " industrious in seeking
out foreign lands, navigable waters and trade." [2]

John Winthrop, although he had been a country squire
before his migration, and in spite of his preference for
agriculture, recognized the necessity of trade as did also
Bradford and Johnson. Bradford welcomed the growth in
trade consequent upon the settlement of Boston by the
Massachusetts Bay Company,[3] but subscribed most heartily
to the principle that trade should be carefully regulated to
prevent " under-trading." [4]   Edward Johnson, who feared
that the activities of traders might be injurious to his ideal
theocratic state, nevertheless recognized the necessity of trade
as a prerequisite for colonial specialization in agriculture and
cattle raising.   " If Merchants' trade be not kept on foot," he
wrote of the Massachusetts settlers, " they fear greatly their
corne and cattel will lye in their hands." [5]   Hubbard also
understood this problem.   Referring to the serious depression
caused by the cessation of immigration into Massachusetts
around 1640, he pointed out that the falling off of the cattle
trade would necessitate more colonial manufacturing.[6]
Gabriel Thomas regarded facilities for trade as one of the
essential requisites of a successful colony,[7] and Archdale
advocated an increase of colonial population because it
would " strengthen the Colony and increase Trade." [8]
Winthrop implied that taxes should be levied in such a
manner that trade would not be restrained.[9]   Thomas Budd
proposed that public granaries should be erected so that

[1] " Extract from a Manuscript Collection of Annals Relative to Virginia."
Printed, *Peter Force Hist. Tracts*, Vol. II., Washington, 1838, p. 5.
[2] Donck. *Representation of New Netherlands*, p. 11.
[3] Bradford, *op. cit.*, p. 361.
[4] *Ibid.*, p. 252.
[5] Johnson, *op. cit.*, p. 211.
[6] Hubbard, *op. cit.*, p. 238.
[7] Thomas, *op. cit.*, p. 325.
[8] Archdale, *op. cit.*, p. 117.
[9] Winthrop. *History of New England*, Vol. II., p. 259.

trade could be extensively developed.[1] Pastorius thought
domestic trade should be encouraged by the establishment
of fairs ; [2] and Beverley lamented that the dispersion of
the Virginia population retarded the growth of trade.[3]
Cotton Mather included the lending of money for the purposes of trade as one of the " pious uses of wealth." [4] In
1693, the Massachusetts legislators, influenced possibly by
the writings of Culpepper or Child, lowered the legal rate of
interest from 8 to 6 per cent., " forasmuch as the Abatement
of Interest hath always been found beneficial to ye advancement of Trade." [5] Throughout the whole century, therefore, and in every American colony, evidence is available to
show the colonial recognition of the necessity and the importance of trade. But a few dissenting voices were raised, and
these must next be heard.

That militant defender of theocracy, Edward Johnson,
although he saw the necessity of trade, was suspicious of
" merchants and traders." For such

" men of trade . . . being so taken up with the income of a
large profit, that they would willingly have had the Commonwealth tolerate divers kinds of sinful opinions to intice men to
come and sit down with us, that their purses might be filled with
coyne." [6]

He did not decry commerce as such, but he did fear that the
quest for profit would induce traders to bring in colonists
who would not harmonize with the religious ideals of Massachusetts Bay. " Let not any merchants, Inkeepers, Taverners and men of Trade in hope of gaine, fling open the gates
so wide," he cautioned,[7] " as that by letting in all sorts you
mar the worke of Christ intended." This excerpt illustrates,
in essence, the seventeenth-century criticism of trade. It

[1] Budd, *op. cit.*, p. 51.
[2] Pastorius, *op. cit.*, p. 9.
[3] Beverley, *op. cit.*, pp. 280–281.
[4] Mather. *Durable Riches*, Part II., p. 7.
[5] Massachusetts Archives, Pecuniary. Vol. I. Quoted by Felt, Joseph B.
An Historical Account of Massachusetts Currency. Boston, 1839, p. 53.
[6] Johnson, *op. cit.*, p. 254.
[7] *Ibid.*, p. 35.

was the perversion of trade that was condemned. There was no belief in any inherent turpitude in trade itself. It is true that the Quaker settlers in Pennsylvania were admonished by their great spiritual leader, " Of cities and towns, of commerce beware. The world is apt to stick close to those, who have lived and got wealth there." [1] But one needs only to glance at the correspondence between Penn and his American agent, James Logan,[2] to discover that Penn's aversion to trade was more rhetorical than real.

II

Although trade was in general warmly encouraged and carefully fostered, the colonial attitude was strangely paradoxical. For whereas the regulation of colonial trade by the mother country was condemned as ultimately injurious and unwise, the several colonial assemblies attempted to regulate their domestic trade by profuse and minute legislation. The outcome is that the word and the deed are constantly at variance. The literature abounds with condemnations of trade regulation and with praises of freedom of commerce. But alongside and contemporaneous with this stands the evidence of the statute books of meticulous control of domestic trade. The study of colonial trade regulation is the province of economic history, but the historian of economic thought must take cognizance of the ripening of ideas into legislation. For this reason, it is necessary to enumerate the types of commercial regulation which were enacted during the seventeenth century. No attempt, however, will be made to catalogue the actual laws themselves.

From New England to Virginia, laws of essentially the same character were attempted. Very often they failed in

[1] Penn, William. Letter to his wife. See Clarkson, Thomas. *A Portraiture of Quakerism*. New York, 1806. Vol. II., p. 44.
[2] " Correspondence between William Penn and James Logan." Philadelphia, 1870. *Publications of the Historical Society of Penna*. Vols. IX. and X.

their purpose ; in fact, the necessity of their re-inactment is proof of their evasion. They reflect the belief which was then current in Europe, and which was a legacy from that great period of social control, the Middle Ages, that trade relations cannot be left to the caprice of the open market. They embody, at the same time, especially in New England, a great many mercantilistic ambitions : regulation of trade with the view of building up an economically self-sufficient political unit.[1] But whether traditional, or politically purposeful, the seventeenth century extensively regulated trade. The export of foodstuffs without licence was forbidden,[2] as was the export of money.[3] Profits were limited by legislative maxima ;[4] markets were established and supervised.[5] The quality of goods brought to market was specified and defined,[6] the " exposure " of defective goods prohibited,[7] and provision was often made for a time limit between the date of importation and the date of sale, so that all prospective buyers might have notice.[8] " Staple " articles for the export trade were defined legislatively by most of the colonies,[9] and export monopolies were created by the colonial assemblies.[10] Attempts were made to create special markets where foreign goods were to be sold,[11] and direct trade between masters of vessels and colonists was repeatedly forbidden.[12] Fairs were established and en-

[1] The inferring of a theory of mercantilism has been considered by the author, for Massachusetts Bay, in an article in the *New England Quarterly* for July, 1928. See Johnson, E. A. J. " Some Evidence of Mercantilism in Massachusetts Bay."

[2] *E.g.*, Massachusetts law of 1631. *Mass. Col. Records*, Vol. I., p. 88.

[3] *E.g.*, Massachusetts law of 1632. *Ibid.*, Vol. I., p. 91.

[4] As in Massachusetts. *Ibid.*

[5] New Netherlands, 1648. See Brodhead, John Romeyn. *History of the State of New York.* New York, 1853, Vol. I., p. 489.

[6] *E.g.*, Pennsylvania, 1682. See Jenkins, Howard M. *Pennsylvania, Colonial and Federal.* Philadelphia, 1903, p. 278.

[7] *Ibid.*

[8] *Ibid.*

[9] *E.g.*, New York, 1638. Brodhead, p. 277. *Cf.* also Massachusetts law of 1640.

[10] *E.g.*, Connecticut, 1644. *Connecticut Colonial Records*, 1644, p. 116.

[11] *E.g.*, Virginia. *Cf.* Bruce, P. A. *Economic History of Virginia in the Seventeenth Century*, Vol. II., p. 363.

[12] *E.g.*, New Netherlands, 1657 ; Massachusetts, 1632.

couraged by law.[1] The Indian trade was carefully regulated,[2] though often for police purposes. Finally, regrating, engrossing and forestalling were prohibited under severe penalties. These laws directed against monopoly reflect essentially similar types of legislation in England, and were more widely enacted than any other regulative measures. In Virginia, a long series of such laws began in 1626, when the purchase of goods for sale at higher prices was forbidden.[3] Plymouth permitted purchases in wholesale lots in order to " retayle the same againe at a reasonable gaine," [4] but forbade regrating and forestalling. New Amsterdam tried to confine trade to settlers who had been resident for at least three years.[5] Laws such as these were the progeny of the theory that trade must be controlled and supervised. Ineffective legislation was from time to time repealed, but through the century a belief persisted that trade should be carefully circumscribed and jealously guarded.

III

Contrary to the foregoing principles is to be found a considerable body of statements which condemn and decry the regulatory activities of England or Holland, and which eulogize the principle of freedom of trade. Liberty, said John Smith, increases trade and trade enriches the state ; [6] in the long run, low customs are more profitable than high duties. Thus the prosperity of Holland and Genoa, Smith conceived to be largely due to their low customs, while the backwardness of Turkey, Sicily and Spain, was attributed to

---

[1] *E.g.*, New Netherlands, 1641 ; Virginia, 1655 ; Plymouth, 1639. The Plymouth law is representative : " It is enacted by the Court that there shalbe a markett kept at Plymouth every Thursday and a faire yearly," etc. *Plymouth Records*, Vol. XI., p. 32.
[2] Plymouth, 1677. *Plymouth Records*, Vol. XI., p. 246.
[3] Bruce, *op. cit.*, Vol. II., p. 359.
[4] *Plymouth Records*, Vol. XI., p. 29.
[5] *Cf.* Brodhead, *op. cit.*, Vol. I., p. 489.
[6] Smith. *Advertisements for the Unexperienced Planters*, p. 60.

their restrictive policies. High duties, Smith held, ultimately impoverish a state although they may enrich the customs collector.[1] He therefore urged, that new plantations should not annoy or discourage commerce by " Pilatage, Boyage, Ancorage, Wharfage, Custome, or any such tricks as hath beene lately used in most new Plantations, where they would be Kings before their folly." [2] The Virginia Assembly, in 1642, passed a " solemn declaration and protestation " against any royal trade monopoly.[3] Such a company, it alleged, would destroy " the freedom of our trade, the blood and life of a commonwealth." [4] Without trade, wrote Donck, " no country is prosperous " ; [5] restrictions upon trade mean economic decay. Strict regulation of trade, said Beverley, makes people " desperate " and leads to revolution.[6] The consequences of any policy which retards trade is diffused to the whole population, said Donck : " The burgher and peasant, the planter, the laboring man, and also the man in service, suffer great injury in consequence " among other reasons, because it retards the growth of shipping. But where shipping is abundant, " everything could be better sold and necessaries be more easily obtained." [7] Monopoly, Donck said, leads to high prices which are not justified ; it restricts the supply, and thereby extorts money from people whose wants must be satisfied.[8] Beverley considered the English restraints on trade as one of the causes of Bacon's Rebellion,[9] and the Navigation Act " seemèd to be of no other use, but to burden the Trade, or create a good Income to the Officers." [10] Donck contended that the regulatory policy of the Dutch West India Company

---

[1] Smith. *Advertisements for the Unexperienced Planters*, p. 60.
[2] *Ibid.*, pp. 59–60.
[3] *Extract from a Manuscript Collection of Annals Relative to Virginia*, p. 5.
[4] *Ibid.*
[5] Donck. *Representation of New Netherlands*, p. 40.
[6] Beverley, *op. cit.*, p. 53.
[7] Donck. *Representation of New Netherlands*, p. 63.
[8] *Ibid.*, p. 40.
[9] Beverley, *op. cit.*, pp. 64–65.
[10] *Ibid.*, p. 66.

had dried up legitimate trade " except a little, which exists pro forma, as a cloak to carry on smuggling." [1]

Roger Williams opposed the policy, advocated by John Cotton, of taking away " Civill priviledges " from those whom the Massachusetts Bay Colony sought to exclude. He understood how trade could be repressed by burdensome duties,[2] and how " the backs of some men, especially Merchants may be broke," by withdrawing civil privileges and " afflicting them in their Purses." [3] Religious belief, he maintained, should have nothing to do with economic privilege. To deprive a man of " any Civill right or Priviledge, due him as a man, a Subject, a Citizen, is to take from Cæsar that which is Cæsar's." [4] Religious persecution, wrote Gabriel Thomas, " knocks all Commerce on the head," as does also " high Imports, strict Laws, and cramping Orders." [5]

Berkeley approved the confining of a colony's trade to the mother country if the Crown was thereby really benefited. But if the benefits were swallowed up by privileged monopolists, it was to be condemned.[6] Increase Mather wrote in his diary, in 1675, " Trade dead, & ye customes in Barbadoes & Virginia very prejudicial to ye Traders of Ye Country." [7] Mather was responsible for the appearance of a London tract in which his ideas were put forth by an English writer. But the ideas were beyond a doubt those of the American colonial agent. This tract eulogized trade as the chief means whereby a nation could obtain riches, greatness and wisdom.[8] State action of some kind, in trade, it was pointed out, is

[1] Donck. *Representation of New Netherlands*, p. 40.
[2] Williams, Roger. " The Bloody Tenant yet More Bloody."   London, 1652. Reprinted, *Publications of the Narragansett Club*, Vol. IV. Providence, 1870, p. 414.
[3] *Ibid.*
[4] *Ibid.*
[5] Thomas, *op. cit.*, p. 329.
[6] Berkeley, *op. cit.*, pp. 6–7.
[7] Mather, Increase.   Diary.   Printed *Mass. Hist. Soc.*, Boston, 1902, p. 5.
[8] *The Humble Address of the Publicans of New England.* London, 1691. Reprinted, *Prince Soc. Andros Tracts*, Vol. II.   Boston, 1869, pp. 251–252.

indispensable. But such action must be based upon knowledge or experience, not chance. It must be purposeful,
definite, and propounded by persons who are intimately
acquainted with the problems.[1]   Liberties and privileges
must be intelligently granted if trade is to prosper, and the
success of the Dutch was explained on this basis ; " Trade
and Tyranny will never agree." [2] The tract was designed
to obtain English support for the contention of the colonial
agent. The commercial privileges of New England, it was
urged, " have been inconsiderable in respect to what other
People who will promote Trade and Plantation have commonly given." [3] Expansion of commerce requires freedom !

IV

On the subject of monopolies there appears to be a distinct difference of opinion between the writers in the charter
colonies and those in royal or company controlled colonies.
In New England, the usefulness and desirability of trade
monopolies were admitted, while in Virginia and New
Netherland, where the direct consequences of controlled
trade were felt, monopoly was decried and opposed. But
this does not mean that the seventeenth-century Virginians
opposed monopoly when it meant larger profits. They
recognized the necessity of concerted action if the tobacco
trade was to be profitable.

The early literature of New England contains repeated
acceptance of the monopoly principle. Governor Bellingham
of Massachusetts advocated the establishment of companies
" in every jurisdiction," and recommended that agreements
should be entered into by the several companies so that trade
would not be " overthrowne." [4] Bradford was distressed
because other traders had " beat down the price " in dealings

[1] *Humble Address of the Publicans of New England*, pp. 251–252.
[2] *Ibid*, p. 252.
[3] *Ibid.*, p. 253.
[4] Bradford, *op. cit.*, p. 462.

with the Indians and "under-traded" the Plymouth settlers.[1]
He maintained that monopoly was necessary to induce
investment in trading projects, and to compensate the
existing investments.[2] Winthrop believed that monopoly
was a valuable means of stimulating young industries and
recorded that the General Court gave a twenty-one year
monopoly to Braintree iron manufacturers.[3] Plymouth, in
1670, granted a monopoly of the tar trade to eight persons
who agreed to buy all the tar made in the colony at fixed
prices ;[4] Connecticut granted an export monopoly of the
colony's wheat, rye, and peas.[5] Such legislative grants
were frequently made in the New England colonies. The
Plymouth grant of 1632 is most interesting. By it, a certain
Stephen Deane was granted the right to set up a "water
worke to beat corne uppon." But his monopoly was a
regulated one indeed. There was to be no usurpation of
valuable sites to hinder future mills ; the grinding toll was
established by law, and the colony reserved the right to
acquire the works when a grinding mill was set up. But
until that time, the establishment was to have a monopoly
right excepting only establishments for private use.[6]

Virginia had witnessed too often the vexatious consequences of royal tobacco monopolies. The outcome was a
wholesome disrespect for any restraint upon trade. From
the very beginning of the tobacco industry, it was recognized
that the greatest prosperity depended upon the widest
market possible. For this reason, every attempt to re-
establish company control over Virginian trade was vigorously opposed. Beverley pointed out that the Navigation
Acts, by decreasing the market, reduced the price of exports
while it "raised the Value of European Goods, to what the
Merchants pleased to put upon them."[7] But Beverley

[1] Bradford, op. cit., p. 252.
[2] Governor Bradford's Letter Book.   Boston, 1906.
[3] Winthrop.   History of New England, Vol. II., pp. 212–213.
[4] Records of the Colony of New Plymouth, Vol. V., p. 46.
[5] Connecticut Colonial Records, 1644, p. 116.
[6] Records of the Colony of New Plymouth, Vol. II., p. 8.
[7] Beverley, op. cit., p. 59.

understood that one could combat monopoly with monopoly, and advocated legislative control over the supply of tobacco to bring the English merchants to terms.[1] In New Amsterdam, Donck was the sharpest critic of the Dutch West India Company's monopolistic policy. He maintained that the high prices of imported goods were not justified by the liability of these goods to depreciation, but were merely extorted by virtue of the intensity of demand.[2]

V

The paper money writers' references to trade were incidental to their inflationist argument. Trade, said Cotton Mather, demands a monetary system which will permit merchants to liquidate their debts.[3] Budd argued that a commodity bank would provide an abundance of money [4] by reducing hoarding. " People of all degrees," said he, " will put in their Moneyes " which the bank will " put out again into Trade to Merchants." The result would be that " Trade is made easie and much convenienced." [5] Woodbridge explained that the reason why trade is facilitated by money is because " no buyer will be bound to one Person, or market." [6] Scarcity of money, he held, leads to high prices, unliquidated indebtedness, slow payments, and the repression of new ventures ; [7] whereas an abundance of money " multiplies Trading " because it " redeemeth Time, Labour and Expence greatly consumed in higling up and down to suit Pay to content." [8] The use of a common standard " abrogatheth the mystery of Trucking," and thereby conserves the time of magistrates which is otherwise spent in settling " wrangling and vexatious Suits upon

[1] Beverley, *op. cit.*, pp. 59–60.
[2] Donck. *Representation of New Netherlands*, p. 40.
[3] Mather. *Considerations on the Bills of Credit*, p. 193.
[4] Budd, *op. cit.*, p. 48.
[5] *Ibid.*, pp. 49–50.
[6] Woodbridge, *op. cit.*, p. 112.
[7] *Ibid.*, p. 113.
[8] *Ibid.*

Debts." In fact the time wasted in legal controversy should rather be spent in " studying the necessary advantages of Trade, and forwarding of Manufacture."[1] Where money is wanting, declared Governor Dudley in 1686, trade is certain to fall into decay.[2] Woodbridge went further, and pointed out that scarcity of money would lead to a restraint of domestic and foreign commerce, accumulation of dead stocks, rigorous competition, and disorganized markets.[3] The author of *Reasons for a Mint in New England*[4] recognized the stagnating consequences which result from the appreciation of a monetary unit : " It would ruyne the Tenant and Debtor, destroy the Trade of that Country, and bring no advantage, but loss to the King." An increase of trade demands an increase of money, wrote John Blackwell. Since specie is " suspected to be insufficient in this age of the world," some substitute must be found if a community is to have " a sufficiency wherewith to manage their increasing trades."[5]

VI

The theory of mercantilism had loyal adherents among the colonial writers on trade. Evidence can be adduced from legislation, from governmental correspondence, from the colonial archives and from histories, pamphlets and tracts to show acceptance of the various elements of the mercantilist philosophy. This situation needs little explanation, for most people are by nature mercantilists. Add to this the popularity of the mercantilist theses from Bodin[6] onward, and

[1] Woodbridge, *op. cit.*, 113.
[2] Massachusetts Archives. "Usurpation," Vol. I. Quoted, Felt, *op. cit.*, p. 46.
[3] Woodbridge, *op. cit.*, p. 114.
[4] In Crosby, Sylvester S. *The Early Coins of America*. Boston, 1875, pp. 92 *et seq.*
[5] Blackwell. *Discourse*, p. 122.
[6] " To abate the custome of marchandise comming in, if the subject cannot passe without them, you must raise the custome of things made by hand, and not to suffer any to be brought out of strange countreys, and not to suffer any rawe stuffs to be carried out of the land, as iron, copper, steele, wool, flaxe, raw silk, etc." Bodin, Jean. *The Six Books of a Commonweale*. Translated by Richard Knolles. London, 1606, p. 663.

the rise of mercantilist dogma as a justification of economic policy. In the American sources one finds the characteristic ideals of mercantilism : praise of a self-sufficient economy, prohibition of the exportation of raw materials and specie, confusion of treasure and wealth, and the balance of trade dogma.

"It is the glory of every Nation," wrote John Hammond,

"to enlarge themselves, to answer their own forraign attempts, and to be able to have of their own, within their territories, as many several commodities as they can attain to, that so others may rather be beholding to them, then they to others." [1]

For this purpose, he said, discovery and colonization have been encouraged. John Smith pointed out that the possession of colonies would make a nation self-sufficient and eliminate a loss of specie.[2] The production of commodities heretofore bought from foreigners, wrote Berkeley, is a "work worthy of a public mark of Honour and Reward," because it keeps specie in the realm.[3] Colonies can provide a nation with such goods and can also provide an export surplus which will "ballance many other forreign necessities." [4] A good colony, said Donck, should import less than it exports.[5]

The author of *A Perfect Description of Virginia* accepted the familiar mercantilist thesis that the purchase of goods from foreigners results in their enrichment, and that a nation loses in her imports. It is the province of the state, he maintained, to encourage industries which will make the state self-sufficient.[6] This duty the several American colonial assemblies accepted, and the legislative records contain a great deal of evidence to show that industry and manufacturing were encouraged to increase the independent status

[1] Hammond, *op. cit.*, p. 6.
[2] Smith. *Map of Virginia*, p. 64.
[3] Berkeley, *op. cit.*, p. 9.
[4] *Ibid.*, p. 10.
[5] Donck. *Representation of New Netherlands,* p. 36.
[6] *A Perfect Description of Virginia.*

of the several colonies.[1] Increase Mather held that the development of manufacturing was necessary in order to retain specie,[2] as did also Pastorius.

"We are also endeavoring to introduce the cultivation of the vine, and also the manufacture of woolen cloths and linens," wrote Pastorius from Pennsylvania,

" so as to keep our money as much as possible in the country. For this reason we have already established fairs to be held at stated times, so as to bring the people of different parts together for the purposes of barter and trade, and thereby encourage our own industry and prevent our little money from going abroad." [3]

Judge Sewall argued that the production of sail-cloth and cordage in Massachusetts would obviate their importation ; would conserve specie, would furnish England with her supplies, and thereby end her dependence upon foreign supply.[4]

The belief in the eminent desirability of the precious metals, together with the peculiar monetary problems in the American colonies, gave rise to a long series of prohibitions against the export of specie. How much of this legislation was motivated by confusion of money and wealth is very difficult to determine. But it is reasonable to suppose that the exaggerated notion of the importance of specie was one of the forces which induced this type of legislation.

The colonial writers understood that if specie was to be accumulated, a favourable balance of trade would have to be obtained. John Smith pointed out that the fishing trade was the means whereby Holland obtained a favourable balance.[5] Edward Johnson enumerated the " staple commodities " which New England could export.[6] In

---

[1] Some illustrative legislation in Massachusetts is to be found in the author's article on " Some Evidence of Mercantilism in the Massachusetts Bay." *New England Quarterly*, July, 1928, pp. 371 *et seq.*
[2] Mather, Increase.   " A Brief Relation of the State of New England," London, 1689. Reprinted, *Peter Force Hist. Tracts*, Vol. IV. Washington, 1838, p. 8.
[3] Pastorius, *op. cit.*, p. 9.
[4] Sewall. *Computation that the Importation of Negroes, &c.*, p. 199.
[5] Smith. *Description of New England*, p. 194.
[6] Johnson, *op. cit.*, p. 247.

reply to the objection that there were no mines in British North America, the author of *New England's First Fruits* answered ; " we have those staple commodities named, they will fetch money from other parts." [1] Very little of the precious metals, he urged, is mined in England ; " How then comes it [money] to abound but by this meane ? " [2]

The paper money writers referred often to the problem of the balance of trade. Most of them understood that the want of specie was due to an unfavourable balance.[3] Mather explained that the colonial inflow of silver resulted from the favourable balance of trade with the West Indies, whereas the drain of specie was due to an unfavourable balance with Europe.[4] A petition from the freeholders of Accomack County, Virginia, declared that money was the " most convenient Ballance for carrying on all Trade and Commerce " and that when other nations draw it away the result is " our Impoverishment and Their Great Advantages." [5] The same opinion is contained in another tract which ascribed the " Real cause of the Scarcity of Moneys " to

" the actual Transporting the Ballance or Over plus of the value of goods imported, above the proportion of the value of the native products exported ; which (Exceedingly) must of necessity be answered by moneys in specie." [6]

Now the interesting aspect of the paper money literature is that it represents the distinct abandonment of the bullionist thesis. The want of specie was explained in the same manner as mercantilists explained it. But the paper money writers, by virtue of their inflationist doctrine, attempted to

[1] " New England's First Fruits." London, 1643. Reprinted, *Old South Leaflets*, No. 51, p. 13.
[2] *New England's First Fruits*, p. 13.
[3] *E.g.*, Blackwell. *Discourse*, p. 123.
[4] Mather. *Considerations on the Bills of Credit*, p. 193.
[5] *Calendar of Virginia State Papers*. Edited by Wm. P. Palmer. Richmond, 1875, Vol. I., p. 53.
[6] " A Model for erecting a Bank of Credit." London, 1688. Reprinted, Prince Society, *Colonial Currency Reprints*, Vol. I. Boston, 1910, pp. 183–184.

solve the unfavourable balance, not by prohibitions of the export specie, nor by the development of manufacturing, but by the substitution of a paper medium in lieu of specie. It is because specie is transportable, said the inflationists, that it is an unsatisfactory medium. A paper currency will not be exported, said Mather. Indeed, the futility of exporting paper currency will mean that goods exports will increase, and thereby correct the unfavourable balance of trade.[1] Blackwell likewise held that while the trade balance is unfavourable, scarcity of currency will persist until a substitute for metallic money is discovered.[2] The inflationist literature of the last quarter of the seventeenth century, to be sure, contains plenty of naïve ideas. But one must admit that it had gone beyond the naïveté of the bullionists. The American bullionists were those optimistic souls who believed an unfavourable trade balance could be corrected by prohibiting the export of specie or by attracting gold or silver by legal over-valuation.

Given an unfavourable trade balance, how then could specie be attracted to a country? To this question a *Petition for a Free Mint*, of 1680, gave answer that were a free mint established, foreigners in the purchase of American goods would " rather choose to send pieces of $\frac{8}{8}$, plate or Bullion then run the hazard of an uncertain market for those goods which they may with less loss send to other parts." [3] A Massachusetts legislative committee, of 1677, came to the conclusion that the only way to attract specie was by " raising the value of our coin . . . or making the mint free." [4] John Hull, the Massachusetts mint-master, diplomatically justified his own seigneurage by his explanation of the causes for the exportation of specie. " If our own

---

[1] Mather. *Considerations on the Bills of Credit*, p. 193.
[2] Blackwell, John. " Some Additional Considerations Addressed unto the Worshipful Elisha Hutchinson, Esq." Boston, 1691. Reprinted, Prince Society. *Colonial Currency Reprints*, Vol. I., p. 203.
[3] " Petition for a Free Mint." Massachusetts Archives, Pecuniary. Quoted by Crosby, *op. cit.*, p. 109.
[4] Mass. Archives, Pecuniary, Vol. I. Quoted, *Transactions and Collections of the American Antiquarian Society*, Vol. III. Boston, 1857, p. 299.

coin be carried out of the country," he wrote in 1680, "it is a sign that it is not so light as it may be, and that it would be for public advantage to make it lighter." [1]

Such were the attempts which the seventeenth century made to deal with the problems of a colony's balance of trade. Vexatious monetary problems, resulting from the necessity which a new nation has of acquiring its share of the world's specie supply, often obscured or confused the trade problems involved. But the problems of the international balance engaged American attention. The monetary aspects of the balance of trade will be considered in the next chapter.

[1] Hull, John. *Trans. & Coll. Am. Antiq. Soc.*, Vol. III., p. 301.

CHAPTER IX

MONETARY PRINCIPLES AND MONETARY PROPOSALS

" Money is that One Thing, which, as a Medium of Trade (for so Solomon's Assertion must necessarily, be understood) answereth All things. For where it is in plenty, no Buyer will be bound to one Person, or Market ; nor purchase Credit at the Grantor's price ; nor be necessitated to become servant to the Lender, if he have money to answer his occasions ; nor will run the hazard of Trusting."

John Woodbridge, *Severals Relating to the Fund*.

CHAPTER IX

MONETARY PRINCIPLES AND MONETARY PROPOSALS

I

ALTHOUGH there is nothing fundamentally new in the American discussion of money, during the seventeenth century, the acute monetary problems of the period constantly stimulated monetary discussion. As a consequence, European ideas on the subject were drawn upon for guidance. The monetary discussion, although frequently confused and obscure, is often lucid and forceful. Specific problems were considered at some length by pamphleteers, and the whole body of thought is far less casual than most of the economic thought of the century. The monetary discussion centres around problems of the origin and function of money, the advantages which result from its use, consideration of the means of acquiring a supply of specie, ways of retaining specie within a colony, coinage, the relation between the quantity of money and prices, the economic consequences of changes in the price level, and the advantages and disadvantages of paper money.

The bulk of the monetary discussion took place during the last quarter of the century, although there are a considerable number of references to monetary problems in the earlier decades. But essentially, it was the paper money propaganda that precipitated a detailed examination of the theory of money. Woodbridge's tract, *Severals Relating to the Fund*, was published in 1682, and from that time onward, the paper money arguments gained ground rapidly. The spirited controversy over the merits of a paper circulation ran on long into the next century, but the fundamental arguments were put forth before 1700.

The issue of government paper by Massachusetts in 1690, gave rise to a whole new set of monetary problems which intensified interest in the theory of money and which called for explanation. The very existence of these troublesome problems led to the consideration of some aspects of money which European writers had not been compelled to deal with. The use of non-metallic money, of course, was not new. The Carthaginians had employed leather money ; in China, paper money had been used, and Cyprus and Leyden are also reputed to have used paper. More important was the card money which had been used in New France, which was an immediate predecessor of the American paper currency.[1] Cotton Mather, for example, referred to the French issues of card money as a reason why Massachusetts should issue paper : " Now if we account ourselves to Transcend the French in Courage, 'Tis a shame for us to come so far short of them in Wit and Understanding." [2]   But while the Americans cannot be said to have been the innovators of paper money, the governmental issues of Massachusetts in the seventeenth century did lead to consideration of a series of monetary problems which had not previously received attention, and to this extent, the American discussion can be said to be in advance of the European. The paper money writers were compelled to defend the thesis that the primary function of money is to pay debts, and that acceptable evidences of indebtedness could perform this task as well as a commodity.

To attempt to state the theoretical legacy which the American writers on monetary subjects had inherited from preceding discussions, is at once unwise and impossible. Medieval notions on economic subjects, as has been shown in the previous chapters, were well diffused in America.

[1] *Documents Relating to Canadian Currency, Exchange and Finance During the French Period.* Edited by Adam Shortt. Ottawa, 1925.
[2] Mather. *Considerations on Bills of Credit*, p. 195.

Aristotle's ideas on money were no doubt known by educated Americans. These monetary ideas had been summarized in the famous Mixt Money Case, decided by the Privy Council in 1604. The decision declared that

" Money is a public measure (mensura publica) intended to obviate the inconvenience and inequity of Barter. There can be no society without exchanges, no system of exchanges without equity and no equity of exchanges without money."

Del Mar took the position that the ideas contained in this decision must have been known in the American Colonies.[1] If they were, it is as likely that they had been obtained from Aristotle or Bodin, as from the Privy Council decision. But whatever the doctrinal genealogy of American ideas may have been, the Colonial writers dealt with monetary theory with a greater degree of competence than they did with most problems.

II

Robert Beverley observed the fundamental principle that a commodity which served the purposes of ornament may be usable for money.
" The Indians," he wrote,

" had nothing which they reckoned riches, before the English went among them, except Peak, Roenoke, and such like trifles made out of the Cunk Shell. These past with them instead of Gold and Silver, and serv'd them both for Money and Ornament."[2]

Most of the American references to the origin of money were concerned with the abstract rather than actual illustration of the emergence of money. Money, wrote John Blackwell, sometime in the remote past " obteyned to be the usual & best known means of Interchange."[3] Its origin was " occaisioned by the experimented inconveniences of

---

[1] Del Mar, Alexander. *The History of Money in America.* New York, 1899, p. 74.
[2] Beverley, *op. cit.*, p. 195.
[3] Blackwell, *Discourse*, p. 122.

Common Barter by Commodities." For barter, he pointed out, required that "both the parties dealing have like occasion reciprocally of each others." [1] Even if such a happy and harmonious coincidence of wants were to be found, barter would not provide an equitable means of exchange, since often "the lesse necessitous over-reached the greater, by imposing ye price of both [commodities] : to his owne advantage, and the others detriment, which was not equal." [2]

A Massachusetts Committee, of 1684, pointed out that money overcame the inconvenience which resulted from the use of "staple commodities" as a means of paying debts. Fish and corn, the committee said, were "so cumbersome and troublesome as could not be borne." [3] Blackwell, in this relation, showed that money facilitated price determination. A fixation of value by public authority, he said, might conceivably overcome the inconvenience of barter. But such a value determination requires a "common standard," and for this, "Money hath obteyned & been admitted as the best ballance of Trade." [4] Cotton Mather, who lived in a period when pounds, shillings, and pence served only as a money of account, turned his great learning to the problems of money, and came to the amusing conclusion that money had its origin "from a general ignorance of Writing and Arithmetic." [5] But popular knowledge of "these Arts" eliminates the necessity of a commodity money. Money, he maintained, "is but a Counter or Measure of Men's Proprieties, and Instituted mean of permutation." If all men had had a knowledge of writing and arithmetic, we must infer from this great mind, all exchange could have been facilitated by keeping accounts !

In spite of the fact that the love of money is the root of all evil, said Mather, in the *Christian Philosopher*, the use of

[1] Blackwell. *Discourse*, p. 122.
[2] *Ibid.*
[3] Report of a Committee (appointed October 30th, 1684), Political MSS., Vol. I. Mass. Archives. Quoted, *Archæologia Americana*, Vol. III., p. 282.
[4] Blackwell. *Discourse*, pp. 122–123.
[5] Mather. *Considerations on the Bills of Credit*, p. 190.

money has had a vast importance to mankind. " Indeed,"
said Mather, " where the Use of Money has not been introduced, men are brutish and savage, and nothing that is good
has been cultivated." [1] More specific was the argument
contained in the Massachusetts Petition, of 1680, for a free
mint. A money economy, it was urged, is eminently
superior to a truck or barter economy, because it saves time
and trouble and because it prevents " many Suits, con-
troversys and inconveniences amongst neighbours and
ffreinds." [2] Moreover, money is the " sinews of war," a
" defense against the designes and power of fforeign or
Intestine Enemies."

John Woodbridge believed that the chief advantage
resulting from the use of money was an economy of time.
For where money is wanting, a great deal of time must be
spent in " higling to suit ends." [3] Waxing more eloquent
in defence of his inflationist programme, he alleged that
money quickens trade, stimulates enterprise, lowers the rate
of interest, increases land values, promotes settlement,
creates an inducement to labour. Lastly, and more scientific,
money " abrogateth the mystery of Trucking, by sinking
barter, and reduceth all bought and sold," to a common
standard. The consequence is, that " wrangling and
vexatious Suits upon Debts " are eliminated, which otherwise exist " to the Scandal of a religious people " and which
consume the time of magistrates which could be better spent
in " studying the necessary advantages of Trade." [4] In
the payment of taxes, said Cotton Mather, money has a
unique advantage over produce, because it provides a
" measure (a thing which Cod allows not)." [5] Moreover,
the receipt of produce for taxes involves greater cost, due
to depreciation. The outcome of produce taxes would be

[1] Mather. *Christian Philosopher*, p. 120.
[2] Massachusetts Archives, Pecuniary. Quoted, Crosby, *op. cit.*, p. 109;
and *Archeologia Americana*, Vol. III., pp. 300–301.
[3] Woodbridge, *op. cit.*, p. 111.
[4] *Ibid.*, p. 113.
[5] Mather. *Considerations on the Bills of Credit*, p. 192.

that the government is rendered " odious by a great noise of taxes, when little comes thereby." [1] In brief, produce taxes are higher taxes than money taxes.

III

The functions of money, according to the American writers, were several : to serve as a medium of trade, to provide a measure of value, to afford a standard of deferred payments. The argument of the paper money writers was that a paper currency could perform these respective functions better than specie. In fact, it was in attempting to prove this thesis that they discussed the function of money in general.

The protracted experience of the American colonists with produce money had clearly demonstrated, that if a commodity were to serve the function of a medium of exchange, it must possess the quality of wide acceptability. For this reason also, the paper money writers were most assiduous in their endeavours to prove that a paper circulation would possess this requisite quality. " Money," wrote Woodbridge, " is that One Thing, which as a medium of Trade (for so Solomon's assertion must necessarily be understood) answereth all things." [2] It generalizes purchasing power, for by its use " no Buyer will be bound to one Person, or Market." [3] It eliminates coercion by sellers or by lenders of goods, since the buyer or the borrower has " money to answer his occasions." [4] Exchange can accordingly be facilitated by bank bills, Woodbridge argued, because coin, when used as money, does not exercise its capacity as a commodity. [5] The function of money, he held, was to provide a medium, for money " does neither Feed nor

---

[1] Mather. *Considerations on the Bills of Credit*, p. 192.
[2] Woodbridge, *op. cit.*, p. 112.
[3] *Ibid.*
[4] *Ibid.*
[5] *Ibid.*, p. 114.

Cloath." A want satisfying power, *per se*, is not necessary, therefore, in a money instrument. Such a quality " is not essential to a thing, meerly good for Exchange." [1] The function of coined money, said Blackwell, in the same vein, is " but to furniss a man with Credit, that he may obtain from his neighbours those Commodities, which he hath occasion for." [2] Here in substance is what Hobbes said in his discussion of " concoction," [3] namely that money sanguifies wealth. Whatever passes as a medium of exchange, concluded Blackwell, will serve the function of money. Produce has performed this work, and paper instruments can also. [4]

As a measure of value, various foreign money had been long employed in the American colonies. The function of money as a measure of value was so evident that abundant consideration was given to it. Money reduces all things bought and sold to a common standard, said Woodbridge, [5] and in this opinion he was seconded by his fellow pamphleteer, Blackwell, who said that " money, whether Gold or Silver, is but a measure of the value of other things." [6] It has become such a measure, he explained, because it has received wide acceptability " for a long Succession of Ages (especially in the civilized & trading part of the world)". As a metal, said Mather, money is a commodity ; " But as Mony, it is no more than what was said," (*i.e.*)" a Counter or Measure of Mens' Proprieties, and Instituted mean of permutation." [7] The Maryland Assembly, in their petition for the right of coinage (1661), declared, that " forasmuch as money being the rule & measure of ye value of Commodities, no trade or commerce can be well managed without it." [8]

---

[1] Woodbridge, *op. cit.*, p. 114.
[2] Blackwell, John. *Some Additional Considerations*, p. 200.
[3] Hobbes. *Leviathan*, p. 168.
[4] Blackwell. *Some Additional Considerations*, p. 204.
[5] Woodbridge, *op. cit.*, p. 113.
[6] Blackwell. *Discourse*, p. 122.
[7] Mather. *Considerations on the Bills of Credit*, p. 190.
[8] Quoted in Crosby, Sylvester S. *The Early Coins of America*. Boston, 1875, p. 126.

The same principle was contained in the paper presented to the English mint in 1686, *Reasons for a Mint in New England*. " Money," according to this paper, " is the measure for the valuation of Houses, Lands, or Goods." [1] The value of money, therefore, depends upon the ratio between the " Stock of Lands and Goods in every Country " and the " Stock of Money." [2]

The author of this address to the officers of the Royal Mint understood as well that money becomes a standard of deferred payments. The appreciation of the " pine tree shilling," which would be involved in bringing it to the English standard, he pointed out, would destroy the capacity of the Massachusetts coin for fulfilling this function. It " would enrich the Landlord and Creditor," he correctly explained, " but it would ruyne the Tenant and Debtor." [3] John Hull, the Massachusetts Mint master, understood that any debasing of a currency renders it impossible for the money unit to serve as a standard of indebtedness. He was optimistic enough, however, to suggest that justice could be provided by an arbitrary separation of old from new debts ; and that the former could be paid in money which obtained at the time the debt was contracted, while the newer debts could be settled in terms of the debased money current.[4]

Of money as a store of value, virtually nothing is to be found, except with reference to the paper money depreciation. To permit the colonial bills of credit to fall to a discount, wrote Cotton Mather, was rank injustice,[5] since thereby the " poor Soldier is horribly injured," because he had looked upon the bills as the equivalent of specie. Blackwell was of the same opinion.[6]

---

[1] " Reasons for a Mint in New England," 1686. Colonial Entry Book, Vol. 61, p. 137. Quoted, Crosby, *op. cit.*, pp. 91–92.
[2] *Ibid.*
[3] *Ibid.*
[4] Hull, John. *Archeologia Americana*, Vol. III., pp. 301–302.
[5] Mather. *Considerations on the Bills of Credit*, p. 194.
[6] Blackwell. *Some Additional Considerations*, p. 201.

IV

Given these several functions of money, what commodity could best perform them ? The colonial answer to this question was limited because many of the seventeenth-century monetary writers attempted to prove that paper would be as satisfactory as a " merchantable " [1] commodity. It was this contention which led to inquiries into the qualities of satisfactory money commodities. Gold is superior to silver for the purposes of money, said John Blackwell, because it can be counted and carried with greater ease ; and, because of its greater value in smaller bulk, there is less risk in transporting or in hoarding gold.[2] But paper money, he argued, is superior to either, since by mere sight one can ascertain the value of a bill, while convenient denominations simplify computation.[3] Bank bills (of his projected commodity bank), he urged, would have still another attractive quality. The risk of loss by theft or destruction could be obviated since the issuing bank could renew the lost or destroyed bill.[4] Cotton Mather recognized that gold was a particularly good money substance because of its ductility and fusibility.[5] Stability of value, he also required of a good money commodity. But as Xenophon had erred with regard to silver, so the devout Mather erred about the constant value of gold and silver. In spite of the " vast Quantities " which have been mined, said Mather, " a surprizing Providence of God " has kept the value of these metals from falling and " so continued them fit materials to make money of." [6] He may, however, merely have meant that in spite of the increased supply of money,

---

[1] Mather. *Considerations on the Bills of Credit*, p. 194.
[2] Blackwell. *Discourse*, p. 132.
[3] *Ibid.*
[4] *Ibid.*, pp. 131–132.
[5] " It is a marvelous thing that Gold, after it has been divided by corrosive Liquors into invisible parts, yet may presently be so precipitated, as to appear in its own golden Form again." Mather. *Christian Philosopher*, pp. 120–121.
[6] *Ibid.*, p. 120.

its value had not fallen because of the increased demand for
it. If this was his meaning, it is incorrect to accuse him of
falling into Xenophon's error.

Although gold and silver are useful monetary substances,
they have also some shortcomings, said Woodbridge, which
render them less satisfactory than paper. In the first place,
treasure " allures an Enemy, and is covetously hoarded
up." [1] Moreover, it is " subject to wear, it is often adulterated, it is ' irrevocably lost ' through fires, robberies,
mistakes, & the like continguencies." [2]   But bank bills
(commodity or land bank) are exempt from these disadvantages, because they are secured by land or commodities which are of " real, durable, & of secure value." [3]
Indeed, since the ultimate function of money is to facilitate
trade, bank bills can perform this function as well as coin,
because coin, when used as money, exercises only its function
as a medium, not its function as a commodity. [4]   The
prejudice in favour of specie, he maintained, was due to an
erroneous belief that a money substance must have " In-
trinsic Value." But this quality, he held, " is not essential
to a thing, meerly good for Exchange ; and serving barely
to procure what One wants, that another abounds with." [5]

The paper money writers were indefatigable in bringing
together arguments to show the advantages of paper money
over specie. To-day, in a world which is ordered on an
elaborate credit system, these arguments seem unnecessarily
prolix. But in the seventeenth century the sympathy of
the reader had to be won by means of elaborately regimented
arguments. Whether the particular propagandist favoured
the colonial bills of credit or a prospective issue of a commodity, or land bank, does not alter the essentials of the
argument. Paper money, it was urged, will perform money
work.

[1] Woodbridge, *op. cit.*, p. 115.
[2] *Ibid.*
[3] *Ibid.*
[4] *Ibid.*, p. 114.
[5] *Ibid.*

Mather, in his defence of the Bills of Credit, argued in this wise : a bill of credit is as valuable as gold or silver if the security for its payment is sufficient ; this condition is bountifully fulfilled in the case of the Massachusetts bills, because their security is no less " than the Credit of the whole Country." [1] The functions of money can be performed by other means than the use of a " Merchantable " commodity. For example, debts may be directly offset against other debts.[2] Or the use of specie may be obviated by the use of bills of exchange.[3] Again, the governmental receipt of its own evidence of debt in payment of taxes, eliminates the use of specie. If bills of credit will perform the function of money between the taxpayers and the government, why can they not do likewise between individuals within the country ? Indeed, private issues of bills have for long periods of time performed money work.[4] Obviously, the security of governmental issues is superior to the security of a private issue. Or can it be, asked Mather ironically, that " the Security of one Plantation Magistrate " is better " than that of all the Massachusetts Representatives ? " [5] Another signal advantage of paper over specie is that a paper currency will not be exported. Its presence will compel *goods* to be exported rather than specie in payment for imports. Paper currency, then, will create a condition which will correct an unfavourable balance of trade.[6] Finally, said Mather, paper money is feasible because the French in Canada have succeeded in circulating an issue of card money.[7]

[1] Mather. *Considerations on the Bills of Credit*, pp. 189–190.
[2] " Is not Discount in Accounts current good pay ? " *Ibid.*, pp. 190–191.
[3] " Do not Bills Transmit to Remote Parts, vast sums without the intervention of Silver ? " *Ibid.*, pp. 190–191.
[4] " 'Tis strange that one Gentlemans Bills at Port Royal for divers years and that among Forreigners ; or another Gentleman's Bills in the western Parts for as many or more years should gain so much credit as to be current pay, among the Traders in those places." *Ibid.*, p. 191.
[5] *Ibid.*
[6] *Ibid.*, p. 193.
[7] For the briefest account of the Canadian Card Money, *cf.* Davis, Andrew MacFarland. *Colonial Currency Reprints*, Vol. I.

John Blackwell, who outlined a theory of land and commodity banking,[1] which will be analyzed in a following chapter, also wrote a pamphlet in defence of the Massachusetts bills of credit,[2] in which he elaborated the advantages of paper money. Merchants' bills, he pointed out, often acquire wide acceptability. In similar manner, a government can acquire credit with the people who compose it.[3] Following the lead of Mather, he argued that rights to receive goods will perform money work. Since bills of credit are a right to receive the services of the Colony (for they are receivable for taxes) they can perform the same function as a commodity money.[4] In this performance they will demonstrate their superiority, because they " have some advantages which Stampt Silver will never have." [5] They are more difficult to counterfeit than silver ; [6] " they are more Portable then Coyn, yet they will not be Exported out of the Land." [7] Neither will paper money be hoarded. Indeed, it will rather " inspire our whole trade with such a vigor as hitherto hath not been seen." [8] It is mere sophistry, said Blackwell, to protest that since bills of credit are mere pieces of paper, they cannot perform money work. As an evidence of debt, they have value. Why, asked Blackwell, " may not Paper-Mony be as good as Tobacco-Mony, Potato-Mony and Sugar-Mony ? " [9] The experience of " Venice, Paris, Leghorn & Amsterdam, and other such trading places " is proof of the superiority of paper money over specie.[10] Paper money issued in these cities has been " less Troublesome and Cumbersome, then Silver would be ;

---

[1] Blackwell, John. *A Discourse in Explanation of the Bank of Credit*, 1687.
[2] *Some Additional Considerations of the Bills of Credit*, 1691.
[3] *Ibid.*, pp. 201–202.
[4] *Ibid.*, p. 202.
[5] *Ibid.*, pp. 202–203.
[6] Woodbridge had brought forth this same argument in favour of bank bills. *Cf.* Woodbridge, *op. cit.*, p. 115.
[7] Blackwell. *Some Additional Considerations*, pp. 202–203.
[8] *Ibid.*
[9] *Ibid.*, p. 204.
[10] *Ibid.*, p. 202.

and more Safe." [1] Such were the advocated advantages of
paper ! A sample dissenting note is found in an Address to
the King, in 1684, justifying the Massachusetts mint. " For
some years," said this address, " paper bills passed for
payment of debts." But these instruments will not satis-
factorily serve the function of money, for they are " very
subject to be lost, rent, or counterfeit." [2]

V

Five ways were advocated for providing and retaining a
monetary supply within a colony : overvaluation of foreign
coins, prohibition of the exportation of specie, establishment
of mints, the substitution of paper for specie money, correction of the unfavourable balance of trade.

That a scarcity of money could be overcome by a legal
overvaluation of foreign coins was a persistent belief of the
seventeenth century. Attempts were made in all of the
colonies to induce an influx of specie by this means.[3] The
theory which underlay this type of legislation is well formulated in a petition of 1697, from the freeholders of Accomack
County, Virginia. Since money is the most convenient
"ballance for carrying on all Trade and Commerce," said
this petition,

" and forasmuch as Experience Informeth us that our Naighbour-
ing provinces & Governments by Inhancing the Vallew of all
foran Quoine, Do Drain and withdraw from this Government
such muneys as by severall opportunity Doth Happen to be
brought amongst us, to our Impoverishment and Their Great
Advantages ; we Tharfore propose That a Certaine Vallew &
Advance may be sett, not only upon Dollers, but upon all sorts
of foran Quoine which may exceed the Vallew of gt. Starling,
That Tharby Incouragement may [be] given for importing, as

---

[1] Blackwell. *Some Additional Considerations*, p. 202.
[2] Address to King, 1684. Quoted, Sumner, W. G. " *Coin Shilling of
Massachusettes Bay,*" *Yale Review*, 1898, p. 249.
[3] The details of the overvaluation by the several colonies are given by
Bullock, Charles J. *Essays on the Monetary History of the United States.*
New York, 1900, pp. 18–19.

well as Keeping the same to Curculate and pass plentifully in this Cuntry." [1]

In Massachusetts, the matter of overvaluation of coin was bound up with seigneurage which was charged by the New England mint. To declare a legal tender value higher than represented by the bullion content, or to coin money in which a considerable amount of alloy has been infused, comes to the same thing. Sumner concluded that the fine silver content of the "pine tree shilling" was only 77·5 per cent. of the English shilling of which it was supposedly the equivalent.[2] The result was that the mint master's seigneurage brought about the same condition as legal overvaluation, *i.e.*, the attempt to circulate money at an exchange value higher than the exchange value of the bullion content. Indeed, the profitableness of the Massachusetts mint was due to the existence of this prevailing opinion that by rating coins above their value they could be retained within a jurisdiction where this augmented value was recognized. Of this theory, John Hull, the Massachusetts mint-master, was a staunch supporter, for it gave a theoretical sanction to his seigneurage. " If our own coin be carried out of the country," he wrote in 1680, " it is a sign that it is not so light as it may be, and that it would be for public advantage to make it lighter." [3] Countries which have no mines, he insisted, must debase their currencies in order to retain money.[4] He maintained that the recoinage of bullion into overvalued coins was the only means of dealing with the problem. To merely overvalue foreign coins by legislation would not suffice. Indeed, such laws will lead to " much loss to the country that so advance it [the foreign coin involved] ; and the gain is only to strangers that bring it in." [5]

Every student of economic history is aware that the usual

[1] *Calendar of Virginia State Papers*, Vol. I., p. 53.
[2] Sumner, W. G. *Coin Shilling of Massachusetts*, p. 252.
[3] Hull, John. *Archeologia Americana*, Vol. III., p. 301.
[4] *Ibid.*
[5] *Ibid.*

consequence of debasement is a corrective increase in general prices. The author of a manuscript in the Massachusetts Archives had an interesting explanation for this phenomenon. The purpose of coining money in New England, he pointed out, was to obtain a domestic currency for managing the domestic trade and was " not Intended to make Returns to other Countries." [1] Debasement of coins by seigneurage, he held, should prevent exportation unless the sellers of goods " doe oppresse & extort in the sale of their goods to make up the said loss." [2] Such practice, it was argued, results from " some men's preferring their owne gaine before the publick good," [3] and the unfortunate consequence is that it " doth bring an undervalue uppon all Commodities Raised among ourselves, and utterly frustrate the end & use of mony amongst us." [4]

Another criticism was made by the author of the *Model of* 1688 against legal overvaluation of foreign coins. If the balance of trade is unfavourable, said he, overvaluation of coins will not correct it. The importer of goods will not be deceived by the legal tender valuation of coins. He will consider the " intrinsique value of the payment, whether it be in money or in goods, and he'll be sure so to deal as to lose nothing by either." [5] In fact, overvaluation will never procure a supply of money in a country which imports more than it exports. The effects of overvaluation, on the other hand, are socially deleterious. The use of foreign coins " Detracts from the sovreign honor," [6] and to increase the legal tender value of such coins " divides the profits of coinage with other Princes." [7] To allow subjects to pay

[1] Massachusetts Archives, Vol. C., p. 46. Quoted, Crosby, *op. cit.*, p. 104.
[2] *Ibid.*
[3] *Ibid.*
[4] *Ibid.*
[5] *Model of* 1688, p. 184. Andrew Mc. F. Davis, the editor of the currency reprints, believed that this tract was written by the same person who wrote Blackwell's *Discourse*. This might have been Blackwell or both might have had a common origin.
[6] *Model of* 1688, p. 182.
[7] *Ibid.*

money contracts in " moneys really less in value " means injustice between debtors and creditors.[1] All those persons who " live upon Pensions, Salaries, Wages ; Civill, Military or Ecclesiastical, Established by Law or otherwise " as well as labourers, will suffer since the " Prices of Victuals, Cloathing, and other Commodities " will rise because this is " an usual consequence of raysing moneys." [2] Finally, all the people would suffer, because " they must all Expect to pay for what imported Goods they need, proportionately to such advance of Coyns." [3] The loss will be caused by the inability to raise the price of exports to parallel the rise in the price of imports. Indeed, " as the Country grows more populous and improved, its products will multiply ; and consequently abate in price." [4] True, an increase in domestic production would tend to correct the unfavourable trade balance. But this would take time and " while the grass grows (as the proverb is) the Steer will starve." [5] Overvaluation of coins would never provide a supply of money, this writer maintained, and paper money was the only solution.

Prohibition of the export of specie was a second means relied upon to provide a colony with specie. The trade with the plantation colonies, and with the Spanish, brought in a considerable amount of coin through the century. The possibility of retaining coin by prohibition of export was a widely accepted theory. A long series of laws give evidence not only of the legislative acceptance of this theory, but also of the futility of the process. Massachusetts forbade the export of specie in 1654,[6] again in 1669,[7] and still again in 1697.[8] The author of a tract in the Massachusetts Archives took the position that a domestic coinage should prevent the

---

[1] *Model of* 1688, p. 182.
[2] *Ibid.*
[3] *Ibid.*, p. 183.
[4] *Ibid.*, pp. 184–185.
[5] *Ibid.*, p. 184.
[6] *Mass. Col. Records*, Vol. III., pp. 353–354.
[7] *Ibid.*, Vol. IV., Part 2, p. 421.
[8] *Acts and Resolves. Province of Mass. Bay*, Vol. I., p. 306.

efflux of specie. But if sellers " oppress " the buyers of goods to the extent of the seigneurage, the export of specie will begin again. When that occurs, there is no other remedy except to prohibit the export of specie.[1]

The third advocated means for supplying a colony with money was the establishment of mints. Massachusetts established its mint in 1652 in hope of coining a uniform, metallic money, sufficiently debased so that it would remain in the colony.[2] Minting of money, said a committee of 1684, was made necessary because the colony " had no staple commodity in our country to pay debts or buy necessaries but fish and corn, which were so cumbersome and troublesome as could not be borne.[3] Paper money, this committee maintained, could not perform the functions of money ; while the consequence of overvaluing " base Spanish money " was that " many people were cousened, and the colony in danger of being undone thereby."[4] The Maryland Assembly, in 1661, petitioned the Lord Proprietor for the right to establish a mint. " No trade or commerce," it was urged, " can be well managed without it " [money].[5] Scarcity of money hinders trade, manufacture and the growth of towns, and the want of money can only be overcome by the establishment of a mint.[6] The burgomasters and schepens of New Netherland petitioned for the right to mint money in the same year, but their request was denied.[7] Increase Mather attempted to justify the Massachusetts mint. Private issues, he alleged, were customary and " the Coyning in Massachusetts Colony was little more than that, and with Design to prevent the great Injuries Merchants and others sustained by base Spanish Money." [8] Moreover,

[1] Mass. Archives, Vol. C., p. 46. Quoted, Crosby, *op. cit.*, p. 104.
[2] Davis, Andrew Mc. F. *Currency and Banking in the Province of Massachusetts Bay.* New York, 1901. Part I., p. 28.
[3] Mass. Archives. Political MSS., Vol. I. Quoted, Crosby, *Archæologia Americana*, Vol. III., p. 282.
[4] *Ibid.*
[5] Crosby, *op. cit.*, p. 126.
[6] *Ibid.*
[7] Brodhead, *op. cit.*, Vol. I., p. 694.
[8] Mather, Increase. "New England Vindicated from Unjust Aspersions."

the mint was set up " when there was no King in England,"
and, in the third place, other colonies and corporations had
coined money.[1]

The merits of recoinage as a means of inducing an inflow
of specie have been considered under overvaluation. The
theory was essentially the same. A mint which charged
seigneurage, it was hoped, would provide a currency which
would not be melted and exported.[2] The " end of Coyning
money within this Commonwealth [Massachusetts] is for the
more easy managing the traffique thereof within itself, &
not Intended to make Returns to other Countries." [3] But
as the author of the *Model of* 1688 well understood, the
consequence of this form of overvaluation would be a
corrective rise in general prices.

Opposition to the seigneurage charged by the New England
mint and a belief that gratuitous coinage would be the means
of attracting money from abroad, are combined in a Massachusetts *Petition for a Free Mint*, of 1680. The impress of a
mint, said this tract, adds nothing to the value of a coin.[4]
Indeed, the charging of seigneurage, deters owners of bullion
from coining it. The result is the hoarding of specie or the
sale of specie " to those that export the same." The New
England mint, it was charged, led to a scarcity rather than
an abundance of money.[5] To overcome this " decay of
Trade and decrease of money," a speedy remedy was
demanded, " and the most probable expedient that offers
is to make the mint free." [6] The advantage of a " free
mint," [*i.e.*, gratuitous coinage as opposed to seigneurage],
it was alleged, would be that it would " convert dead
treasures into currant coin," because owners of bullion or coin

London, 1688. Reprinted, Prince Society, *Andros Tracts*, Vol. II. Boston,
1869, pp. 115–116.
  [1] *Ibid.*
  [2] *Cf.* Del Mar, *op. cit.*, p. 77.
  [3] Mass. Archives, Vol. C., p. 46. Quoted, Crosby, *op. cit.*, p. 104.
  [4] " Petition for a Free Mint." Mass. Archives, Pecuniary. Quoted,
Archæologia Americana, Vol. III., pp. 300–301.
  [5] *Ibid.*
  [6] *Ibid.*

" will finde the mint their surest and highest market." [1]
Still more important was the second advantage advanced in
favour of gratuitous coinage : " Strangers from forreign
parts " who wished to buy the products of New England,
will " rather choose to send peices of $\frac{8}{8}$, plate or Bullion, then
run the hazard of an uncertain market for those goods which
they may with less loss send to other parts." [2] For the mint
would provide the highest and best market for holders of
monetary material. This in turn would decrease goods
imports, while the exports would tend to increase.

Between the advocates of overvaluation and the
advocates of gratuitous coinage, was a most interesting
clash of opinion. The ideas of the *Petition for a Free Mint*
had been set forth in a Report of a committee, in 1677.[3]
The advocates of overvaluation believed that by means of
legal tender declaration, bullion and specie could be attracted.
Both groups held forth a solution for the want of money.
The advocates of gratuitous coinage believed that legal
tender laws were not only futile, but defeated the purpose
which they set about to accomplish. Only by providing a
market where bullion and foreign coin could be transformed
into full weight colonial coins, said this group, could a
monetary supply be attracted. For this reason no charge
of coinage should be collected by the mint. The cost of the
mint should be " levyed by some easy rate, or by Excise
upon some of those unprofitable Commodities which are
consumed to nourish lust and vice." [4] The benefit of the
mint, it was held, would " far Surmount the charge," [5]
because the mint would increase the quantity of money and
prices would rise. But here the logic of the argument, which
had been so satisfactory, suddenly ends. For the rise of
prices, produced by an abundance of money, it was argued,

---

[1] " Petition for a Free Mint." Crosby, *op. cit.*, p. 109.
[2] *Ibid.*
[3] Mass. Archives. Pecuniary MSS., Vol. I. Quoted, *Archæologia Americana*, Vol. III., p. 297.
[4] " Petition for a Free Mint." Crosby, *op. cit.*, p. 110.
[5] *Ibid.*, p. 109.

would cause a decline in the quantity of goods imported and correct the adverse balance of trade.[1] Against the reasoning in this " Petition," John Hull, who had long profited from seigneurage, was obdurate. Gratuitous coinage, he insisted, would provide a currency which would be as certain to be exported as bullion, by virtue of being full weight. The merchant, he maintained, " may as well transport the coined money as the bullion ; and then you have no money left in the country." [2]

The paper money writers did not believe that any of the foregoing methods would ever provide an adequacy of currency. There must be a correspondence between the quantity of money and the amount of business. This can never be obtained " till we can light on something Equivalent to Coyn," [3] and something which will not " Bleed away in vast summs by every vessel that goes to forreign parts." [4] Specie money is insufficient, said Blackwell, to cope with the enlarged trade.[5] This shortage may be due to the failure of mines to produce a sufficiency, or to an unfavourable balance of trade. But whatever the cause,

" 'tis now so hard to come by, for the carrying on of trade, to answer the vastness of men's attempts & aymes of increase in Merchandize, as that it's suspected to be insufficient in this age of the world." [6]

This relative scarcity, said he, has led to a search for other media. " Divers persons & countreys " sought for some more satisfactory medium until some " happily pitch't upon That, of Banks, Lumbards & Exchange of Moneys by Bills." [7] Something of this nature must be set on foot, said Blackwell, to supply the want of money. He then proceeded to outline

---

[1] " Petition for a Free Mint." Crosby, *op. cit.*, p. 109.
[2] Hull, John. *Archæologia Americana*, Vol. III., p. 302.
[3] Blackwell. *Some Additional Considerations*, p. 203.
[4] *Ibid.*
[5] *Ibid.*, p. 123.
[6] *Ibid.*
[7] *Ibid.*

a means whereby bank bills could be issued against a deposit of land or commodities.

Woodbridge had outlined a similar scheme and Budd elaborated a banking project in Pennsylvania. Receipts from public warehouses, said Budd, will serve as money,[1] and will be sufficient for the needs of trade.[2] Cotton Mather, who ardently defended the colonial Bills of Credit, was convinced that a paper currency would not be exported. It is " an abiding Cash," he wrote, " for no man will carry it to another country." [3] Since paper currency cannot be exported to pay for imports, " only the Growths of the Country will be carried off." This, he assured his readers, would be a distinct social advanatge. A sufficiency of money is necessary, said the paper money men, not only for trade, but for the payment of taxes.[4] Since specie is exported, said Mather, to require men to pay their taxes in specie, is like requiring men to " make bricks without straw." [5]

The paper money writers were eloquent and extravagant in their prophecies concerning the manifold advantages which would result from the inflation which could be provided by bank bills or bills of credit. Scarcity of money, said Woodbridge, leads to a scarcity of goods, to indebtedness, slow payments, extortionate dealings in money, repression of enterprises, business corruption and extortion.[6] But an abundance of money quickens trade, stimulates manufacture, increases land values, promotes settlement of new areas, creates an inducement to labour, decreases litigation, lowers the rate of interest, and leads to general well-being.[7] For the state, paper money provides purchasing power,[8] while for the citizens, it provides a means for the payment of taxes.[9]

[1] Budd, *op. cit.*, pp. 40–41.
[2] *Ibid.*, p. 48.
[3] Mather. *Considerations on the Bills of Credit*, p. 193.
[4] Blackwell. *Some Additional Considerations*, p. 200.
[5] Mather. *Considerations on the Bills of Credit*, p. 192.
[6] Woodbridge, *op. cit.*, p. 113.
[7] *Ibid.*
[8] Blackwell. *Some Additional Considerations*, p. 203.
[9] Mather. *Considerations on the Bills of Credit*, p. 192.

Strangely enough, although many of the seventeenth-century writers understood that the primary reason for the scarcity of specie was the existence of an unfavourable balance of trade, very few writers considered the possibility of correcting this trade balance. Rather, most of the monetary writers seemed to look upon this as an inevitable situation which could not be helped, and which would have to be overcome by the several means which have been enumerated above. New England, said Mather, is fed with silver from the West Indies and loses silver to Europe : [1] " Silver in New England is like the water of a swift Running River, always coming, and as fast going away." It was this situation, he insisted, which demanded paper money. Blackwell admitted that the cause of the lack of specie was the unfavourable balance of trade,[2] and the author of the *Model of* 1688 pointed out that " the real cause of the Scarcity of Moneys " was " the Actual Transporting the Balance or Overplus of the value of goods imported, above the proportion of the value of native goods exported." [3]

The advocates of paper money, it is clear, would not admit the feasibility of correcting this unfavourable trade balance. The author of the *Model of* 1688, however, did consider the matter. Among the proposed remedies for the want of specie, he included the proposal of " Ballancing the importations of such Commodities as are most useful, with the exportation of the manufactures and Products of the Country." [4] This, he proposed to effect by " sumptuary and Trading Laws." But for the most part, it was the critics of the paper money inflationists, in the first quarter of the next century, who showed that the only permanent solution for the want of money was the correction of the unfavourable balance of trade. A few seventeenth-century writers, however, saw this point. Sewall, for example, held that the domestic production of sail cloth and cordage would

[1] Mather. *Considerations on the Bills of Credit*, p. 193.
[2] Blackwell. *Discourse*, p. 123.
[3] *Model of* 1688, pp. 183–184.
[4] *Ibid.*, p. 185.

tend to decrease the efflux of specie.[1] Pastorius realized that manufacturing was necessary to keep specie from being carried out.[2] and Increase Mather maintained that New England did not have a twentieth part of the amount of manufacturing which would be necessary to prevent " returns " from being made in specie and bullion.[3]

VI

The value of money was considered by the colonial writers to some extent before the paper money agitation. Winthrop, for example, recorded that, in 1640, " the scarcity of money made a great change in all commerce." [4] The price of land and of cattle declined rapidly in Massachusetts. This depression was not entirely the consequence of a decrease in money circulation, to be sure, but the cessation of immigration cut off an important source of specie, and curtailed the demand for colonial products. Yet Winthrop recognized that there was an essential connection between the level of prices and the quantity of money.[5] Money changes in small communities are more apparent than in larger, and where there is no credit mechanism, monetary problems are bound to be intensified. Bradford also understood that an increase in the quantity of money, other things equal, brings a fall in its value. The use of wampum as money, he pointed out, led to an increase in its quantity, and as a consequence, he said, " it may prove a drugg in time." [6]

The monetary discussion during the decade from 1680 to 1690, definitely brought out colonial ideas about the value of money. The advocates of a free mint argued that an increase in the supply of species would lead to a rise in prices.[7] " It is very observable," said these petitioners,

---

[1] Sewall. *Computation that the Importation of Negroes, &c.*, p. 199.
[2] Pastorius, *op. cit.*, p. 9.
[3] Mather, Increase. *Relation*, p. 8.
[4] Winthrop. *History of New England*, Vol. II., p. 18.
[5] *Cf. Ibid.*, pp. 7, 21.
[6] Bradford, *op. cit.*, pp. 282–283.
[7] " Reasons for a Mint in New England." See Crosby, *op. cit.*, pp. 91–92.

" that in all Countrys' where money abounds, the prices of all
Commoditys' and provisions of their place advances, and the
goods imported abate proportionably." [1]

The paper money writers argued that the expansion of trade
demanded an increase in the supply of money.[2] Scarcity
of money, said Joseph Dudley, causes a decay of trade.[3]
But an abundance of money, wrote John Woodbridge,
" inciteth to the purchasing of land, and heighteneth its
value." [4] The enlargement of trade, wrote Blackwell, has
been so vast that the demand for money thereby is so great
that a substitute for specie must be found.[5] But Cotton
Mather, although he was an ardent advocate of the Massachusetts Bills of Credit, did not accept the theory that the
quantity of money influenced its value. " A surprizing
Providence of God," said this theologian, has kept up the
value of gold and silver, " notwithstanding the vast Quantities dug out of the earth in all ages." [6] It was this divine
means which had " continued them fit Materials to make
Money of." [7] Perhaps the " surprizing Providence " was
merely the demand for money.

The consequences of changes in the value of money upon
the various classes in a community, have already been considered under the function of money as a standard of deferred
payments. The appreciation of the " pine tree shilling," as
was suggested by the English mint in 1686,[8] was opposed
because it would enrich landlords and creditors while it
would impoverish tenants and debtors.[9] John Hull
recognized that a change in the value of money led to
inequality between debtors and creditors. But this, he
believed, could be overcome by an arbitrary separation of

[1] Mass. Archives.   Crosby, *op. cit.*, p. 109.
[2] See Davis.   *Colonial Currency Reprints*, Vol. I.
[3] See Felt, *op. cit.*, p. 46.
[4] Woodbridge, *op. cit.*, p. 113.
[5] Blackwell.   *Discourse*, p. 123.
[6] Mather.   *Christian Philosopher*, p. 120.
[7] *Ibid.*
[8] Davis.   *Currency and Banking in the Province of Mass. Bay*, Vol. I.,
pp. 32–38.
[9] " Reasons for a Mint in New England."   Quoted, Crosby, *op. cit.*, p. 92.

those debts where the old currency would apply, from those where the new would apply, or, by an equal division of the loss.[1] The demonetization of sewan, said Cornelius Tienhoven, would fall heaviest upon " labourers, boors, and other common people," since they had no other money.[2] Similarly, Mather argued that to allow the Massachusetts Bills of Credit to fall to a discount, would mean injustice to the soldiers who ventured their lives in public service. Indeed, such depreciation would make the Government " contemptible as not worthy to be trusted." [3] Blackwell held that to discriminate against the bills of credit was oppression since they were receivable for taxes.[4] The author of the *Model of* 1688 maintained that the overvaluation of foreign coins disturbed the relations between debtors and creditors, since creditors would be " paid in other moneys really less in value ; which carries great injustice in it." [5] All those who live on pensions, salaries, or wages, he pointed out, would suffer, for whereas their incomes would not expand, " the Prices of Victuals, Cloathing, and other Commodities " would rise.[6] More than that, an arbitrary change in the legal tender value of money would lead to a rise in the price of imports. But the price of exports, he held, could not be raised in proportion because considerable time would be required to change the " wonted known prices ". [7]

VII

Several aspects of the theory of paper money circulation have been considered in the various topics above. One problem, peculiar to paper money, calls for separate treat-

[1] *Archæologia Americana*, Vol. III., pp. 300–301.
[2] Tienhoven, Cornelius Van. " Brief Answer to Representation of New Netherlands." MSS. The Hague, 1650. Printed as appendix to Donck. *Representation of New Netherlands.* New York, 1849, p. 82.
[3] Mather. *Considerations on the Bills of Credit.* p. 194.
[4] Blackwell. *Some Additional Considerations*, p. 201.
[5] *Model of* 1688, p. 182.
[6] *Ibid.*
[7] *Ibid.*, pp. 184–185.

ment : the matter of depreciation. The circulation of paper currencies is never a simple procedure, and for the seventeenth-century Americans, who had little experience to go by, the problems of depreciation were perplexing indeed. Much was written, as a result, about the ways and means of making paper circulate at its face value.

The advocates of paper attempted, first, to show that paper would circulate because of its advantage over specie. Paper bills, they said, would involve no necessity for weighing or assaying ; mere sight of a bill would indicate its value.[1] The function of coined money, said Blackwell, is merely to furnish a man with credit,[2] and governmental paper should be the means, *par excellence*, of providing such credit.[3] But when actual depreciation set in, the reason why these advantages did not manifest themselves had to be accounted for.

In the issue of government paper, said Mather, a legislative act, levying a tax to be collected in the future, becomes the equivalent of a fund which makes the instruments passable.[4] Government issues, said Blackwell, " are founded on the acknowledgement which the Country hath made of their being so much in Debt, and their Resolution of raising what is owing." [5] A small issue of bills, he thought, could be circulated even if " that Fund, be never so Tottering." [6] Mather believed that if the issuing government were well established, and the legislation, designed to sink the issue, were enforced, paper should be more valuable than specie.[7] Paper money, wrote Blackwell, has been known to rise to a premium ; in Venice, for example, " such was the usefulness of these Bills that they would not be parted with for Mony." [8] It is lack of confidence that leads to depreciation of paper

[1] Blackwell. *Discourse*, p. 132.
[2] Blackwell. *Some Additional Considerations*, p. 200.
[3] *Ibid.*, pp. 201–202.
[4] Mather. *Magnalia*, p. 190.
[5] Blackwell. *Some Additional Considerations*, p. 202.
[6] *Ibid.*
[7] Mather. *Magnalia*, p. 191.
[8] Blackwell. *Some Additional Considerations*, p. 202.

money, said Mather [1] ; and this lack of confidence is
unwarranted. Indeed, only if " we are reduced to Hobs
his state of Nature " where there would be " no Magistrates,
no Government, and by Consequence . . . no Security for
anything," only then would there be justification for lack
of confidence. [2]

But in spite of these arguments which were designed to
prove that paper should pass at its face value, the bills of
credit depreciated and the paper money theorists were
compelled " to examine, what it is that clogs the passing of
our bills." [3] The arrested circulation, Blackwell recognized,
was due to their depreciation ; " the debasing of them, so
that twenty shillings in a Bill can scarce find Credit for
fourteen or fifteen shillings of stampt silver." [4] Four
methods were recommended to bring about a circulation of
the bills of credit : voluntary agreements to accept them ;
circulation at a discount ; withdrawal and cancellation ;
punitive taxation.

Mather believed that the circulation of paper could be
guaranteed if business men would agree to accept them in
payment for goods without advancing prices. [5] If leading
merchants would agree to give " a just Reputation to
our Bills, The Whole Country must and will joyn with
them in it." [6] If influential merchants, therefore, would
show " how willing they themselves are to pay and also to
take Bills at a due Price, doubtless it would much promote
the Cure of this Distemper." [7] Blackwell thought acceptability could be facilitated by moral suasion, and bank bills,
he believed, would circulate as money if there were an agreement among traders to receive them. [8] If paper were only
made generally acceptable, said Mather, the credit of Massa-

[1] Mather. *Magnalia*, p. 191.
[2] Mather. *Considerations on the Bills of Credit*, pp. 191–192.
[3] Blackwell. *Some Additional Considerations*, p. 204.
[4] *Ibid.*
[5] Mather. *Magnalia*, pp. 191–192.
[6] Blackwell. *Some Additional Considerations*, p. 205.
[7] *Ibid.*
[8] *Ibid.*, pp. 125–126.

chusetts " will rise to the utmost height of its ability." [1]
But if the government issues are allowed to depreciate,
" who will hereafter serve the Country in their greatest
Dangers ? " [2]

The second means of circulating paper, that is, of allowing
it to fall to a discount, was therefore unworthy of consideration. By " selling them [bills] at under-rates " soldiers
are defrauded who " adventured their lives in publick Service." [3] A government which allows its obligations to its
defenders to decrease in value, is " made contemptible as
not worthy to be trusted." [4]

A third cure for depreciation was suggested by Blackwell
which was as ingenious as it was naïve. " Let the Publick
Rates be vigorously Raised," said he, so that all extant
bills will be paid into the treasury [5] ; then cancel all the
returned bills. This wholesale withdrawal of bills, he maintained, would at once prove to the people that the country
must have currency. The people would then demand a new
supply and desist from depreciating the bills. Mather, whose
theology led him to believe in the efficacy of punishment,
proposed another remedy. Punitive taxation, said he,
should be employed against those who are " debasing the
Credit of your bills either by purchasing them with little
money, or selling commodities for them at excessive dearer
Rates." [6] Blackwell also subscribed to this remedy. If
the government can discover those who have discriminated
against the bills of credit, said he, " they ought to advance
the Rates of such people to procure a Reparation to them
that have been wronged." [7] Mather's punitive programme
was more extensive. In addition to the imposition of
differential tax rates, he recommended that the Government
require the taxes of all " refusers " of bills to be paid in

[1] Mather. *Considerations on the Bills of Credit*, p. 193.
[2] *Ibid.*
[3] *Ibid.*, p. 194.
[4] *Ibid.*
[5] Blackwell. *Some Additional Considerations*, p. 205.
[6] Mather. *Considerations on the Bills of Credit*, p. 194.
[7] Blackwell. *Some Additional Considerations*, p. 201.

silver ; " nor Let them have the benefit of paying them, who will not also Receive them." [1] His final proposal, to force the circulation of paper, was that the government should withdraw the support of the courts from those who refused to receive the bills at their face value.[2] For why should the government concern itself with the recovery of private debts, when the creditors seeking legal help will not accept the evidences of public debt ?

[1] Mather. *Considerations on the Bills of Credit*, p. 194.
[2] *Ibid.*, pp. 194–195.

LOMBARD BANKS AND LAND BANKS

"Obj. 1. Will you not be bound to give me ready money for
the Bankbills I have, when I have occasion for Money ?
Ans. 1. This Bank is not Proposed to be a Bank of moneys
(wch is liable to un-expressible & un-foreseen hazards)
but a Bank of Credit, to be given forth by Bills, to
supply such as cannot get money (by reason of it's
scarceity) with what so ever may be had for moneys."

John Blackwell, *A Discourse in Explanation
of the Bank of Credit.*

CHAPTER X

LOMBARD BANKS AND LAND BANKS

I

C O L O N I A L ideas on banking were by no means original, since the issue of bills secured by personal credit or by a deposit of goods or land mortgages had both theoretical and practical precedents.[1] In England, the seventeenth century witnessed the appearance of a long series of proposals for banks, ranging from " montes pietatis," to land and commodity banks which could issue circulating notes.[2] The idea of depositing a mass of heterogeneous coins as a basis for bank money, which had been successfully accomplished at Amsterdam and other continental trading centres, was expanded, in theory, to comprehend first goods and then land (by means of mortgages).[3] The success of the Bank of England, however, crushed the hopes of the land bank advocates in England. But the seventeenth century discussion of land banks gave birth to the American project of 1740.[4] The colonial literature of banking was, therefore, a counterpart of the English discussion. But whereas the bulk of English proposals were put forth in the seventeenth century, the American discussion began definitely in the last two decades of the century and continued long into the next.

American banking discussion during the seventeenth century was, with few exceptions, confined to the writings

[1] Cf. Davis. Currency and Banking in the Province of Mass. Bay, Vol. II., Chapters 1–3.
[2] A number of these tracts have been brought together by Shaw, W. A. Select Tracts and Documents Illustrative of English Monetary History, 1626–1730. The several proposals are briefly summarized in Davis, op. cit., Vol. II., Chapters 1–3.
[3] Davis, op. cit., Vol. II., p. 2.
[4] Ibid., Chapter III.

of three persons : John Woodbridge, John Blackwell, and Thomas Budd. Each proposed the establishment of a bank of issue, and each, in turn, drew upon previous English proposals for their ideas. John Winthrop, Jr., had outlined a banking project for the Royal Society (of which he was a member), but what his plan actually was we do not know. The plan may have been the one later set forth by John Blackwell.

Each of the three American writers on banking drew directly upon English theories. John Woodbridge, for example, referred to William Potter, who had outlined a theory of banking in the *Key to Wealth* (1650), as " an intimate friend." [1] He also had in his possession a copy of Potter's book, so the direct influence of Potter's theories is evident. Blackwell, the second American bank promoter, had been a member of the English Parliament in 1656, and treasurer of the army under Cromwell. He came to Boston, in 1684, bringing the English banking theories, then current, to more receptive atmosphere. Thomas Budd reproduced the proposal that Andrew Yarranton had espoused in England. [2] The three American projects, therefore, represent essentially an outgrowth from the English seventeenth-century discussion.

II

Money, said John Woodbridge, [3] in a tract which he published in 1682, " is that One thing . . . which answereth all things." Where money abounds, no person is restricted to a single person or market. Neither is there any extortion on the part of sellers or lenders. A sufficiency of money increases trade and manufacture, lowers the rate of interest, increases land values, eliminates waste of time, reduces litigation, and overcomes the disadvantages of barter. The

[1] Woodbridge, *op. cit.*, p. 110.
[2] Yarranton, Andrew. *England's Improvement by Sea and Land.* London, 1677.
[3] Woodbridge. *Severals Relating to the Fund*, p. 112.

want of money, which stagnates enterprise, can be overcome by the establishment of a " Fund " which can provide credit to be circulated by " book and Bills." This credit would be able to perform all the functions which are performed by specie.[1]

Indeed, the function of money does not require a monetary substance which has " intrinsique value." The purpose of money is merely to provide a means " to procure what One wants, that another abounds with." [2] The use of specie is beset with difficulty, because it allures enemies, it is hoarded, it is subject to wear, it is adulterated, and it is destroyed by means of " fires, robberies, mistakes, & the Like Contingencies." But a " Fund, or Deposit in Land," can be created which will become the foundation of credit which will perform all the functions of money ; and such a fund or deposit would be of " real, durcable, & of secure value." [3]

The fund, thus accumulated, could become the basis of a credit circulation in three ways : the use of book entries, the use of bills of exchange, and the use of " change bills." [4] Book entries were intended to balance the accounts between the members of the " fund," and payments between these persons would thereby be effected in " fund credit " instead of money. In fact, the pamphlet which Woodbridge wrote, described the operation of such a " fund " which was set up by a group of Boston merchants in 1681. At the outset, it appears that the use of " fund credit " was to be limited to the " Funders " or the actual contributors to the fund. But it was hoped that the reputation of the project would soon induce other persons to accept " fund pay " for ordinary money purposes. The " bills of exchange " were intended to make " great payments," while the " change bills " were designed to provide " running cash." [5] It was the latter which was to provide a circulating medium for the public.

---

[1] Woodbridge. *Severals Relating to the Fund*, pp. 112–114.
[2] *Ibid.*, p. 114.
[3] *Ibid.*
[4] *Ibid.*, pp. 115–117.
[5] *Ibid.*, p. 112.

These " change bills," said Woodbridge, " may be so contrived as to pass with facility and without counterfeiting." [1] The " change bill " must have been similar to the modern letter of credit.[2] The acceptor of " credit " in payment of an account noted the amount on the bill itself. In turn, the acceptor was supposed to obtain a transfer of a similar amount of credit to his account at the office of the " Fund."

Further details of the plan are not necessary to explain the theory involved. The scheme as outlined was hopelessly cumbersome, but it must be said that it recognized the principle which is the basis of modern banking : the offsetting of debts against debts. John Woodbridge must be considered as the first American exponent of the clearance principle.

The author of *Severals Relating to the Fund* did not claim any originality for the project. In fact, he admitted in the pamphlet that his " intimate friend," William Potter, of London, had imparted " a Designe for the Accomodation of Commerce " [3] to him, in 1649. Potter's Scheme [4] was one designed to furnish credit based upon " personal credit, by a considerable number of able Men Ingaging," or upon the " depositing of Goods, in the nature of a Lumber of Merchandise." [5] Woodbridge possessed a copy of Potter's book, and the details of Potter's scheme were thoroughly familiar to him. The theory of the " Fund " must therefore be considered to be simply the translation of an English scheme of essentially the same nature, to America.

III

Five years after the appearance of Woodbridge's tract, another banking project was set on foot at Boston. It was approved by the more prominent men of the Massachusetts

[1] Woodbridge, *op. cit.*, p. 115.
[2] *Cf.* Davis, Andrew Mc. F. *Colonial Currency Reprints*, Vol. I. Introduction, p. 7.
[3] Woodbridge, *op. cit.*, p. 110.
[4] *Key to Wealth.* London, 1650.
[5] Woodbridge, *op. cit.*, p. 110.

Bay Colony, including Joseph Dudley, then the president of the Council. In support of this project, an elaborate prospectus was prepared by John Blackwell,[1] and this tract contains the theoretical arguments in favour of the scheme. The history of this banking project forms an interesting chapter in the economic history of the century. But the concern of this chapter is with the banking theories advanced during the seventeenth century, rather than institutional matters.

Whether or not Blackwell was the author of the manuscript, which outlined the theory of this bank of 1687, is uncertain. True, the manuscript is in his handwriting, but the publication of a pamphlet [2] in London, in 1688, which is essentially similar, has led to the conjecture that Blackwell was the author of both, or more probable, that both had a common original, of which Blackwell may or may not have been the author.[3] But Blackwell's manuscript represents the second source of banking theory among the seventeenth-century Americans.

Like Woodbridge, John Blackwell held that specie money is insufficient to satisfy the demands of trade.[4] This scarcity of money " hath put divers persons & countreys upon contrivances, how to supply that deficiencie, by other mediums." Three solutions, said Blackwell, had been found : " Banks, Lombards & Exchange of Moneys by Bills." [5] The first two plans had " been sett on foot in divers Countreys." They had been the means of enriching countries, he said, and have been " of greater value than the Species of Gold and Silver." The " Exchange of Moneys " had been attempted by merchants " to their great advantage also." [6]

---

[1] " A Discourse in Explanation of the Bank of Credit." Printed, *Colonial Currency Reprints*, Vol. I.

[2] *A Model for Erecting a Bank of Credit with a Discourse in Explanation Thereof.*

[3] For a discussion of the problem of authorship, see Davis, Andrew Mc. F. *Colonial Currency Reprints*, Vol. I. Introduction, pp. 8–21.

[4] Blackwell. *Discourse*, p. 123.

[5] *Ibid.*

[6] *Ibid.*, p. 24.

These three methods, said Blackwell, could be accommodated to the needs of New England. The foundation of the systems, however, should be commuted from either

" an Imaginary being or presence of the Species of Gold and Silver moneys lodged in such Banks (which this place hath not in such plenty as to deposit for such a purpose) into Reall and Substantiall Lands & goods of un-questionable title and value (which this Countrey hath)." [1]

Such a bank would not be a " Bank of Moneys," but a " Bank of Credit," and the bills which could be issued against these lands and commodities, " Bank Bills of Credit."

Thus far, the theory of the project appears to be essentially the same as the " Fund." Woodbridge, for example, had pointed out that the advantage of a land bank over a bank of money was that " those Founded on Money, had only their defect, of a possibility to break ; which this fixed on Land, was not capable of." [2] But Blackwell's project contained an item not countenanced in the " Fund." Whereas under Woodbridge's scheme, the only security for the credit which was intended to circulate as money, was the land or goods deposited, Blackwell's scheme comprehended the provision of additional security in the form of the liability of the " sayd Managers and partners." These persons were to

" Deposit moneys, & other estates in the Bank as a stock or Fund : which will be a further security and obligation upon them for their upright dealing, for, thereby every of themselves, and the whole partnership become personally Interested and concerned to be carefull in every thing : and the whole society liable to answer the damages." [3]

The ideal of this project as well as that of Woodbridge, was to eliminate the dependence of trade upon a substance not found in New England, and to establish " the trade and wealth of this Country . . . upon its owne Foundation, &

[1] Blackwell. *Discourse*, p. 124.
[2] Woodbridge, *op. cit.*, p. 112.
[3] Blackwell. *Discourse*, p. 137.

upon a medium or Ballance arizing within it selfe." [1] This foundation should be the " Lands & Products " of the country deposited " in fitting places " determined by the Managers. Against this deposit, bank bills would in turn be issued to the extent of one half or two thirds of the value of the hypothecated property.

The bank bills issued against such deposited land mortgages or " staple un-perishable goods & merchandises " could circulate as money, providing " a considerable number of persons, some of each trade, calling & condition agree voluntarily to receive [them] as ready moneys." [2] They should be signed by the partners and would represent, therefore, both a claim upon the hypothecated property and the liability of the signers. They would become the means of converting goods or land into purchasing power, and would consequently stimulate all manner of economic pursuits. There would be no need of making these bills convertible into specie at the bank, said Blackwell, [3] because their advantages over gold or silver would make them not only convertible into gold and silver in the market, but convertible at a premium. For whereas gold is superior to silver as a money means, so bank bills would be superior to gold. The mere sight of a bank bill would show its value [4]; there would be no need of weighing or assaying. Risk of loss could be obviated because the issuing bank could replace all lost or destroyed bills. In the third place, said Blackwell, a premium would soon emerge on bank bills.

The issue of bank bills was to be entrusted to a committee of the partners. This committee was to receive the applications of the public for credit, determine the proportion of credit to be granted on the hypothecated property, draw up the instruments requisite for the deposit of the goods or land in question, have custody over the pledged property, and see to it that the security for the bank bills was maintained.

[1] Blackwell. *Discourse*, p. 144.
[2] *Ibid.*, p. 125.
[3] *Ibid.*, p. 131.
[4] *Ibid.*, p. 132.

The management of the bank by this committee, in turn, was to be inspected by a body of " Assessors " who should have " oversight & Comptroll of the whole affayre." [1]

Blackwell's prospectus pointed out that the success of the project depended upon an honest *clientèle* which would build up the good will of the institution, abide by the rules, and pay the interest rates charged for credit extension. Matured loans could be extended at the discretion of the managers except those based upon perishable commodities. The depositor of goods was to have access to the hypothecated goods to see that they were intact, and for showing them to prospective buyers. The project was promised not to be suddenly terminated, if ever, but due time for the disposal of pledged property was to be provided.

The benefits which the community would receive from such a " bank of credit " were set forth with elaborate profusion. The trade of the country would be established upon a medium arising within the country and dependence upon specie would be obviated [2]; the bank would tend to augment production and thereby permit an increase in immigration ; oppression and extortion in prices would end ; fishing and navigation would be developed, and royal revenues would accordingly be increased.[3] The price of land and land rents would rise, due to an increase in quantity of purchasing power, and a fall in interest rates. High interest rates, said the promoters, impoverish " many Landed persons," [4] but the bank would provide relief by accommodating them " on better terms, and without danger of being worm'd out of their Lands & Estates." [5] The bank would facilitate the better marketing of goods since the " storehouses " would serve as continuous open markets.[6] Manufacturers could therefore buy materials advantageously, while working

---

[1] Blackwell. *Discourse*, p. 136.
[2] *Ibid.*, p. 144.
[3] *Ibid.*
[4] *Ibid.*, p. 134.
[5] *Ibid.*
[6] *Ibid.*, p. 129.

capital would be provided in abundance by bank credit. As a consequence of the increase in manufacturing, exports would increase and thereby give rise to a " Returne of Bullion, Moneys or other useful goods." [1] " Montes pietatis " could also be conveniently joined to the bank ; " A Lumbard for ye Poore ".

Such were the manifold benefits of the proposed bank ! A report of a committee, selected under the government of Joseph Dudley, to investigate the merits of the scheme, came to conclusions no less optimistic. [2] Such a bank, said the Committee, would be " very useful and conduceable to the encourageing of Trade, navigation, manufacturers, planting and improving of lands and estates, increasing of his Majesties revenues, facilitating the payment thereof, and of other debts, and removing the present greatest obstruction thereto." But it must be recalled that these worthy members of the committee were financially interested in Blackwell's bank.

How far the " bank bills " of Blackwell's scheme differed from the " change bills " proposed by Woodbridge, cannot be said with certainty. There is evidence, however, which leads one to believe that Blackwell's " bank-bills " were to be issued in denominations rather than receive their amounts from endorsement by acceptors. In outlining hypothetical cases to illustrate the use of the bank's credit, Blackwell said that " chapmen " would receive bank bills " of several values from 20s. and so upward." [3] This reference leads one to believe that it was not intended to issue bills of a lower denomination than 20s., and it seems clear that the purpose of the bank was to provide a denominational paper currency which would take the place of a specie coinage. Blackwell's proposal must therefore be considered as an important stage in the evolution of the conception of paper money. [4] The " bank bills " represent a distinct improvement over Wood-

[1] Blackwell, *Discourse*, pp. 129–130.
[2] *Massachusetts Archives*, Vol. 126, No. 104.
[3] Blackwell. *Discourse*, p. 126.
[4] *Cf.* Davis. *Colonial Currency Reprints*, Vol. I. Introduction, p. 15.

bridge's " change bills," since they would be in convenient denominations ; would be protected by the security held by the bank, and by the liability of the partnership of " persons of known integrity, prudence, and estate." [1]

Like Woodbridge his predecessor, Blackwell could lay no claim to originality for his projected bank. His discussion of the attempts which had been made to overcome the want of money by money banks, lombard banks, and land banks, shows that he was conversant with the existing European banking literature. His suggestion that a " mons pietatis " could be a " handmayd " of the bank of credit shows that he was acquainted with this means of providing loans. In England, several projects similar to Blackwell's had been put forward before 1686. The idea of establishing warehouses for the storage of goods, where merchants might make deposits and obtain advances, was set forth in 1676.[2] The next two years saw the appearance of four pamphlets on the same subject by Mark Lewis. He recommended the establishment of a loan office for commodities, and the issue of certificates which could pass as money.[3] An anonymous pamphlet, of 1683, urged that goods and land were the most solid foundation for credit, and that convertibility into gold or silver was not necessary to make bills passable.[4] A tract of 1685 proposed the erection of " Mounts of Piety " to overcome oppression in interest. All these tracts antedated the bank proposed by Blackwell, and all but one had been published before he came to Massachusetts, in 1684.

IV

In comparison with the elaborate scheme outlined by Blackwell, the proposals of Thomas Budd [5] were naïve and

[1] Blackwell. *Discourse*, p. 124.
[2] Davis. *Currency and Banking in the Province of Mass. Bay*, Vol. II., p. 33.
[3] *Ibid.*, pp. 42–43.
[4] *Ibid.*, p. 47.
[5] Budd, Thomas. *Good Order Established in Pennsylvania and New Jersey*. Philadelphia, 1685.

visionary. In order to overcome the inconvenience caused by lack of specie, and in order to promote the rapid settlement of Pennsylvania, Budd proposed three schemes. The first was that of a Lombard bank. Public storehouses should be erected for the storing of flax, hemp or linen, and public granaries for the storing of corn. The commodities should be here deposited and preserved intact for a small charge. The owner should have the right to withdraw, sell, or assign the deposited goods. When such commodities were received, their quantity, quality, and value should be recorded in a public register and a receipt issued by the storehouse keeper. These notes, said Budd, would then pass from hand to hand, and facilitate the exchange of goods between farmers, manufacturers and merchants without the use of money. As long as goods of any stage of manufacture would be on deposit, the notes would be extant, while when the notes were surrendered and the goods withdrawn, the notes would be " filed up as Waste Paper." [1]

Budd's second suggestion was the establishment of a " Bank of Monies and Credit." The assembly should set the interest rate, said Budd, " at 8*l*. per cent. the year." All money lent at interest should then be represented by " Bills and Bonds." These should be entered upon a " publick Registry " and declared assignable by an act of the Assembly. By this means, these notes would become " Bills of Exchange," and one " Bond or Bill would go through twenty hands, and thereby be as ready Monies." [2] The plan was merely the legalization of personal notes for legal tender purposes.

Budd's third plan was borrowed almost word for word from Yarranton's *England's Improvement by Sea and Land* (1677). It provided that all lands and houses should be registered with an account of their value, and how the properties were occupied or tenanted. A prospective borrower would present a " particular " of his lands and

[1] Budd, *op. cit.*, pp. 40–42, 50–52.
[2] *Ibid.*, p. 48.

houses together with his application for credit. This
" particular " would then be compared with the public
register, and, if it coincided, a loan to about two-thirds of
the value of the property would be made. What the plan
amounted to, therefore, was a discount of land or houses.
But " such an Anchorage, Fund or Foundation " as land or
houses, said Budd, " will then bring out the Monyes un-
employed from all Persons in these Provinces, even people
in all degrees will put in their Monyes, which will put [them]
out again into Trade to Merchants." [1]

These roseate pictures of Thomas Budd scarcely compare
with the projects of either Blackwell or Woodbridge. For
while " change-bills " and " bank-bills " were attended
with important theoretical limitations, it must be admitted
that both Woodbridge and Blackwell had made serious study
of the various banking projects advanced by their English
contemporaries, and had conscientiously attempted to
circumvent the economic difficulties involved. The same,
unfortunately, cannot be said for Thomas Budd.

In England, the success of the Bank of England tended to
eclipse the commodity and land bank proposals. In
America, the seventeenth-century literature on banking was
only the beginning of a long series of proposals and disappointing experiments. The American colonial literature
of land and commodity banks has been carefully brought
together by Andrew MacFarland Davis, and fills four stout
volumes.[2] The persistence of the American inflationist
programme, however, is not hard to explain. Scarcity of
money was a necessary concomitant of colonial expansion ;
English mercantilism and the need of new communities for
capital tended to maintain an unfavourable balance of trade.
The banking proposals represent the colonial hopes of
circumventing the inconveniences which economic imma-
turity had imposed upon the American colonies.

[1] Budd, *op. cit.*, p. 49.
[2] *Colonial Currency Reprints.*

CHAPTER XI

WAGES AND USURY

" Quest.   What rule must wee observe in lending ?
Ans.   Thou must observe whether thy brother hath present
or probable or possible means of repaying thee, if there
be none of those, thou must give him according to his
necessity, rather than lend him as he requires ; if he
hath present means of repaying thee, thou art to look
at him not as an Act of Mercy, but by way of Commerce
wherein thou arte to walk by the rules of Justice."

John Winthrop, *A Modell of Christian Charity*.

WAGES AND USURY

I

A l t h o u g h colonial America was hampered by both the scarcity of labour and the want of capital, strikingly divergent views were held regarding governmental control of wages and of usury. The rise of wages was condemned as "oppression," while the taking of interest was accepted as legitimate and necessary. The first part of the century was characterized by a persistent effort to control wages. But the ever present opportunity for labourers to become agriculturalists gradually undermined and weakened this medieval survival. By the close of the seventeenth century, powerful institutional forces had modified America's economic heritage. Perhaps no better illustration can be found in American economic thought of the moulding influence of environment.

The American doctrine of wages, at the beginning of the century was essentially medieval in character. Preacher and pamphleteer reiterated the traditional view while the law-makers attempted to curb the demands of wage-earners. The medieval theory of wages proceeded from the scriptural "law of labor," the theory of classes, and the doctrine of "just price." The necessity of labour was designated as a consequence of divine law. Labour was conceived as the "providential arm" which served man in his struggle for existence.[1] Labour was not only necessary, but honourable and an obligation upon every member of society. Wealth was necessary as a means whereby men could accomplish their several ends ; labour was the means whereby wealth

---

[1] *Cf.* Brants, *op. cit.*, p. 75.

might be obtained. But the tasks which must be performed in society are many and dissimilar, and must be distributed according to ability and aptitude. For this reason, said the medieval philosophers, only a part of society must apply itself to manual labour.[1] Yet those individuals who are to perform these tasks must look upon them as duties imposed upon them by divine providence. The Christian should accept his duties with resignation. There should be no striving to escape from the class into which a person has been placed ; neither should there be imitation of those who have been designated by providence to fulfil other duties and live in another class. Inequality of fortune or of incomes was not a chance phenomena, but rather a manifestation of God's benevolence, and man should not presume to distort this divine process by avaricious conduct.

The wages of the labourer must be adjusted in relation to his status in society. They should be sufficient to provide him with the requirements of his class. For the labourer to ask exorbitant wages was dangerous, because it disturbed social organization. More than that, it would be a violation of the doctrine of " just price," since the price of labour must be determined in the same manner as the price of other saleable commodities. The duties of the parties to a labour contract, were, accordingly, bilateral. It was an act of justice for the hirer of labour to give a " just price." [2] The seller of labour, on the other hand, must arrive at the " just price " by endeavouring to set a price which would reasonably compensate him for the sacrifice he has made, and one which will provide for his temporal and spiritual needs.[3]

The medieval theory of wages was somewhat modified at the hands of the mercantilists before the seventeenth century. A complaint about high wages characterizes the mercantilist attitude toward labour.[4] The medieval principle that wages must be regulated, was accepted, not as a means of com-

[1] Brants, op. cit., p. 76.
[2] Aquinas. Summa Theologica, II., 2, 114, 1.
[3] This rule was formulated by Langenstein. Cf. Brants, op. cit., p. 119.
[4] Hales, op. cit., pp. 15 and 98.

pelling hirers of labour to pay a " just price," but to prevent
labourers from charging too much.[1] High wages were
believed to result in excesses in expenditures, in drunkenness
and idleness. This modified medieval doctrine was the
heritage which the seventeenth-century Americans received,
and this heritage they tried to defend by word and law.
But another important factor also played a part in the
American wages discussion : the constant scarcity of
labourers in a new country. John Smith pointed out, for
example, that a successful colony depends upon good
labourers,[2] but Berkeley complained that skilled labourers
were difficult to attract, and that very high wages were
necessary to induce them to migrate.[3] Only when the
phenomenon of labour scarcity is considered together with
the medieval and mercantilist theories of wages, does the
colonial attitude toward wages become understandable.

Winthrop recorded that, in 1633, " the scarcity of workmen had caused them to raise their wages to an excessive
rate, so as a carpenter would have three shillings the day, a
labourer two shillings and six pence." [4] The consequence,
he pointed out, was that all who had goods to sell, advanced
their prices. The Court was compelled to take notice of the
" general complaint," as well as " further evils, which were
springing out of the excessive rate of wages." Legislation
was enacted which established a maximum wage, which
carpenters, masons and other labourers could charge. The
law also stipulated that " no commodity should be sold at
above four pence in the shilling more than it cost for ready
money in England." [5]

Winthrop's complaint bespeaks the colonial philosophy of
wages. Here is the medieval doctrine, modified by the
mercantilist prejudice and conditioned by the economic fact
that labourers were scarce. The " just price " aimed at was

[1] *E.g.*, Petty, *op. cit.*, p. 274.
[2] Smith. *Advertisements for the Unexperienced Planters*, p. 15.
[3] Berkeley, *op. cit.*, pp. 4, 7–8.
[4] Winthrop. *History of New England*, Vol. I., p. 116.
[5] *Ibid.*

one which would prevent " excessive " wages, rather than secure a proper subsistence to the labourer. This does not indicate a rejection of the medieval principle, but it does indicate that because wages were high, only the restrictive aspect of the medieval wage philosophy came into play. Ten years later, Winthrop referred, in his *History*, to a servant who " took great wages above others," and by this means " scraped together about 25 pounds and then returned with his *prey* into England." [1] Hubbard accepted as a matter of course, the necessity of regulating wages. The first Court of Assistants (1630), he said, found it necessary to prescribe wages because " it being commonly found that men, gotten from under the reins of government, are but like cattle without a fence, which are thereby apt to run wild and grow unruly." [2] Referring to the legislation of 1633, Hubbard agreed with Winthrop that scarcity of labourers had caused the rise in wages. " Many new Plantations going on at this time," he wrote, " made labourers very scarce, and the scarcity made workmen demand excessive wages." But the labourers excused their conduct, said Hubbard, by pleading that the prices of commodities had risen and that their wage demands were in proportion. The Court saw fit, however, to attempt to restrain both wages and prices. " But these good orders," lamented Hubbard, " were not of long continuance, but did expire with the first and golden age in this new world." [3]

The spiritual leader of this " golden age," John Cotton, vigorously advocated the fixation of prices and wages. " To the intent that all oppression in buying and selling may be avoided," he wrote in his proposed code of laws, the judges should " set reasonable rates upon all commodities and proportionably, to limit the wages of workmen and laborers." [4] Like the mercantilists, Edward Johnson also

[1] Winthrop. *History of New England*, Vol. II., pp. 98–99 (italics mine).
[2] Hubbard, *op. cit.*, pp. 146–147.
[3] *Ibid.*, p. 158.
   Cotton. *Abstract of the Laws of New England*, p. 180.

complained about high wages,[1] contending that high wages retarded manufacturing in New England, and lead to excessive consumption.[2] Hubbard considered " oppression and extortion in prices and wages " to be " injustice done to the public," [3] and approved of severe punishment for such offences. He cited with approval the case of Edward Palmer, who asked " an excessive price for a pair of stocks which he was hired to frame," and who " had the honor to sit an hour in them first himself." [4] The Boston Synod of Churches included in their list of social evils the fact that " Day Labourers and Mechanicks are unreasonable in their demands." [5]

Maintenance of " fair wages " was attempted by legislation, by prosecution and by a dependence upon the individual to set wages which coincided with the " *communis estimatio*." Abundant wage legislation characterized the early period in the American colonies. Massachusetts, for example, set maximum wages in 1630, and provided a fine for both those who gave or received wages above these rates.[6] From 1631 to 1633, wage contracts were to be " left free and at liberty as men shall reasonably agree." [7] But in 1633 the legal definition of fair wages was renewed because of the " great extortion used by divers persons of little conscience " and because of the great disorder caused by " vain and idle waste of much precious time " which had been caused by " immoderate gains." [8]

Legal prosecution of those who charged high wages also characterized the early period. A certain Francis Godson, for example, was haled before the General Court of Massachusetts for changing " too great wages," in 1634.[9] After

---

[1] Johnson, *op. cit.*, p. 246.
[2] *Ibid.*, p. 211.
[3] Hubbard, *op. cit.*, p. 248.
[4] *Ibid.*
[5] *Necessity of Reformation*, p. 7.
[6] *Mass. Col. Records*, Vol. I., p. 74.
[7] *Ibid.*, p. 84.
[8] *Ibid.*, p. 111.
[9] *Ibid.*, p. 123.

the laws prescribing specific wage rates had been repealed in
Massachusetts, the General Court dealt with the wages
problem by declaring that those who took excessive wages
should be punished by fine or imprisonment according to
the "quallity of the offence."[1] Winthrop ultimately
admitted the futility of attempting to outlaw a rise in wages,
and recognized that the possibility which labourers had to
become agriculturalists was the primary cause for the
persistent wage increases.[2] He recorded that the Court
abandoned its attempt to regulate wages, for the whole
colony, and charged the "several towns to set down rates
among themselves."[3] An interesting piece of evidence on
the colonial theory of just wages is found in the Massachusetts records for 1641. In that year, the court "taking
into consideration the general fall in prices," declared that
labourers and workmen should "be content to abate their
wages according to the fall of the commodities wherein their
labours are bestowed."[4] Labourers should be content to
share in the "present scarcity," it was argued, since they
had shared in the "plenty of former times."[5]

Like the mercantilists, the seventeenth-century Americans
believed that high wages demoralized labour. Winthrop
complained, for example, that in consequence of high wages
"1. Many spent much time idly &c. because they could get
as much in four days as would keep them a week. 2. They
spent much in tobacco and strong waters &c. which was a
greate waste to the Commonwealth."[6] This statement is
merely a sample of the great number of similar complaints
in the colonial records. The persistent belief that high wages
were socially and morally dangerous continued through the
seventeenth century and far into the eighteenth, until it was
answered with extraordinary ability by Adam Smith. His

[1] *Mass. Col. Records*, Vol. I., p. 160.
[2] Winthrop. *History of New England*, Vol. II., p. 25.
[3] *Ibid.*   *Cf. Mass. Col. Records*, Vol. I., p. 183.
[4] *Mass. Col. Records*, Vol. I., p. 327.
[5] *Ibid.*
[6] Winthrop. *History of New England*, Vol. I., p. 116.

answer was that high wages, as a general rule, stimulate
rather than repress industry.[1] Only a minority of 'the
labourers are tempted to idleness by high wages ; and when
this does occur, it is usually the " excessive application
during four days of the week " which is the " real cause of
the idleness of the other three, so much and so loudly complained of." [2] It is true, of course, that backward people,
with inflexible standards of living may be tempted to idleness by high wages, but the general mercantilist fallacy had
no such anthropological basis.

The American wages discussion toward the close of the
century shows considerable advance in thought. In the
various colonies, strict regulation of wages was gradually
abandoned, first by the colonial assemblies, and then by the
towns. The existence of free land played a most important
part in rendering wage legislation futile. Winthrop remarked
on this, as early as 1640. The consequence of legal regulation
of wages, he said, was merely that labourers " would either
remove to other places where they might have more, or else
being able to live by planting, and other employments of
their own, they would not be hired at all." [3] Wage regulations were therefore turned over to the towns, and by
" persuasion of the Elders and example of some who led the
way," labourers were " brought to more moderation than
they could be by compulsion." [4]

But it appears that it was not only the futility of wage
regulations which altered the colonial ideas. Gabriel
Thomas's remarks on wages lead one to believe that he
understood the influences of differences in the productivity
of the soil as a cause of differences in wages. " The chief
reason why wages of Servants of all sorts is much higher,"
in Pennsylvania, said he, " arises from the great fertility

[1] " The liberal reward of labour . . . increases the industry of the
common people." Smith, Adam. *Wealth of Nations* (Cannon Edition),
Vol. I., p. 83.
[2] *Ibid.*, p. 84.
[3] Winthrop. *History of New England*, Vol. II., p. 25.
[4] *Ibid.*

and Produce of the Place." Moreover, he pointed out that
" if these large stipends were refused them, they would
quickly set up for themselves." [1] The cheapness of the
land, the fertility of the soil, the good market for grain by
the " great and quick vent into Barbadoes and other
Islands," [2] and the low taxes were the cause of the high
wages in Pennsylvania. Thomas claimed that Pennsylvania
wages were three times as high as those of England or Wales.[3]
He realized also the influence of the supply of labour. The
" Reason why Womens wages are so exhorbitant," said
Thomas, is because " they [women] are not yet very
Numerous, which makes them stand upon high Terms for
their several services." [4] The authors of the *Present State
of Virginia* [5] saw also in the matter of supply, one explanation of high wages. Because of the " want of towns, markets
and money, there is little encouragement for tradesmen and
artificers, and therefore little choice of them, and their
labour is dear in the country." [6] But, in general, the
extensive use of indented servants explains the paucity of
wage discussion in the Virginia literature of the seventeenth
century. In Pennsylvania, Thomas Budd pointed out the
connection between high prices and high wages.[7] The
domestic manufacture of cloth and cordage, he urged, would
be highly profitable since it could be sold in competition
with imported cloth and cordage. The Pennsylvania manufacturers would have no transportation charges to pay, and
" it appears that at those prices [foreign cost plus trans-
portation] we shall have double for our labor." [8]

Aside from the type of ideas outlined above, only a few
other colonial references are to be found regarding wages.

[1] Thomas, *op. cit.*, p. 328.
[2] *Ibid.*, pp. 328–329.
[3] *Ibid.*, pp. 319, 326.
[4] *Ibid.*, p. 329.
[5] Hartwell, Blair and Chilton. *An Account of the Present State and
Government of Virginia*, 1698.
[6] Hartwell, Blair and Chilton, *op. cit.*, p. 128.
[7] Budd, *op. cit.*, p. 42.
[8] *Ibid.*, p. 47.

The paper money writers, to be sure, held that scarcity of money holds down wages,[1] and that overvaluation of specie would diminish the amount of commodities which labourers could buy.[2] Demonetization of small commodities, Tienhoven said, would injure wage-earners,[3] while Mather recognized that depreciation of paper money would injure labourers who looked upon these instruments as a store of value.[4] It is, however, the very absence of references to wages in the closing decades of the century which is significant. The medieval-mercantilist philosophy had been reiterated. But the expansion of this philosophy into policy had been unsuccessful. The old doctrines had been tried and found inapplicable.

II

The discussion of usury by the seventeenth-century Americans had a quite different flavour from the discussion of wages. In England and Holland the usury problem was settled by the opening of the century. The writings of Molinaeus, Calvin, and Salmasius had refuted the canonist theories which had been adduced to prove that usury must be prohibited, while the growth of commerce and industry had led to expanding demands for credit. The taking of interest had been sanctioned by public opinion, and in England after 1545, by the Crown. The last prohibition of interest taking was removed during the reign of Elizabeth in 1571.[5] To the American colonists, therefore, the usury problem was no longer a moral issue. Capital was admittedly productive ; trade, colonization and agriculture demanded credit which in turn required the payment of interest. Indeed, so generally was the righteousness of interest or usury (in America the terms were synonymous in the seventeenth century) admitted, that the staunchest defenders of

---

[1] *E.g.*, Woodbridge, *op. cit.*, pp. 113–114.
[2] *Model of* 1688, p. 182.
[3] Tienhoven, *op. cit.*, p. 82.
[4] Mather. *Considerations on the Bills of Credit*, p. 194.
[5] Böhm-Bawerk, Eugene V. *Capital and Interest*, p. 43.

the Mosaic code found no fault with the receipt of such an income, providing there was no oppression of the poor.[1] As contrasted with the great number of laws concerning wages, the total absence of usury laws, in the American colonies, signifies the complete acceptance of the idea that interest was a necessary remuneration. Outside of admonition that lending should be tempered with charity, the scholastic and canonist denunciation of usury had no echo in the American colonies.

The necessity and the justice of usury was frankly admitted. Winthrop sanctioned usury in his *Modell of Christian Charity*,[2] as did also John Cotton.[3] Roger Williams considered usury an evil practice, but admitted interest taking because its prohibition would lead to greater evils " as stealing, robbing, murthering, perishing of the poore, and the hindrance or stop of commerce and dealing."[4] Jonathan Mitchell charged the state to suppress " biting usury," not all usury.[5] The " several pastors " of the Massachusetts churches declared that usury involved no " intrinsick turpitude," and was " justified by the law of necessity and utility,"[6] while Cotton Mather held that lending was one of the " pious uses of wealth."[7]

"What rule must be observed in lending ? " asks an imaginary questioner of John Winthrop. That depends, answered he, upon whether the borrower " hath present or possible or probable means of repaying thee." If he has neither, then the Christian should not lend but give. On the other hand, if the borrower has the ability to repay, then the Christian may " look at him not as an Act of Mercy, but by way of Commerce."[8] And such, in substance, was the

---

[1] *E.g.* Cotton, John. *Abstract of the Laws of New England* (originally called Moses, his Judicials).
[2] Winthrop. *Modell of Christian Charity*, p. 37.
[3] Cotton. *Abstract of the Laws of New England*, p. 180.
[4] Williams. *Bloody Tenant*, p. 169.
[5] Mitchell, *op. cit.*, pp. 3-5.
[6] "Thirty Cases," &c., in Mather's *Magnalia*, Vol. II., p. 259.
[7] Mather. *Durable Riches*, Part II., p. 8.
[8] Winthrop. *Modell of Christian Charity*, p. 37.

theory of usury from Winthrop to Mather. "Lending" was to be confined to those who could repay. It involved a legitimate charge for usury, and should be governed by the "rules of Justice." But lending should be carefully distinguished from "giving" or "forgiving." The poor should be objects of mercy and there should be no taking of usury from those who are deserving of charity.

Lending, said Winthrop, should be confined to those who have "possible means of repaying."[1] "Our Lending," said Cotton Mather, "should be to such ; as are likely to come into a way of what they may call their own."[2] The lending of means for the purposes of trade was, therefore, one of the "pious uses" of wealth.[3] But lending to those "Idle Vagrants and Varlets" who do not intend to repay is one of the "indiscreet abuses of our Estates."[4] While usury was approved as a legitimate reward on productive loans, it was under no circumstances to become a means of oppressing the poor. The poor should be an object of mercy. "If any of thy brethren be poor &c.," wrote Winthrop, "thou shalt lend him sufficient."[5] Indeed, this is not lending, but giving or forgiving. To the poor man, the Christian "must give him according to his necessity."[6] Or, if a loan has been made, "whether thou didst lend by way of commerce or in mercy, if he hath nothing to pay," the Christian must forgive the debt.[7] The only exception which was allowed was where a "pledge" had been given for a loan.[8] But even here, the law of love should modify the lender's activity. "The lender," said Cotton, "shall not make choice of what pledge he will have, nor take such a pledge as is of daily necessary use unto the debtor, or if he does take

[1] Winthrop. *Modell of Christian Charity*, p. 37.
[2] Mather. *Durable Riches*, Part II., p. 8.
[3] *Ibid.*, Part II., p. 7.
[4] *Ibid.*, Part II., p. 8.
[5] Winthrop. *Modell of Christian Charity*, p. 37.
[6] *Ibid.*
[7] *Ibid.*, p. 38.
[8] *Ibid.*

it, he shall restore it again the same day." [1]   When the
" Hand of God " has made a borrower unable to discharge
his debt, " 'Tis among the Pious uses of our Estates " to
forgive the obligation.   It is this, said Mather, that the
" Word of God recommends unto us in Ezek. xviii. 7 and
elsewhere, under that Expression of Restoring the Pledge." [2]
And so the famous grandson of John Cotton, laid down the
same rules regarding usury as had his famous grandfather.

Merchants and men of affairs had nothing to say on the
question of usury, because there was no occasion for them to
do so.   Interest was given and received.   Only the ministers
who were concerned with impressing upon the people their
duties as Christians, touched upon the subject.   This discussion of the subject was incidental to their expounding
the duties of Christian charity.   It was in this relation that
Winthrop touched upon it, and Mitchell and Mather.   " Tho'
usury be lawful," wrote Cotton Mather, " there are some
Hard Usages in the Usury, between the Creditor and Debtor
among ourselves, which the Law of Love will never justify." [3]
Where insolvency was caused by " bad courses," there
should be no forgiving of debts, nor any relinquishing of
interest.   Indeed, such persons

" should undergo whatever Lash the Law will help their Creditor
to inflict upon them ; for they are a sort of Cheats and Thieves,
the punishment of whom is a thing very Soveraign and wholesome for the whole Body Politick." [4]

But, when the " pure Frowns of God " have made the
debtor unable to pay, both interest and principal should be
forgone.[5]   Indeed, said Mather, this is the true meaning of
the scriptural charge in Luke vi. 35 : " Lend, Hoping for
Nothing again."   The Christian should " Lend, with a
Disposition to call for nothing again, in case the Hand of

---

[1] Cotton.   *Abstract of the Laws of New England*, p. 180.
[2] Mather.   *Durable Riches*, Part II., p. 9.
[3] Mather, Cotton.   *Fair Dealing between Debtor and Creditor.*   Boston,
1716, p. 27.
[4] Mather.   *Durable Riches*, Part II., p. 10.
[5] *Ibid.*

God, should impoverish the borrower." [1] The Greek word, Mather pointed out, means to despair ; " When we lend, we should suppose that the Debt may become Desperate ; and be ready to Release Principal as well as interest, if Divine Providence make it so." [2]

An extraordinary exposition of the colonial theory of usury was set forth in 1699, by the pastors of the churches adjacent to Cambridge, Massachusetts.[3] The whole subject was carefully analyzed and " resolved with evidence of Scripture and Reason." Usury, said these pastors, arises from anything lent " by contract." [4] It is not confined to a return upon money, but may arise from anything " lent upon usury." The real difference between receiving usury and " other ways of dealing " lies in " the owners not running the risque of the principal." [5] Usury is lawful for the Christian, because of several reasons. Some usury is permitted by divine law ; for example, the Levitical law permitted lending to strangers upon usury. Such permission could never have been given by the Scriptures " if usury had in it any intrinsick turpitude." [6] Indeed, in the Old Testament prohibition of usury " there are clauses in the context which seem to intimate as if the *poor* brother only were intended in the prohibition." [7] Even so, Gentiles are exempted from the prohibition, and the words of Christ in the New Testament, gave " countenance, in Matt. xxv. 27, unto a man's receiving his own with usury." John the Baptist likewise, " forbade not unto the publicans the usury which their condition of life led them unto." [8]

Turning from the Scriptural attitude, the Massachusetts

---

[1] Mather. *Durable Riches*, Part II., p. 10.
[2] *Ibid.*
[3] " Thirty Important Cases, resolved with Evidence of Scripture and Reason. By Several Pastors of Adjacent Churches meeting in Cambridge, New England." Boston, 1699. Printed in Mather's *Magnalia Christi Americana*, Vol. II., p. 259.
[4] *Ibid.*
[5] *Ibid.*
[6] *Ibid.*
[7] *Ibid.*
[8] *Ibid.*

pastors next examined the reasonableness of interest. Usury, said they, is a necessary for the welfare of society ; " Humane society, as now circumstanced, would sink, if all usury were impracticable." [1] In addition to being " justified by the law of necessity and utility," usury is justified by the " law of equity." It is only fair that the lender should partake in the benefits which " his estate procures for another man." [2] Indeed, it is sinful for the borrower not to share his gain with the lender. Usury, then, cannot be sinful, for it cannot be sinful for the lender to receive that which it is the duty of the borrower to give.[3] Again, usury is justified by the " law of parity." Money is as " improveable a thing " as any other commodity. Money and goods are, therefore, on a par as far as the righteousness of usury is concerned.[4] Neither is usury contrary to the " law of charity." When the use of property is relinquished, the owner has a right to expect an income " for the profitable use which other men may make of those things whereof he is himself the proprietor." [5]

Charity, to be sure, must " regulate our usury," lest it be carried unto a " biting extremity." One person must not " make his own advantage by adding to his neighbour's misery." [6] The right to claim usury must not supersede the Christian obligation to relieve a necessitous neighbour. For this reason, it is sinful to demand usury from the poor " when we accomodate them for their mere necessary sustenance and subsistence." So is it also sinful to refuse to help the poor because a person wishes to satisfy his own desires for luxury.[7] " Hire " must be distinguished from " lending upon usury." To charge as much for usury, where there is no " risque of the principal," [8] as for hire, is sinful.[9]

---

[1] " Thirty Important Cases." *Magnalia*, Vol. II., p. 259.
[2] *Ibid.*
[3] *Ibid.*
[4] *Ibid.*
[5] *Ibid.*
[6] *Ibid.*, pp. 259–260.
[7] *Ibid.*
[8] *Ibid.*, p. 259. These writers were evidently considering secured loans.
[9] *Ibid.*, p. 260.

Finally, usury which gives rise to idleness, must be condemned, for then, usury " is justly become a thing of evil
character." [1]

These were the arguments which the New England pastors
adduced in favour of interest taking. The scriptures, which
for so many hundred years had been relied upon to justify
the condemnation of usury, were now used to justify interest.
All the rules of reason were likewise shown to support this
income. " All these things being thus considered," declared
the pastors, " the severe declamations of the ancients against
usury, must be of no further account with us." [2]

Aside from these extraordinary ecclesiastical pronounce-
ments, virtually nothing more on the subject of usury is to
be found. The paper money writers, to be sure, promised
that their projects would lead to lower interest rates.[3] One
interesting bit of evidence, however, is to be found in the
Massachusetts Archives, for 1693. The legal rate of interest
was, in that year, reduced from 8 to 6 per cent., " Forasmuch
as the abatement of the Interest hath always been found
beneficial to ye advancement of Trade and improvement of
lands by good husbandry." [4] Here is a single piece of
evidence of the probable influence of the fallacy of Culpepper [5] and Josiah Child.[6] It is not unlikely that this
reference is an American reflection of this theory.

III

In addition to the discussion of wages and usury, a few
statements regarding the rent of land are to be found in the
American literature of the seventeenth century. So abundant
is land in America, wrote John Smith, that " here every man
may be master of his owne labour and land." As a conse-

---

[1] "Thirty Important Cases." *Magnalia*, Vol. II., p. 260.
[2] *Ibid.*
[3] Blackwell, *op. cit.*, p. 134 ; and Woodbridge, *op. cit.*, p. 113.
[4] Mass. Archives, Pecuniary, Vol. I.
[5] *A Tract Against Usurie.* London, 1621.
[6] *Brief Observations Concerning Trade and Interest of Money.* London,
1668.

quence, said he, there " are no Landlords to racke us with high rents." [1] The same idea was contained in a letter which William Hilton wrote from Plymouth plantation in 1621. " We are all free-holders," he advised prospective colonists, " the rent day doth not trouble us." [2] Robert Cushman contrasted the economic opportunities in Plymouth with those in England. While Plymouth held forth a promise of plenty, England " groaneth under so many closefisted and unmerciful men," that colonization only could correct the " straitness of the land." [3] While " the rent-taker lives on sweet morsels," Cushman continued, " the rent-payer eats a dry crust often with watery eyes." [4] There is more land in America, said John Smith, than " all the people in Christendom " can use ; " And shall we here [England] keep such a coyle for land, and at such great rents, and rates, when there is so much of the world uninhabited ? " [5] Such were the ideas of the colonization writers. High rents persisted in Europe and were the result of a scarcity of land. The abundance of land in America would make high rents impossible, and this elimination of rent would increase the prosperity of the settlers. But John Cotton understood that rent would emerge in spite of the sheer abundance of land. In outlining his proposed tax system, he recommended that if, by inheritance, the lands of any town should become " alienated from the townsmen," the non-resident owners could be made to contribute to the town income if " a reasonable rent charge " were laid upon such alienated land. [6]

No further reference to rent has been found before the paper money pamphlets appeared. John Blackwell said that if a bank, such as he sponsored, were established, " The Rents of Landed men will be increased, and the payment of

[1] Smith. *Description of New England*, pp. 195–196.
[2] Young, *op. cit.*, p. 250.
[3] *Ibid.*, p. 249.
[4] *Ibid.*, p. 248.
[5] Smith. *Advertisements for the Unexperienced Planters*, p. 22.
[6] Cotton. *Abstract of the Laws of New England*, pp. 177–178.

them . . . facilitated." [1] Just how the rise of rents would take place, he unfortunately did not explain. He only added, as another promised benefit of more money, that the " Purchase value of Lands will rise." *The Model of* 1688, which Blackwell either wrote or copied,[2] was no clearer on this issue :

" The Rents of Land, yea the purchase value thereof, will rise ; For the Plenty of Money, or a valuable credit equivalent thereunto and the Lowering of Interest, must necessarily have that effect." [3]

The writers on monetary problems, however, did understand one important point about rents : that the appreciation of a monetary unit would make money rents more burdensome. " The Rents of Houses and Lands," wrote the author of *Reasons for a Mint in New England,* " have been paid, and all Goods bought and Sold for many years in New England, by this measure [pine tree shilling] and the altering of it, and bringing it to the standard of Old England, would enrich the Landlord and Creditor, but it would ruyne the Tenant and Debtor." [4] The author of the *Model of* 1688, was of the same opinion. The overvaluation of Spanish coins, it was urged, would carry " great injustice in it " for all those who had made long time contracts such as those who receive " Rents on Leases." [5]

There is an even greater scarcity of references to profits, than to rent. A great deal of the colonial theory of profits, to be sure, is bound up with the theory of " just price." Complaints about " oppression in prices " were complaints about high profits. Massachusetts Bay Colony, for example, limited profits to " ffoure pence in the shilling more than the cost " in England, by legislation of 1633.[6] This act was repealed, in 1635, but unreasonable profits were to be

[1] Blackwell, *op. cit.,* p. 144.
[2] Davis. *Colonial Currency Reprints,* Vol. I. Introduction, p. 16ff.
[3] *Model of* 1688, p. 177.
[4] Reasons for a Mint. Crosby, *op. cit.,* p. 92.
[5] *Model of* 1688, p. 182.
[6] *Mass. Colonial Records,* Vol. I., p. 111.

punished by fine or imprisonment " according to the quallity of the offence." [1] Plymouth Plantation regarded a 50 per cent. advance over cost unreasonable.[2] In the case of John Barnes, already mentioned, the Plymouth Court held that an advance in price of 25 per cent. was extortion, not *per se*, but because the commodity was sold " *without adventure* or *long forbearance* in *one and the same place*." [3] Gross profits were therefore recognized to compensate risk, interest and costs of transportation. A similar idea is found, much later, in the pronouncement of the Massachusetts ministers on usury. The " main difference of usury from other ways of dealing," said they, " is the owners not running the risque of the principal." [4] " Hire " apparently was compensation for waiting combined with risk.

A few opinions are to be found regarding the relation between wages and profits. William Wood expressed the thesis, that high wages are not a subtraction from profits :

" Whereas it is generally reported, that servants and poore men grow rich, and the masters and Gentrie grow poor ; I must needs confesse that the diligent hand makes rich . . . but I cannot perceive that those that set them aworke are any way impoverished by them ; peradventure they have lesse money by them, but never the lesse riches ; a mans worke well done being more beneficiall than his monie, or other dead commodities, which otherwise would lye by him to no purpose." [5]

John Winthrop recognized that the level of profits in agriculture was one of the causes for the height of wages in Massachusetts,[6] and Gabriel Thomas pointed out that unless wage-earners were paid " large stipends," they would " quickly set up for themselves." [7] John Cotton urged that if sellers used unjust weights and measures, " the profit so

[1] *Mass. Colonial Records*, Vol. I., p. 160.
[2] *Records of Colony of New Plymouth*, Vol. I., p. 137.
[3] *Ibid.*, Vol. I., p. 5 (italics mine).
[4] " Thirty Important Cases." *Magnalia*, Vol. II., p. 259.
[5] Wood, *op. cit.*, p. 51.
[6] Winthrop. *History of New England*, Vol. II., p. 25.
[7] Thomas, *op. cit.*, p. 328.

wickedly and corruptly gotten," should be " forfeited to the public treasury of the Commonwealth." [1]

The colonial ideas on wages, usury, rent and profits, therefore, represent a curious admixture of medieval, mercantilistic, and relatively modern ideas. The usury theory presents the most systematic approach which the seventeenth century made to an explanation of any form of income. But although the colonial ideas on wages, rents or profits are more fragmentary, they reveal more definitely the influence of circumstance upon ideas. The sheer impossibility of repressing wages in a country where land was abundant and labour scarce reveals a significant aspect of American history and American civilization. The new world, as Professor Wertenbaker has said, made new men. Among the influences, which have created a difference between European and American habits of thought, the economic have not been least significant !

---

[1] Cotton. *Abstract of the Laws of New England*, p. 180.

THE CONDEMNATION OF COMMUNISM

" When our people were fedde out of the common store and laboured jointly in the manuring of the ground, and planting corne, glad was that man that could slippe from his labour, nay the most honest of them in a generall businesse, would not take so much faithfull and true paines in a weeke, as now he will doe in a day, neither cared they for the increase, presuming that howsoever their harvest prospered, the generall store must maintain them, by which meanes we reaped not so much corne from the labours of 30 men, as three men have done for themselves."

Ralphe Hamor, *A True Discourse of the Present Estate of Virginia.*

THE CONDEMNATION OF COMMUNISM

IN the colonial appraisal of private property and communism, theological reasoning is blended with pragmatic considerations. Communism was repudiated both on theological grounds and because of the disappointing experiments in Plymouth plantation and in Virginia. One phase of the colonial antipathy toward common ownership was traditional; the other was a product of experience. Since the theological opposition to communism was inherited from the medieval logicians, it may be well to briefly recapitulate the doctrines of the Schoolmen before presenting their American counterparts.

God gave the earth to men, said the medieval writers, that His servants might use it for His glory. In the state of innocence, men lived and had all in common. But sin ruined this perfect plan of the Creator, and private property has become a necessary institution in a fallen world. Private acquisition, therefore, is the consequence of man's degeneracy and a divine concession to human weakness. Given a world composed of imperfect ethical beings, private property is necessary because it brings results which redound to God's glory. It facilitates the production of that amount of wealth which is necessary for each person to maintain his status in society, it increases human industry, and reduces contention and social disharmony. It makes possible that degree of charity which Christians must observe, and it provides for the support of all the institutions which God has ordained. At its worst, then, private property is a superior alternative to a communism of individuals who have fallen from that state of ethical perfection

which would have made communism possible. But God's
ideal for men was a communism wherein the sons of
Adam might have lived in love and harmony together,
enjoying the bounty of God's providence. Communism
was conceived to be an ideal for ideal men and
private property an alternative caused by man's corruption.[1]

The American writers echoed the medieval belief of the
impossibility of realizing ideal communism. The original
tenure of the earth, said John Winthrop, was one of commonage.[2] " The first right to the earth was *natural* when
men held the earth in common every man soweing, and
feeding where he pleased." [3] But this commonage did not
outlive the period of man's innocence (the period analogous
to the Golden Age of the Ancient Greeks). For whereas
" Adam in his first estate was a perfect modell of mankinde,"
and whereas then, love was the sole principle of human
relations ; " Adam rent himselfe from his Creator " and
thereby " rent all his posterity allsoe one from another."
In consequence of this moral degeneration, " every man is
borne with this principle in him to love and seeke himselfe
onely." [4] It is this self-love, innate in man's nature, which
makes communism impossible. Communism, said Governor
Bradford, leads to a destruction of mutual respect. But
some may answer, he said, that this is a result of man's
corruption and not the fault of communism. His reply
reiterated the medieval belief : " I answer, seeing all men
have this corruption in them, God in His wisdom saw another
Course fitter for them." [5] Only ideal men, therefore, can
aspire to an ideal distribution of goods. Robert Cushman
urged the Plymouth settlers to approximate this ideal plan

[1] These ideas are to be found in the writings of Lactantius, St. Augustine,
Gratian, St. Ambrose, and St. Thomas Aquinas. The ideas on communism
of the church Fathers has been carefully analysed by Hubbard, Joseph.
Economic Thought in Patristic Literature. Harvard University Thesis.
[2] Winthrop. *Conclusions,* p. 6.
[3] *Ibid.*
[4] Winthrop. *Modell of Christian Charity,* p. 41.
[5] Bradford, *op. cit.,* p. 164 (italics mine).

as nearly as possible. " Nothing in this world," he declared,
" doth more resemble heavenly happiness, than for men to
live as one, being of one heart and one soul," [1] while nothing
" more resembles hellish horror, than for every man to shift
for himself." [2] Indeed, " if it be a good mind and practice,
thus to affect particulars, mine and thine, then it should be
best also for God to provide one heaven for thee and another
for thy neighbour." [3] But Winthrop understood that it was
self-love which made earthly communism impossible, and
that communism could not obtain " till Christ comes and
takes possession of the soule and infuseth another principle." [4] Till man is raised from his fallen estate, communism is impossible, and God in His wisdom has sanctioned
another plan of social organization ; a system of private
property and inequality.

" God Almighty in his most holy and wise providence,"
said Winthrop, " hath soe disposed of the condition of
mankind, as in all times some must be rich, some poore,
some high and eminent in power and dignitie ; others mean
and in submission." [5] Inequality, then, is no chance
phenomenon ; it is the means whereby various duties
have been imposed upon men by the Creator. The unequal
distribution of wealth serves several important divine
purposes. It reveals the glory of God's wisdom " in the
variety and difference of the creatures " ; [6] it serves the
purpose of " moderating and restraining " the avaricious
natures of men, " soe that the rich and mighty should
not eat upp the poore nor the poore and dispised rise upp
against and shake off theire yoake." [7] In other words,
inequality teaches the favoured mercy and justice, while the
poor it teaches resignation. But Aristotle had set forth the
principle that where only two classes exist in society, the

---

[1] Young, *op. cit.*, p. 266.
[2] *Ibid.*
[3] *Ibid.*
[4] Winthrop. *Modell of Christian Charity*, p. 41.
[5] *Ibid.*, p. 33.
[6] *Ibid.*, pp. 33–34.
[7] *Ibid.*

state can never have tranquillity. One class, said he, cannot
obey, and can only rule despotically, while the other must
be ruled like slaves.[1] Winthrop, on the contrary, believed
that the very existence of inequality would lead to the moral
improvement of society by a distribution of duties.   Every
one would then come to realize that he has " need of others,
and from thence they might be all knitt more nearly together
in Bonds of brotherly affection."   Indeed, men must come
to realize that

" noe man is made more honorable than another or more wealthy,
&c. out of any particular and singular respect to himselfe, but
for the glory of his Creator and the common good of the creature,
man." [2]

Wealth was designated as a loan from God,[3] entrusted to
individuals, upon whom corresponding duties devolve.

Inequality was conceived to be an evidence of God's
purposes.   Since men have " this corruption in them," [4]
inequality is superior to any communism of imperfect
ethical beings. God " is the Maker both of the rich and the
Poor," [5] and men should reconcile themselves to their
places in the divine plan.   Pride, which causes " Servants
and the poorer sort of People " to spend excessive amounts
of money on apparel, and thereby " goe above their estates
and degrees," is a transgression of both the laws of God and
man.[6] This was the doctrine which Jonathan Mitchell set
forth in his election sermon of 1667 : " Keep Order, keep in
your places, acknowledging and attending the Order that
God hath established in the place where you live." [7]
Winthrop recognized only two classes in society.   " All
men," said he, are " ranked into two sortes, riche and poore."
Under the first he included all those " as are able to live

---

[1] Aristotle.   *Politics.*   Edition cited, pp. 168–169.
[2] Winthrop.   *Modell of Christian Charity*, p. 34.
[3] Mather.   *Durable Riches*, Part II., p. 2.
[4] Bradford, *op. cit.*, p. 164.
[5] Mather.   *Durable Riches*, Part II., p. 2.
[6] *Necessity of Reformation*, pp. 2–3.
[7] Mitchell, *op. cit.*, p. 26.

comfortably by their own means duely improved " ; [1] all others were classed as " the poore." Aristotle had classified the members of society into three groups, the " very rich," the " very poor," and a mean between the two.[2] A city which is composed of the middle class, said the Greek philosopher, is the most satisfactory. " Great then is the good fortune of a state in which the citizens have a moderate and sufficient property."

The colonial writers not only believed property to be theologically justified, but they believed property was also sanctioned by natural law. Here is another appearance of medieval theory. Thomas Aquinas had argued that private property was perfectly compatible with natural law [3] ; that it was natural, legitimate, and necessary. John Winthrop, it will be recalled, had said that " God hath given to the sonnes of men a double right to the earth " ; " a natural right and a Civill right." [4] The civil law was an addition to the medieval canon law, but the two were considerably fused by the end of the fifteenth century. It was the civil law which was relied upon by the Americans to justify their taking up land in America,[5] but they recognized that the first right to land (the right which the aborigines had) was a " natural right." In the acquisition of land, said Winthrop, " the end is Double morall & natural." [6]

The American comparison of the virtues of communism as opposed to private property was precipitated by the necessity of concerted action in founding colonies, and by the obligations which were imposed upon two colonies, at least, by the English merchants who financed the ventures. The Virginia settlement began with the use of a common

---

[1] Winthrop. *Modell*, p. 34. " Duely improved " in all probability means duely improved at interest. *Cf.* Oxford English Dictionary. The same phraseology appears in " Thirty Important Cases." *Magnalia*, Vol. II., p. 259.

[2] Aristotle. *Politics*, pp. 168–169.

[3] Aquinas. *Summa Theologica*, II., 2, 66, 2.

[4] Winthrop. *Conclusions*, p. 6.

[5] *Cf.* Cotton. *God's Promise to His Plantation* ; *cf.* also, Cushman in Young, *op. cit.*, p. 244.

[6] Winthrop. *Conclusions*, p. 5.

stock as did also Plymouth. These situations, fortunately, produced written criticisms which form a chief source of our knowledge of the American ideas of communism. The general belief was that communism was attended with so many disadvantages that it could under no circumstances provide the degree of well-being which would be forthcoming under a *régime* of private property.

By far, the most important critic of communism was that great and courageous leader of Plymouth plantation, William Bradford. His thankless task it was, for three years, to regulate the labour of the community and distribute the scanty proceeds. Not only was he compelled, during this enforced communism, to be the overseer of work and the foreman in the fields, but the storekeeper, who apportioned the common supplies.[1] With Plato's praise of communism he was familiar, but the sad experiment at Plymouth taught him most of what he later laboriously wrote of communism in his history.

In 1623, when it became evident that something must be done to improve the economic situation at Plymouth, Bradford was reluctant to give up common cultivation, not because he favoured communism in itself, but because of the contract which the Plymouth leaders had made with the London merchants. But

" at length after much debate of things, the Govr (with the advise of ye cheeftest amongst them) gave way that they should set corne every man for his owne perticular, and in that regard trust to themselves ; in all other things to go on in ye general way as before." [2]

The consequence, he recorded, was an extraordinary increase of activity. The individual use of land " made all hands very industrious, so as much more corne was planted than other waise would have beene by any means ye Govr or any other could use." [3] Nor were the causes for this increased planting difficult to discover ;

[1] See Usher, *op. cit.*, p. 204.
[2] Bradford, *op. cit.*, p. 162.
[3] *Ibid.*

" The women now wente willingly into the feild, and took their little ons with them to set corne, which before would aledge weakness, and inabilitie ; whom to have compelled would have been thought great tiranie and oppression." [1]

Here is a classic statement. Communism reduces economic activity by making labour more disagreeable and irksome ; it breeds discontent and a feeling of injustice and oppression. More concisely, it creates subjective conditions which increase the real costs of production.

Nor is this all. The experience with communism, wrote Bradford,

" tried sundrie years, and that amongst godly and sober men,[2] [the experiment he meant, was a fair one], may well evince the vanitie of that conceite of Plato & other ancients, applauded by some of later times ;—that ye taking away of propertie, and bringing in communitie into a comone wealth, would make them happy and flourishing ; as if they were wiser than God." [3]

For instead of bringing happiness, as the apostles of communism had predicted, the Plymouth experiment, " was found to breed much confusion & discontent, and retard much imployment that would have been to their benefite and comforte." [4] Instead of happiness, unhappiness ; instead of harmony, confusion ; instead of abundance, dearth ! For Bradford, the explanation was not difficult :

" For ye yong-men that were most able and fit for labour and service did repine that they should spent their time & striength to work for other mens wives and children, without any recompence." [5]

Here arose one complaint of injustice. " The strong, or man of parts, had no more in divission of victails & cloaths, then he that was weake and not able to doe a quarter ye other

---

[1] Bradford, *op. cit.*, p. 162.
[2] *Ibid.*, p. 163.
[3] *Ibid.*
[4] *Ibid.*
[5] *Ibid.*

could ; this was thought injuestice." [1] But these two classes of the community were not the only groups to complain ; " The aged and graver men to be ranked and equalized in labours and victails, cloaths &c. with ye meaner and yonger sorte, thought it some indignitie & disrespect unto them." [2] Finally, and by no means least important, " for mens wives to be commanded to doe service for other men, as dressing their meate, washing their cloaths &c., they deemed it a kind of slaverie, neither could many husbands well brooke it." [3]

One would have to search long for such a damning criticism of communism, or such a penetrating analysis of the causes for its failure as a practical expedient. It restricts production by increasing the real costs involved ; it breeds confusion and discontent ; it creates a feeling of injustice in the minds of the young and old, the strong and weak, the married or unmarried. More than that, said Bradford,

" Upon ye poynte all being to have alike, and all to doe alike, they thought themselves in ye like condition, and one as good as another ; and so, if it did not cut of those relations, that God hath set amongst men, yet it did at least much to diminish and take of ye mutual respects that should be preserved amongst them." [4]

Bradford was not the only critic of the communist experiments. Next in importance was the Virginian, Hamor, whose criticism John Smith incorporated into his *Generall Historie*. Communism, said Hamor, leads to indifference. Work is avoided and even the most honest persons labour with very low intensity. "When our people were fedde out of the common store," wrote Hamor,

" glad was the man that could slippe from his labour, nay the most honest of them in a generall business, would not take so

---

[1] Bradford, *op. cit.*, p. 163.
[2] *Ibid.*
[3] *Ibid.*
[4] *Ibid.*, pp. 163–164.

much faithfull and true paines in a weeke, as now he will do in a day." [1]

Moreover, under communism, the size of the jointly produced product does not appear to interest the members of the community. " Neither care they for the increase," said Hamor, " presuming that howsoever their harvest prospered, the generall store must maintain them." [2] But private property stimulates enterprise. Under communism, said Hamor, " we reaped not so much corne from 30 men, as three men have done for themselves." [3] Edward Winslow, who had been a witness to the Plymouth experiment, supported Bradford as a critic of communism. Self-love, said Winslow, makes communism impossible, as does also " the base disposition of some drones." [4] The reason why communism does not induce men to labour, he said, is because governors have nothing to give and therefore cannot command labour. [5] He believed, as did his medieval predecessors, that communism is feasible only with ideal men. But imperfect beings require an inducement to labour, and private property provides that stimulus.

These criticisms of communism were not new. Aristotle had pointed out that under private property men will not complain, they will make more progress by attending closely to their own affairs. [6] Self-love, he said, is implanted by nature, and although excessive self-love is to be condemned, a reasonable self-love makes men industrious. [7] Thomas Aquinas held that private property was necessary for three reasons : because every man is more careful to procure what is for himself alone than that which is common to all ; because, under private property, human affairs are conducted in a more orderly fashion ; and because private property

[1] This passage is reproduced in Smith almost verbatim. Smith. *Generall Historie*, p. 516.
[2] *Ibid.*
[3] *Ibid.*
[4] Young, *op. cit.*, p. 347.
[5] *Ibid.*, p. 346.
[6] Aristotle. *Politics*, p. 62.
[7] *Ibid.*, pp. 62–63.

brings social peace by eliminating quarrels over the division of product.[1]

The communism, which was advocated and accepted as desirable by the American writers, was a modified Aristotelian communism of use. This was the sort of communism that Cushman defended, that Winthrop referred to as a " community of perill," and that the New England clergy accepted as the basis of Christian charity. All individual ownership, said Cushman, was caused by Satan [2] ; sin has made God's intended communism impossible. Yet while private property is a necessary form of organization, particular situations require temporary communism. " It is yet too soon to put men to their shifts," Cushman preached at Plymouth, in 1621 ; " Israel was seven years in Canaan before the land was divided into tribes, much longer before it was divided into families." [3]

Communism may be temporarily necessary ; if so, men must " cheerfully, as with one heart, hand and shoulder " go about their work " both in wars, building and plantations." [4] Indeed, under such circumstances, if " every man seeks himself, all cometh to nothing." [5] Moreover, declared Cushman,

" It wonderfully encourageth men in their duties when they see the burden equally born ; but when some withdraw themselves, and retire to their own particular ease, pleasure or profit, what heart can men have to go on in their business ? " [6]

Here was the argument for temporary communism, a means of dealing with a particular situation. To accomplish a particular purpose of this nature, Cushman insisted that the proper attitude must be acquired, and if such an attitude could be developed, then communism would work. The

---

[1] Aquinas. *Summa Theologica.* II., 2, 66, 2.
[2] " Who I pray thee, brought this particularizing first into the world ? Did not Satan, who was not content to keep the equal state with his fellows, but would set his throne above the stars." Young, *op. cit.*, p. 266.
[3] *Ibid.*, pp. 265–266.
[4] *Ibid.*, p. 265.
[5] *Ibid.*
[6] *Ibid.*, pp. 264–265.

example of the industrious, he said, will put the slothful to shame, but if holding forth glory and credit will not curb idleness, then it must be curbed by withholding food.[1]

Cushman's theory of temporary or circumstantial communism was essentially the same as Winthrop's " community of perill." Winthrop laid down first, a theory of social relations. Originally, said he, man's relationship to his fellow man was determined by the law of nature. This required two things : that every man help his fellow man " in every want or distresse," and that " hee performe this out of the same affection which makes him carefull of his owne goods." [2] But this " law of nature " could only have application in " the estate of innocency." [3] Therefore, after man's fall, the law of nature must be supplanted by " the law of the Gospell." The obligation which the Gospel law lays upon man varies between " seasons and occasions." [4] " There is a time," said Winthrop, " when a Christian must sell all and give to the poor, as they did in the Apostles time." [5] There are times when Christians " must give beyond their ability." Finally, there is a " community of perill " which calls for " extraordinary liberality." To Winthrop, therefore, the sharing of goods was a requirement of God, although the extent of the sharing required depended upon circumstances. In the first place, all sharing of goods, Winthrop carefully pointed out, must be subsequent to the provision for one's family of the " means of comfortable subsistence." [6] The Gospel law, then, requires circumstantial communism ; a " community of perill " may require an almost complete sharing of goods. The primitive church, said Winthrop, was a " community of perill " when the early Christians, " sold all, had all in common, neither did any man say that which he possesed was his owne." [7] In like

---

[1] Young, *op. cit.*, p. 267.
[2] Winthrop. *Modell of Christian Charity*, pp. 34-35.
[3] *Ibid.*
[4] *Ibid.*, p. 35.
[5] *Ibid.*
[6] *Ibid.*, pp. 35-36.
[7] *Ibid.*, p. 38.

manner, the return from captivity because " the worke was great " and the " danger of enemies common to all," demanded a greater sharing of goods than ordinarily was necessary.[1]

The colonial theory of communism, it is evident, converges with the theory of the use of wealth. Winthrop set forth the duties of giving, lending, and forgiving, which Mather elaborated again at the close of the century. These duties were the consequence of a divine distribution of property, and true Christians were to accept and fulfil them. " The care of the publique must oversway all private respects," wrote Winthrop, for " particular Estates cannot subsist in the ruin of the publique." [2]   Private property must be limited by enforced circumstantial communism on occasions of danger ; and by public interest, love and Christian charity at all times. This was exactly the theory of the medieval writers.[3]

The upshot of the colonial discussion of communism was a recognition of the superiority of private property as long as men are not ideal by nature. Private property in land, wrote the author of the *Essay on the Laying out of Towns*, stimulates enterprise because of the desire for emulation.[4] Bradford, although he lamented the dispersion of the Plymouth population, recognized that the continuous use of land, and the right to acquire land stimulated industry.[5] John Smith urged that the promise of rights to land in fee simple was the greatest inducement for labourers,[6] and for this reason he cautioned leaders of colonies not to

" stand too much upon the letting, setting or selling those wild countries, nor impose too much upon the commonalty either by your Maggazines, which commonly eat out all poore mens labours, nor any other too hard imposition for present gaine." [7]

---

[1] Winthrop. *Modell of Christian Charity*, p. 38.
[2] *Ibid.*, p. 45.
[3] *Cf.* Brants, *op. cit.*, p. 55.
[4] *Essay on the Laying out of Towns*, pp. 478–479.
[5] Bradford, *op. cit.*, p. 201.
[6] Smith. *Advertisements for Unexperienced Planters*, p. 41.
[7] *Ibid.*, p. 40.

The civil right to land, said Cotton, gives men a right to occupy empty lands [1] ; Winthrop had expressed the same opinion.[2] John Cotton held that inheritance was sanctioned by the law of nature [3] ; while Roger Williams admitted the legitimacy of private property in his re-statement of the Christian doctrine of the trusteeship of wealth.[4]

[1] Cotton. *God's Promise to His Plantation*, p. 5.
[2] Winthrop. *Conclusions*, p. 5.
[3] Cotton. *Abstract of the Laws of New England*, p. 178.
[4] Williams. *Bloody Tenant*, p. 254.

CHAPTER XIII

THE SUPPORT OF GOVERNMENT

"Till matters come to a settled government, no man is ordinarily sure of his house, goods, lands, cattle, wife, children or life."

"No government is maintained without tribute, custom, rates, taxes &c."

The Letters of Roger Williams.

THE SUPPORT OF GOVERNMENT

I

THE Aristotelian principle that a state must have wealth was accepted by the seventeenth-century Americans. The righteousness of moderate amounts of wealth for the individual found a complementary thesis in the right of the state to appropriate some wealth for common purposes. But in spite of the host of contingencies which demanded group action, colonial governmental expenditures were few and simple.[1] The support of the governor and the salaries of a few other executives were the chief costs of colonial government. Expenses of colonial agents were additional but unusual expenses. Defence was facilitated by local militia except in rare emergencies. Few public improvements were undertaken and the sphere of government had not yet been extended to include important expenditures for humanitarian purposes.

But although the province of governmental undertaking was comparatively small, logic and experience had convinced colonial leaders that government was indispensable. Government, said Roger Williams, " is the Ordinance of the Most High for the peace and good of mankind." [2] Like Plato, Williams declared that no group can maintain itself which does not submit to some form of government ; " Even robbers, pirates and rebels themselves cannot hold together but by some law among themselves." Unless a " settled government " is provided, neither security of property nor

---

[1] For a convenient summary of colonial expenditures, *cf.* Dewey, D. R. *Financial History of the United States.* New York, 1922.

[2] Williams. *Letters*, p. 401.

of person can obtain.[1] Williams compared government to a "tyrant in peace" who is much to be preferred to the absence of authority "where every man is a tyrant."[2]

Since government is theologically approved, socially indispensable, and economically useful, it must be maintained. Taxation is the means of its existence. "No government," said Williams, "is maintained without tribute, custom, rates, taxes, &c."[3] A state, said John Cotton, in his recommended code of laws, must have revenue; "No commonwealth can maintain either their authority at home, or their honor and power abroad, without a sufficient treasury."[4] Laws must, therefore, be devised which will provide public income. Since voluntary contribution is an uncertain means of obtaining income, taxation is necessary.[5] In simple communities, public contribution might be merely a compulsory accumulation of goods. Thus Cotton suggested that a "magazine, or storehouse be erected, and furnished in every town." Here a

"provision of corn, and other necessaries may be laid up at the best hand, for the relief of such poor as are not members of the church : and that out of it such officers may be maintained, as captains and such like, who do any public service for the town."[6]

But whereas contribution of commodities might suffice for local taxation, the commonwealth must have a "treasury." Blackwell explained the necessity of taxation on the same grounds as did Roger Williams. The failure to provide a public income out of which public charges could be defrayed, would not only "dissolve all Government but all Society."[7] Taxes must be levied and must be paid ; to complain about

---

[1] " Till matters come to a settled government, no man is ordinarily sure of his house, goods, lands, cattle, wife, children or life." Williams, *Letters*, p. 401.

[2] *Ibid.*, p. 402.

[3] *Ibid.* This classification is essentially the same as Bodin's. A government, said Bodin, obtains treasure from revenues, conquest, gifts, tribute, traffic, merchants, and imports. Bodin, *op. cit.*, Book VI., Chapter 2.

[4] Cotton. *Abstract of the Laws of New England*, p. 176.

[5] Bradford, *op. cit.*, p. 178.

[6] Cotton. *Abstract of the Laws of New England*, p. 177.

[7] Blackwell. *Some Additional Considerations*, p. 197.

taxes " is a Piece of unreasonable and abominable Baseness." [1]

The payment of taxes for the support of government was construed to be a legitimate charge upon any political group. The support of government, the ministry and all " public servants " is a Christian duty, said Cotton Mather, and one " which our Estates are to be put unto." [2] Only by recognizing and fulfilling this duty can the citizens of a community make their public servants " Capable to Discharge what obligations we have laid upon them." [3] Taxes, said Roger Williams, are " the reward or wages which people owe for such a worke." Magistrates supply public peace and they facilitate and protect commerce. Their " wages " consist of " tribute, toll, custome " and should be payable by all persons, " Natives and Forreigners who enjoy the same *benefit* of public peace and Commerce." [4]

Here is a clear cut benefit theory of taxation. Just where Williams got his ideas on taxation, it is impossible to say. Hobbes, who has been considered by Seligman [5] as the first exponent of the benefit theory, did not publish his *Leviathan* until 1651, whereas Roger Williams published the *Bloody Tenant* in 1644. Williams may have obtained the idea of a benefit theory from Hobbes's earlier Latin writings or possibly from the writings of Hugo Grotius. Grotius, however, applied a benefit theory only to dues and tolls for the use of roads [6] ; general taxes, he held, could not be imposed upon foreign merchants. But Grotius did mean that any governmental service enjoyed ought, if possible, to be charged for, to the extent of the benefit derived. In all probability, the benefit theory is much older than Hobbes ; Williams's acceptance of it as a basis of taxation, appears to bear out this point. Cotton Mather, later in the century, referred to

[1] Blackwell. *Some Additional Considerations*, p. 197.
[2] Mather. *Durable Riches*, Part II., p. 5.
[3] *Ibid.*
[4] Williams. *Bloody Tenant*, p. 355 (italics mine).
[5] Seligman, E. R. A. *Progressive Taxation in Theory and Practice*, 1894, p. 87.
[6] Grotius, *op. cit.*, Book II., Chapter II., Sec. 14, par. 1.

the benefits, which government provides, as the explanation of the justice of taxation. " All the Inhabitants of the land, taken as one Body," said he, " are the Principals, who *Reap the Benefits* and must bear the Burdens." [1] A country must pay its debts, said Mather, regardless of changes in government. This imposes an obligation upon all the people who have reaped the benefits, not upon " the Gentlemen who Administer the Government, who are but the Countries Agents in this Affair." [2]

The benefits which citizens derive from government were not carefully classified by the seventeenth-century Americans. But sufficient references exist to show that these were understood to consist primarily of public tranquility and order, together with protection from foreign enemies. A few writers included other governmental functions, such as the support of schools or the operation of a mint. Roger Williams appears to have followed reasoning similar to that of Hobbes. The function of government, said he, was to provide social peace and harmony.[3] Jonathan Mitchell admonished " Good Rulers " to insure " Tranquility, Quietness (or Peace) in the enjoyment of all those (both Religious and Civil good things)." [4] Cotton held that the commonwealth must maintain its " authority at home," and its " honor and power abroad." [5]

Colonial defence, though largely provided for by militia, nevertheless frequently demanded taxation. " Without great charges," wrote John Blackwell, " it is impossible to pay the just wages of them that hath bin in the Publick Service ; to defraud whom would not only be an Imprudence, which must in a little time leave us without all defense, but also an Injustice that would cry in the Ears of the Lord of Hosts." [6] William Wood, early in the century,

---

[1] Mather. *Considerations on the Bills of Credit*, p. 190 (italics mine).
[2] *Ibid.*
[3] Williams. *Letters*, p. 401.
[4] Mitchell, *op. cit.*, pp. 4–5.
[5] Cotton. *Abstract of the Laws of New England*, p. 176.
[6] Blackwell. *Some Additional Considerations*, p. 197.

pointed out that as a colony grows in wealth, provision for defence becomes necessary.[1] Blackwell alleged that the fall of Constantinople was due to a refusal to levy sufficient taxes for defence.[2] Opposition to taxes, said he, is caused by " covetousness." Failure to provide revenue for purposes of defence was, to his mind, the " worst ill Husbandry." [3] A government, said Cotton Mather, must provide security ; only if " we are Reduced to Hobs his state of nature, which (says he) is a state of War," is this otherwise.[4] The defenders of a colony, said Blackwell, must have support and reward.[5] But defence requires taxation, since voluntary contributions can never take the place of taxes. Voluntary contributions would not bring in enough revenue ; moreover, they " would lay the burden upon those that are the most willing, but not the most able." [6]

II

The question of the kinds of taxes which should be levied in order to accomplish these several purposes or functions of the state received but little attention. Roger Williams and Cotton Mather indicated that a tax system should levy charges in proportion to the benefits which were derived (which would mean progressive taxation). Blackwell denied that voluntary contributions could ever be a satisfactory means of acquiring revenue because contributions would not be adjusted in accordance with individual ability to pay. It is because of the paucity of statements, in the colonial literature, regarding the forms of taxation, that one is compelled to turn to the colonial laws to discover this aspect of the theory of taxation.

Systems of taxation varied between different colonies, and

---

[1] Wood, *op. cit.*, p. 57.
[2] Blackwell. *Some Additional Considerations*, p. 198.
[3] *Ibid.*
[4] Mather. *Considerations on the Bills of Credit*, pp. 191–192.
[5] Blackwell. *Some Additional Considerations*, p. 203.
[6] *Ibid.*, pp. 197–198.

between groups of colonies. In New England, chief reliance
was placed upon the poll tax and the general property tax.
The property tax was fairly well adjusted to an economic
section in which a wide distribution of property existed.
Property was mainly in land, buildings and cattle, and
consequently easy to assess.[1] The poll tax, although
primitive, was easy to administer, and became a fundamental part of the New England tax system. Supplementary
to the property and the poll tax was a faculty tax levied upon
artisans. This, however, was not a true income tax since
the assessments were arbitrarily determined. To some
extent, indirect taxation was employed in New England,
together with a limited use of license taxes.

The Southern colonies relied chiefly upon indirect taxation,
and upon poll taxes. The poor classes protested against the
poll tax, while the property tax was opposed by the planters.
The middle colonies were characterized by a mixed system
of taxation. New Netherlands introduced indirect taxes
and excises in imitation of the Dutch fiscal policy. Among
the several colonies, therefore, the forms of taxation employed during the seventeenth century were : the property
tax, the poll tax, the faculty tax, import and export duties,
excises and, to a limited extent, license taxes. A new form
of concealed taxation came into being with the issue of the
Massachusetts Bills of Credit, in 1690.

The general property tax, so extensively employed in New
England, was, in reality, an extension of the right of trading
corporations to levy assessments against their stockholders.[2]
Property taxes were common in England when the New
England colonies were first settled. As a consequence
nothing was said about the theory underlying the property
tax. " Rates " were voted by the New England governments with apparent confidence that a property tax was a
satisfactory way of obtaining revenue. A " rate " although

[1] See Dewey, op. cit., p. 11.
[2] Osgood, Herbert L. The American Colonies in the Seventeenth Century.
New York, 1904, Vol. I., p. 470.

originally a lump sum, soon came to mean a proportion of the taxpayer's " visible estate." [1] The application of the property tax was simple. The General Court of a colony determined the needed amount of income. This amount was next apportioned between the towns. An effort was made to discover " the true value of every town and so to make an equal rate." [2] To do this the towns were instructed to assess " every man according to his estate, and with consideration [of] all other his abilities whatsoever, and not according to the number of his persons." [3] Exemptions were allowed on account of illness or infirmity. Minimum amounts of property were exempted in the case of magistrates [4] or ministers. In a few cases, certain industries were temporarily relieved of taxes as the fishing trade, [5] or iron manufacturing. [6]

But whereas New England accepted the property tax, as a reasonable means of raising revenue, the Southern property owners took quite a different attitude. The property tax was first used in Virginia, in 1645, [7] as a supplement to the poll tax. But the principle of a property tax was not accepted in this legislation. Indeed, the law of 1654 was really a temporary concession wrung from the wealthy land holders (who controlled the assembly) by the small land owners who were beginning to feel that poll taxes were compelling them to pay a disproportionate share of taxation. One defence made by the large holders of land in the Southern colonies was that land paid its proportion of the public burden through quit-rents. [8] The authors of *The Present State of Virginia* held that poll taxes were to be preferred to property taxes. Land, said they, " pays tax

---

[1] *E.g.*, In Massachusetts after 1646.
[2] Massachusetts Law of 1636.
[3] *Mass. Colonial Records*, Vol. I., p. 168.
[4] *Ibid.*, Vol. II., p. 101.
[5] *Ibid.*, Vol. I., p. 257.
[6] *Ibid.*, Vol. II., p. 62.
[7] Ripley, William Z. *The Financial History of Virginia.* New York, 1893, p. 25.
[8] Hartwell, Blair and Chilton, *op. cit.*, p. 156.

enough in quit-rents" and as for cattle and horses, the planters can turn them "to so little account, that they think it not reasonable to lay a tax upon them." [1] But the quit-rents, as Ripley has pointed out, were not designed as a fiscal measure.[2] They were a recognition of the ultimate sovereignty of the king, and essentially feudal dues. The real objection to the property tax arose from an unwillingness on the part of the wealthy planters, who controlled the assemblies, to bear their share of the tax burden. The opposition of the small farmers to the poll tax, combined to create an opposition to all forms of direct taxation in the Southern colonies. The patroons of New Netherlands took the same attitude toward the property tax as did the large landholders of the Southern colonies.

The poll tax, as Dewey has pointed out, was complementary to the property tax. In Massachusetts, for example, every adult male was valued at a property sum, and the poll tax was a proportion of the sum. The apportionment of the poll tax was similar to that of the property tax, and was one of the means whereby the towns raised the amount of taxes assigned to them.[3] The valuation of each person was a principle which, in practice, gave comparatively little trouble in New England as compared with Virginia. But even in New England the poll tax led to complaints. For when the "rates" voted by the General Courts were doubled or trebled, the poll taxes were similarly increased. The consequence was that the tax burden, involved in the poll tax, tended to increase or decrease disproportionately, depending on whether the taxpayer possessed more or less than the average amount of property.[4] It was the reduplication of the poll tax, rather than the poll tax itself, which led to complaints in New England. "In respect of polle money," wrote Boston petitioners, in 1653, "we apprehend its

[1] *Perfect Description of Virginia*, p. 9.
[2] Ripley, *op. cit.*, p. 47.
[3] See Douglass, C. H. J. *Financial History of Massachusetts.* New York, 1892, p. 29.
[4] Douglass, *op. cit.*, p. 30.

parallel is not in any country where the sword is not drawn in offensive or defensive war." [1]

The attitude of the Southern colonies toward the poll tax is exemplified by Virginia. Before 1645 public charges had been met by a simple poll tax.[2] But this form of taxation, said the property tax act of that year, " hath been found inconvenient, and is become insupportable for the poorer sorte to beare." [3] The property tax, however, was repealed in 1648, leaving the poll tax to fall with unfortunate inequality upon the small landowners. As a consequence, a long struggle arose between the small and the large landowners, which led to violence in Bacon's Rebellion. Beverley said, in his history, that the poll taxes of fifty pounds of tobacco levied in 1674 to pay the expenses of colonial agents " fell heaviest on the poor People," who began to become " desperately uneasy." [4] The Burgesses, in 1658, even though they represented the landed classes and opposed any property tax, admitted that a poll tax was a " burthensome and unequall waie of layinge taxes." [5] But the Virginia legislators did not pose as advocates of a poor man's cause. They were interested in abolishing all direct taxation. The poll tax was continued in spite of the protest of the small farmers and tenants, and was used throughout the century. As late as 1693, Hartwell, Blair and Chilton could write : " taxes in Virginia have always been laid in this fashion, viz., not upon lands, houses, stocks of horses, cattle, trade, &c., but the number of titheables." [6] In the middle colonies the poll tax and the property tax were commonly combined. This was the case in Pennsylvania,[7] for example. But in proprietary colonies the poll tax generally gave way to a property tax.[8] Even in Maryland and Virginia, where the

---

[1] Mass. Archives, Vol. 100, p. 44.
[2] Ripley, *op. cit.*, p. 25.
[3] Hening's Statutes, Vol. I., p. 305. Quoted Ripley, *op. cit.*, p. 25.
[4] Beverley, *op. cit.*, pp. 65–66.
[5] Hening's Statutes, Vol. I., p. 491. Quoted, Ripley, *op. cit.*, p. 28.
[6] Hartwell, Blair and Chilton, *op. cit.*, p. 156.
[7] Osgood, *op. cit.*, Vol. I., p. 348.
[8] *Ibid.*, p. 349.

poll tax was used, its assessment upon servants and slaves tended to make it approximate a property tax.

In New England, the presence of an artisan class led to a form of taxation known as the " faculty tax." Although in theory an income tax, its arbitrary administration tended to make it equivalent to a poll or a property tax. Individuals were assessed at fixed amounts according to their occupations. The Massachusetts Act of 1646, for example, divided the persons liable to " faculty " taxation into two classes on the basis of their incomes. The faculty tax was essentially an assessment upon an arbitrary capitalized value of wages.[1] Massachusetts introduced the faculty tax in 1646,[2] and it soon became a part of the tax systems of all the New England colonies. Later the principle was introduced into Pennsylvania, Delaware and Maryland.[3] It represents the colonial attempt to impose some portion of the burden of taxation upon people who would not be reached by property taxes.

Indirect taxation was as unimportant in New England as it became usual and customary in the Southern colonies. Throughout the seventeenth century, New England relied chiefly upon direct taxation, while excises and custom duties were introduced only as a means of easing the tax burden.[4] New York, on the other hand, introduced the property tax as a means of decreasing the burden of indirect taxation which had grown up during the Dutch period and which had been continued after the conquest. The Southern colonies, where the separation of two great classes had created opposition to both the property and the poll tax, were compelled to rely chiefly upon indirect taxes for revenue.

The most important forms of indirect taxation were import and export duties. " The vicious ruinous plant of Tobacco," wrote Berkeley, " I would not name but that it brings more money to the Crown, then all the Islands in

---

[1] Douglass, *op. cit.*, p. 31.
[2] *Mass. Col. Records*, Vol. II., p. 173.
[3] Dewey, *op. cit.*, pp. 11–12.
[4] Douglass, *op. cit.*, p. 32.

America." [1] But if tobacco was important to the Crown, it was scarcely less important to the Southern colonies. Curiously, however, the fiscal importance of export duties on tobacco was not early recognized, in Virginia.[2] It was not until 1661 that an export duty was laid upon tobacco primarily for fiscal purposes [3]; but this legislation became a model for later acts. This first act, however, explained that one of the purposes of the export duty on tobacco was to create " an encouragement to men to produce other useful and beneficial commodities." [4] Berkeley put the arguments in favour of an export tax with clarity and insight. In his address to the Crown, in which he asked for permission to increase the export tax on tobacco, he pointed out, that such a tax would create an income which would " pay all the publick charges of the Countrey." [5] It would be the nearest " way to a publick unquarrelled contribution " that could be found since its ultimate incidence would be upon the producer. " Who pays for this," asked Berkeley, " but the poor Planter, whose Tobacco must sell for lesse." [6] His argument, in brief, was that an export tax falls ultimately on the producer. It provides revenue with the least trouble, and this is well, because " never any Community of people had good done to them, but against their wills." [7] South Carolina followed the example of Virginia and Maryland, and levied an export tax in 1691.[8]

In New England export duties were unimportant. Very often, when export duties were levied, the purpose was not fiscal. Connecticut, for example, laid heavy duties on the export of lumber in order to compel conservation of building material.[9] The same theory may have motivated the

[1] Berkeley, *op. cit.*, p. 2.
[2] Ripley, *op. cit.*, p. 57.
[3] *Ibid.*, p. 58.
[4] Hening's Statutes, Vol. I., p. 413. Quoted, *ibid.*, p. 57.
[5] Berkeley, *op. cit.*, p. 8.
[6] *Ibid.*
[7] *Ibid.*
[8] Osgood, *op. cit.*, Vol. I., p. 360.
[9] Dewey, *op. cit.*, p. 15.

Plymouth legislation of 1662 which laid export duties on timber, barrel staves, tar and oysters.[1] But the number of items taxed leads one to believe that revenue was also a significant item.

Import duties, although extensively used in the Southern colonies and in New Netherlands for revenue, were often used in New England to regulate or alter consumption or production. Wine merchants, wrote Hubbard,

" filled the country with that commodity, to the overflowing of luxury and other evils, whereas, had there been a greater impost laid thereon, it might have turned the stream of traffic into another channel, that might have been more beneficial to the place." [2]

Sumptuary regulation was most frequently effected by excise taxes, although sometimes an import duty was combined with the excise for this purpose.[3] By 1668, in Massachusetts, import duties were levied on liquors, money, plate, bullion, and merchandise in general, at an *ad valorem* rate of 2 per cent.[4] Even in Virginia, where indirect taxation was favoured, both by the rich and poor, import duties were designed almost as much for sumptuary purposes as for fiscal. This was true, for example, of the law of 1661, which imposed duties on rum and sugar.[5] It was not until late in the century that import duties on liquors were advocated primarily for revenue purposes.[6] Import duties on slaves did not become of significant importance in the seventeenth century.[7]

The Dutch, at New Amsterdam, were the only colonists who levied high import taxes primarily for revenue purposes and in this they followed the fiscal policy of Holland. Duties varying in height from 10 per cent. in 1642, to 16 per cent.

[1] *Records of Colony of New Plymouth*, Vol. XI., p. 132.
[2] Hubbard, *op. cit.*, p. 520.
[3] As in Massachusetts, in 1645.
[4] *Mass. Col. Records*, Vol. V., p. 138.
[5] *Hening's Statutes*, Vol. II., p. 212.
[6] Ripley, *op. cit.*, pp. 69–70.
[7] *Ibid.*, p. 73.

in 1658, were laid upon a long list of commodities. Moreover, specific duties were assessed against goods intended for Indian trade. Adrian Van der Donck alleged that the heavy taxation of New Netherlands was the explanation for its tardy economic development.[1] The Dutch colonists, said he, are so burdened by taxes that they " are not able to appear beside their neighbours of Virginia or New England, or to undertake any enterprize." Indirect taxes were continued in New York after the conquest, and the Dutch use of specific duties was also followed.[2]

Besides import and export duties, several other forms of indirect taxation came into use. Most of the colonies, for example, levied tonnage duties at one time or another. Sometimes provision for colonial defence was assisted by requiring shipowners to turn over powder in proportion to the ship's tonnage. Of such nature was the Virginia law, of 1631,[3] and such a duty was included by Cotton in his recommended code of laws for Massachusetts.[4] Later in the century the powder duties were commuted into cash.[5]

More important than tonnage duties, were excises, which became especially significant in New Netherlands. An excise etymologically and actually is " something cut off " ; that is to say, by its imposition, the state cuts off for itself a share of the selling value of the taxed commodity. This mode of indirect taxation was translated from Holland to New Netherlands as a part of the fiscal policy of the Dutch West India Company. Here it was well adapted to the economic situation since the patroon landowners were hostile to property taxes. Excise taxes were first levied in New Netherlands in 1644, and were imposed upon beer, wine, brandy and beaver.[6] But while the excise was fiscally more important in this colony, it was by no means restricted to

---

[1] Donck. *Representation of New Netherlands*, p. 64.
[2] Osgood, *op. cit.*, Vol. II., p. 360.
[3] *Hening's Statutes*, Vol. I., p. 176.
[4] Cotton. *Abstract of the Laws of New England*, pp. 176–177.
[5] Dewey, *op. cit.*, p. 15.
[6] Osgood, *op. cit.*, Vol. II., p. 356.

New Netherlands. Plymouth resorted to the excise in 1646 with taxes upon wine, " strong waters " and tobacco.[1] The occasion for this change in the tax system, according to this law, was that the " comon charge " had increased and the colony was " unwilling to defray the same by way of Rate but rather by way of Excise." This language suggests, although it does not prove, that the excise was adopted for fiscal expediency. From New Netherlands the excise was passed on to the English colony of New York, but with the change in government came a development of the property tax as a fundamental part of the tax system. From New York the excise expanded into the other middle colonies, for example, into East New Jersey, in 1692, and into Pennsylvania in 1700. Since an excise tax falls on the consumer, commodities such as beer, ale, or wine, were selected for taxation. William Kieft, who introduced the excise tax into New Netherlands, proposed " to impose some duties on those wares from which the good inhabitants will suffer the least inconvenience." [2] The collection of the beverage excise was accomplished by dividing it between the brewer and the tapster.[3]

Together with the excise on liquor went the license tax. In New Netherlands, an extensive system of tavern regulation was necessary to enforce the excise.[4] But the license tax was not necessarily tied up with the excise. New Netherlands, for example, charged license fees from those who slaughtered domestic cattle [5]; Massachusetts beginning in 1644, charged a license tax for every butt of wine drawn by vintners [6]; Plymouth began to collect fishing license taxes from foreigners in 1646,[7] while retailers of wine or liquors, after that year, were required to pay license taxes as a part

---

[1] *Records of the Colony of New Plymouth*, Vol. XI., p. 51.
[2] Brodhead, *op. cit.*, Vol. I., p. 394.
[3] Tienhoven was not entirely correct when he wrote, " the beer excise . . . is paid by the tapster and not by the burgher." Tienhoven, *op. cit.*, p. 86.
[4] Osgood, *op. cit.*, Vol. II., p. 357.
[5] *Ibid.* (in 1656).
[6] *Mass. Colonial Records*, Vol. II., p. 82.
[7] *Records of Colony of New Plymouth*, Vol. II., p. 103.

of the excise system.[1] Licenses were also required for the operation of bridges and ferries.[2]

Government paper money began a new method of public finance with the issue of the Massachusetts Bills of Credit, in 1690. The act which provided for taxes, to be collected in the future, according to the paper money advocates, " was a *fund*, on which the credit of such a sum should be rendered passable." [3] Had the bills continued to circulate at their face value, it is quite true that they would have been merely a means of anticipating taxes. But depreciation soon altered the situation. The paper money writers soon realized that the bills were depreciated. Cotton Mather took the naïve position that certain people were responsible for the depreciation of the bills of credit. As a result of their fall in value, said he, " the poor soldier is horribly injured." [4] Inflation had produced an unfair form of taxation which fell heaviest upon the innocent recipients of the bills.

Mather understood that by the circulation of depreciated paper, the burden of the taxation or confiscation involved would fall on the poorer classes. The bills of credit could be made to circulate, he said, by " Selling them at Under-Rates," which is a " way found out by poor men's necessities." [5] But if the bills could be restored to a purchasing power equal to their face value, argued Mather, there would be no injustice involved. Since he had ascribed the depreciation to the diabolical activities of persons, it was easy for him to provide as naïve a remedy :

" Raise the Rates of those above the common Standard, whom you catch tardy in Debasing the Credit of your Bills, either by purchasing them with little money ; or selling commodities for them at Excessive dearer Rates." [6]

[1] See also act of 1677, with regard to collecting of fines for the sale of liquors " without lycence." *Records of the Colony of New Plymouth*, Vol. XI., p. 247.
[2] *E.g.*, New Netherlands. Brodhead, *op. cit.*, Vol. I., p. 575.
[3] Mather, Cotton. *Magnalia*, p. 190.
[4] Mather. *Considerations on the Bills of Credit*, p. 191.
[5] *Ibid.*, pp. 193–194.
[6] *Ibid.*, p. 194.

In other words, correct the injustice resulting from depreciation by punitive taxation of the depreciators. Would that
it were so simple ! John Blackwell said that for anyone to
discriminate against the bills of credit was " crying oppression." [1] He agreed with Mather " that if the Government
can find out any " who have depreciated the bills, it " ought
to advance the Rates of such people to procure a Reparation
to them that have been wronged." [2] Such taxation, not
only would punish the depreciators, but also correct the
injustice resulting from depreciation. What a beautiful
prospect this must have been to soldiers and wage-earners !

III

The final question regarding colonial taxation theory is
concerned with the distribution of tax burdens. Roger
Williams and Cotton Mather referred to a benefit theory of
taxation, but it cannot be said that the colonial tax systems
attempted to apply a benefit theory as a basis of tax distribution. Blackwell pointed out that voluntary contributions
could never replace taxation for the support of government [3]
because the willing contributors would be penalized. " The
burden," said Blackwell, would fall " upon those that are
most Willing but not the most able." [4] It cannot be said
that colonial taxes were apportioned either according to the
benefits derived (which would involve progressive taxation)
or on the basis of ability to pay. To be sure, there was some
approximation of ability to pay in the combined property,
poll and faculty tax system of New England. But the controversy between the large landowners and the small landowners, in Maryland, Virginia or New Netherlands, bespeaks
the failure of the tax systems to even roughly approximate
taxation according to ability to pay. The one guiding
principle of colonial tax distribution was simply that of

[1] Blackwell. *Some Additional Considerations*, p. 201.
[2] *Ibid.*
[3] *Ibid.*, pp. 197–198.
[4] *Ibid.*

fiscal expediency. Economic conditions and institutional traditions combined to develop one system in New England, another in New Netherlands and others in the Southern colonies. In so far as any of the tax systems conformed to any ideal scheme, this was, to a large extent, accidental rather than contemplated.

Still the literature of the century contains quite a number of references to what a tax system should be, and to the consequences of ill-devised systems. Complaints about unfair taxation were legion. To recite these would be a tedious repetition of like grievances. The colonial governments were compelled, however, to take cognizance of these complaints and modifications of the tax laws often resulted. Plymouth, for example, was compelled, in 1668, to seek " some more equal and just way and course " of levying taxes in order that some men " be not oppressed." [1] Donck argued that New Netherlands was so heavily taxed that the people were unable " to undertake any enterprize." [2] Roger Williams alleged that Puritan Boston attempted to exclude persons, who did not harmonize with the religious beliefs of the Boston people, by the use of penalties. This form of taxation he denounced as invidious. " A great Load," said he, " may be made up by Parcels and particulars, as well as by one masse or bulke." [3] Beverley alleged that the heavy taxes in Virginia was one of the causes for Bacon's Rebellion. [4]

Only a little constructive advice about taxation can be gleaned from the colonial literature. John Smith, for example, cautioned prospective leaders of new colonies to be moderate in imposing duties. [5] " Have a care," he wrote, that those who come to trade " be not troubled with Pilatage, Boyage, Ancorage, Wharfage, Custome, or any such tricks as hath beene lately used in most of new Planta-

---

[1] *Records of Colony of New Plymouth*, Vol. V., pp. 4–5.
[2] Donck. *Representation of New Netherlands*, p. 64.
[3] Williams. *Bloody Tenant yet more Bloody*, p. 414.
[4] Beverley, *op. cit.*, pp. 64–65.
[5] Smith. *Advertisements for the Unexperienced Planters*, pp. 59–60.

tions." [1] Nothing " inricheth a Commonwealth than much
trade," said Smith, and there are " no means better to
increase [trade] than small custome." [2] The prosperity of
Holland, Genoa and Leghorn, Smith ascribed to low customs,
while the backwardness of Turkey, Spain and Sicily, he
attributed to their restrictive indirect taxes. The moderate
rate of taxation in Pennsylvania, Gabriel Thomas signalized
as one of the causes of high wages.[3] Winthrop argued that
when tax rates are changed, notice must be given to those
who will be required to pay the new taxes.[4] He recorded
how importers were offended by the new customs duties of
1646, since a " due course " had not been " taken to give
notice thereof to foreign parts." All dealings, said Cotton
Mather, in a country " that hath been by the help of God so
extraordinarily signalized " should be ordered on the basis
of " extraordinary equity." [5] He exhorted his listeners to
" deal fairly in bargains ; deal fairly in taxes." [6] Unfortunately, the learnèd Mather did not explain how this
" extraordinary equity " might be infused into a tax
system.

The failure to defray public charges, said John Blackwell,
would dissolve all government.[7] But the colonial writers
understood that a tax system must be devised which will
decrease the burdensomeness of this necessary taxation.
To collect taxes in the form of commodities, said Mather,
increases the tax burden, because risk and depreciation is
necessarily involved. The consequence, he said, would be
that the government is rendered " odious by a great noise
of Taxes, when little comes thereby." [8] Yet taxes must be
payable in something that is available. Since specie money
is very scarce, said Mather, in defence of the colonial bills,

[1] Smith. *Advertisements for the Unexperienced Planters*, pp. 59–60.
[2] *Ibid.*, p. 60.
[3] Thomas, *op. cit.*, p. 329.
[4] Winthrop. *History of New England*, Vol. II., p. 259.
[5] Mather. *Boston Ebenezer*, pp. 15–16.
[6] *Ibid.*
[7] Blackwell. *Some Additional Considerations*, p. 197.
[8] Mather. *Considerations on the Bills of Credit*, p. 192.

" to require the Country to pay their Taxes in Silver " is akin to forcing men " to make Bricks without Straw." [1] Since specie is scarce, and commodity taxes are unwise, said Mather, paper money is necessary if people are to pay taxes.[2] The defence of a country, said Blackwell, demands money. But a sufficient amount cannot be obtained by taxation because men are covetous and oppose taxation.[3] For this reason resort to paper money was necessary; indeed, " a better way could not be thought upon, than the Bills of Credit now passing." [4] In other words, the use of paper money was the expedient which led to the least complaint.

Colonial taxation theory was pragmatically concerned with the ways of obtaining revenue with the least opposition. Although a desire for a fair system of taxation is apparent throughout the century, fiscal expediency overshadowed the quest for justice. To some extent taxation was also regarded as a means of changing the economic activity of the colonists. Taxes on tobacco were designed to provide revenue, but also to encourage the production of " useful and beneficiall " commodities [5]; import duties were levied for income, but also to deter the importation of undesired commodities [6]; industries like fishing or iron manufacturing were exempted from taxes in order to stimulate their growth.[7] Excise duties were levied for the double purpose of creating public income and repressing intemperance or luxury.

[1] Mather. *Considerations on the Bills of Credit*, p. 192.
[2] *Ibid.*
[3] Blackwell. *Some Additional Considerations*, p. 198.
[4] *Ibid.*, p. 200.
[5] Ripley, *op. cit.*, p. 57.
[6] Hubbard, *op. cit.*, p. 520.
[7] Winthrop. *History of New England*, Vol. I., p. 307 ; II., pp. 212–213.

THE FRUITS OF ECONOMIC PHILOSOPHY

" The People of New-England shewed the world, that Necessitie and Freedome could do Wonders : for in a few years, they grew to such a height and greatness that they brought more Spirit, Virtue, Riches, Industry, Glory and Honour, to the English Nation, than ever any Collony did."

The Humble Address of the Publicans of New England.

CHAPTER XIV

THE FRUITS OF ECONOMIC
PHILOSOPHY

I

W I T H pride and veneration can Americans turn through
the pages of colonial history. With loving care, the antiquarian can assemble the evidences of craftsmanship,
literature, and architecture, which America's first century
produced. Yet these are but the evidences which have
been preserved for us of the extraordinary substantial
combination of economic and moral purpose which characterized the colonial era. The hardships of the seventeenth
century have yielded abundant fruit ; the millions who have
inherited the new carth have indeed come to a " bride feaste
wher all things are provided for them."

Of all the manifold forces which have combined to produce
America's institutional and intellectual legacy, the crude
economic ideas of a century of pioneers are not least important. A philosophy, of course, is not a prime mover ; but a
philosophy is a maker of some of a nation's fundamental
patterns. Future generations may alter or improve these
patterns, but they do not obliterate all traces of the original
designs. Two centuries and more have indeed modified the
economic patterns which were cut out with Puritan stern-
ness. But many centuries will elapse before they are effaced.

Historians have faithfully recorded the political contributions of colonial America ; moralists have appraised
the religious leaven. Only the history of the economic ideas
of the founders of the American nation has been neglected.
Indeed, if one were to believe the biographers of the seventeenth-century Americans, it would seem that the courageous

men who laid the foundations of American life entertained no economic ideas whatsoever! Such happily is not the case. Exactly what theories, concerning economic life, heritage and circumstance produced, it has been the purpose of this essay to classify, illustrate and define. Rather than hazard generalization, it has seemed wise to resort frequently and abundantly to the actual words of the colonial writers. In retrospect, however, amid the diversity of economic ideas, an harmonious theme is to be found. Fragmentary in origin, the thought of seventeenth-century America is not devoid of structural unity.

Private property and a degree of freedom in the acquisition of wealth were regarded as necessary in a world composed of individuals actuated by self-love and incapable of accomplishing the ideal communism which might have been possible in a society of ideal men. Wealth was, therefore, accepted as necessary both for the individual and for the state. But wealth ought not to become an end in itself; it should rather be a means of accomplishing the destiny of mankind which was conceived to be the realization of the Christian life and salvation. For this reason, the use of wealth was believed to require regulation, and the state was charged with surveillance over the wealth-getting and wealth-using activities of men. This economic circumscription was a logical corollary of the doctrine that the production of wealth was not wholly a matter of man's volition. For the original source of wealth was the bounty of a gracious God or a generous nature. Man's *rôle* in production was to appropriate this bounty through the application of labour.

Since labour was a chief means of obtaining a necessary supply of wealth, idleness was branded as socially and morally undesirable. In New England, slavery was conceived to be economically inferior to a system of free labour. In the southern colonies, slavery was of little importance until the eighteenth century. Although labour received chief attention as a productive force, capital was regarded as an important assisting means. As a result, the receipt of interest was considered not only legitimate and necessary, but compatible with Christian life. Since economic differentiation demanded means for the exchange of wealth, markets, fairs and trade facilities were created and encouraged by government. Freedom of trade was frequently lauded and approved despite the traditional belief that trade relations between individuals could not be left unregulated. A fear lest the innate self-love of each individual would lead to untoward social consequences nurtured a policy of economic control. To some extent, the medieval doctrine of " just price " was reproduced ; for a time, the state was charged with the duty of determining " fair wages " and " just prices." But the modifying influences of new conditions, abundant resources and the quest for freedom, gradually tended to qualify the medieval heritage. With the weakening of the influence of the clergy is correlated an expansion of economic liberalism.

The exchange of wealth was understood to require a monetary mechanism in order to function properly. The invention of money was attributed to the necessity of overcoming the inconvenience of barter. As a medium of exchange, a measure of value, and a standard of deferred payments, money was regarded as a requisite for economic well-being. The manifold advantages of money demanded that the new world should provide means for obtaining a money supply. Ordinarily such a supply could be obtained through international trade. But if, for any reason, a favourable balance of trade could not be secured, other ways must be devised for this purpose. Over-valuation, recoinage with seigneurage, gratuitous coinage, and the issue of paper money were, in turn, advocated as means whereby a colony could provide itself with a sufficiency of currency. Scarcity of money was believed to result in business stagnation and economic distress, while an abundance of currency was regarded as a cause of well-being. For these reasons, a system of currency capable of great expansion was advocated.

Two avenues for providing such an elastic currency were heralded as great discoveries : the issue of bills of credit by a government, and the issue of bank notes on the security of land or merchandise. The *rôle* of banks was to provide an abundance of currency.

The exchange of wealth, which money facilitated, like other economic matters, was examined from the ethical point of view. " Excessive wages " were believed to lead to excessive consumption. Immoderate consumption tended to upset an inequality in the personal distribution of wealth which was considered theologically just and socially desirable. For inequality, to the colonial mind, was not a chance phenomena but a manifestation of God's designation of certain persons to perform certain duties. Private property and inequality were regarded as the consequence of man's corruption and as necessary alternatives since true communism could only be realized in a society of ideal men. In an imperfect society, communism was branded as impracticable. Many indictments indeed were levied against common ownership : it restricted production, bred disrespect, and produced contention by creating a persistent feeling of injustice. One duty of government, therefore, was to institute laws for the protection and maintenance of private property. To fulfil this function, the state must have revenue. Good taxation systems should obtain maximum revenue with a minimum of complaint. Fairness in taxation was fitting and right and an ideal tax system should combine fiscal efficiency and economic justice. But although the clergy admonished rulers to guarantee justice in taxation, the actual tax systems can scarcely be said to have attained this worthy goal.

II

In its emphasis upon ethical considerations, American economic thought lagged behind contemporary European economic thought. In its emphasis upon the necessity of a larger measure of economic freedom for the individual, it foreshadowed the "natural rights" philosophy of the eighteenth century. The reactionary qualities of colonial thought are not difficult to explain. Enforced pre-occupation with comparatively small economic problems, scarcity of institutions of learning, the predominance of agriculture, the permeating influence of a theology which turned back to Scripture as the sole source of guidance, all these forces and others combined to canalize economic thought in traditional channels. But at the same time, the encompassing natural resources provided unparalled economic opportunity. The presence of opportunity together with the selective influence of migration fostered an independent turn of mind which refused to suffer restraint. In reality, the seventeenth century is a remarkable history of a succession of tentative compromises between social control of economic activity and economic individualism.

As the frontier expanded, with its subtle moulding of pioneer psychology, more liberal compromises became imperative. The sea-board tended to cling to the doctrine of social control. Meantime the frontier demand for economic freedom became more insistent. Yet the frontier could not wash away all the influences of early American economic philosophy. Strong ethical traditions lingered and moved with the pioneers. The clergyman was no longer the law-giver, but the frontier church was neither mute nor unimportant. The dignity of labour, the sanctity of property and the virtue of saving were preached as eloquently in the frontier village as they had been in the brick churches of Boston.

Throughout the eighteenth and the nineteenth centuries, the pioneers echoed the economic principles which the seventeenth century had propounded. The labour doctrine of property justified continued pressure upon Indian tribes and vindicated the demands for "squatter sovereignty." The frontier demanded industry and frugality. The pioneers were emotionally in sympathy with rules of conduct which glorified labour and made frugality a virtue. The continuation of economic conditions, similar to those of the seventeenth century sea-board, gave an expanded area of acceptance for a Puritan economic philosophy.

But whereas continuity of some colonial economic principles has characterized America's growth, the modification of other principles (already begun during the seventeenth century) became even more pronounced. The futility of governmental control of wages in a dynamic society became increasingly apparent since dissatisfied wage-earners could easily become farmers. Freedom to buy and sell, freedom to establish mercantile or industrial businesses, occupational mobility, all these became inseparable phases of American economic liberty. Freedom of international trade came, in time, to mean license to evade the English Navigation Laws. The wise policy of " salutary neglect " was a concession to a trend in American economic ideas whose roots are imbedded in the seventeenth century.

Monetary theory represents perhaps the best illustration of the continuity of colonial ideas. The paper money propaganda, which Blackwell and Woodbridge had fomented, precipitated a veritable flood of eighteenth-century pamphlets. Proposals led to experiment and experiment to the rise of class consciousness on monetary issues. Continental Bills of Credit, Shay's Rebellion and " Free Banking," are only a few consequences of the inflation doctrine ; bimetallism and the Populist cause continued the tradition. In the realm of public finance, America's heritage is no less distinct. The general property tax has spread over a continent. But less willing to change than even stubborn Puritans, twentieth-century Americans have clung to an ill-adapted, outworn institution. Fairness in taxation, which received lip service in the seventeenth century, receives but little more in the twentieth.

The complex of traditional ideas and enforced compromise, which characterized America's first century, bespeaks the economic policy of America. The Puritans tried earnestly to set up economic institutions which would be compatible with a theological code of morals. In this they were unsuccessful. Stubborn facts would not conform, economic circumstances bred rebellion. Yet back of this stern and futile experiment lay the belief that ethical considerations in economic affairs were indispensable. Circumstances, however, demanded compromise and reluctantly the seventeenth-century moralists tempered their idealism with pragmatism. There is this much similarity between the seventeenth century and the twentieth : each period was or is doubtful of the automatic emergence of maximum welfare in the economic sphere. Perhaps the modern dilemma is the greater. The Puritan found a test for economic institutions and economic conduct in the Mosaic law. Secularization has destroyed this touchstone, although the want of ethical canons in matters economic is to-day a signal problem. But ethical considerations can have meaning only in terms of ideals. Unfortunately, modern society does not and cannot agree on its ideals. Even if it did agree, the modern age would find compromise as necessary as did an age that is past.

BIBLIOGRAPHY

No attempt has been made to list all the materials used in the preparation of this volume. The following list includes only the more important books and source materials to which reference has been made in the documentation. Editions referred to are indicated by asterisks in all cases where several editions exist.

ARCHDALE, JOHN. A New Description of Carolina. London, 1707. *Reprinted, *Hist. Coll. S. C.*, Vol. II., pp. 85–120. New York, 1836.

ARISTOTLE. *Politics.* Translated by Benjamin Jowett. *Oxford University Press Edition. Oxford, 1920.

ASH, THOMAS. Carolina. London, 1682. *Reprinted *Hist. Coll. S. C.*, Vol. II., pp. 58–85. New York, 1836.

BACON, FRANCIS. Of Plantations. London, 1625. *Reprinted in Brown, *Genesis of the United States*, pp. 799–802. Boston, 1891.

BEER, GEORGE LOUIS. *The Origins of the British Colonial System*, 1578–1660. New York, 1908.

BERKELEY, SIR WILLIAM. *A Discourse and View of Virginia.* London, 1663. *Reprinted, Norwalk, Conn., 1914.

BEVERLEY, ROBERT. *The History of Virginia.* London, 1705. *2nd Edit., 1722.

BLACKWELL, JOHN. (1) Some Additional Considerations Addressed unto the Worshipful Elisha Hutchinson, Esq. Boston, 1691. *Reprinted, Prince Society, *Colonial Currency Reprints*, Vol. I., pp. 197–206. Boston, 1910.
(2) A Discourse in Explanation of the Bank of Credit. MSS. Winthrop Papers. Mass. Hist. Soc. Printed *Pro. Mass. Hist. Soc.*, 2nd Series, Vol. XVIII., pp. 62–81. *Reprinted, Prince Society, *Colonial Currency Reprints*, Vol. I., pp. 122–146. Boston, 1910.

BLISS, LEONARD. *The History of Rehoboth.* Boston, 1836.

BODIN, JEAN. *The Six Books of a Commonweale.* Translated by Richard Knolles. London, 1606.

BÖHM-BAWERK, EUGEN V. *Capital and Interest.* Translated by William Smart. London, 1890.

BRADFORD, WILLIAM. (1) *Governor William Bradford's Letter Book.* Boston, 1906.
(2) *Of Plimoth Plantation.* Boston, 1856. *Commonwealth Edition, 1898.

BRANTS, VICTOR. *Ésquisse Des Théories Économiques Des XIIIe et XIVe Siècles.* Louvain, 1895.

BRODHEAD, JOHN ROMEYN. *History of the State of New York.* New York, 1853.

BROWN, ALEXANDER. *The Genesis of the United States.* Boston, 1891.

BRUCE, PHILIP ALEXANDER. *Economic History of Virginia in the Seventeenth Century.* New York, 1896.

BUDD, THOMAS. *Good Order Established in Pennsylvania & New Jersey in America.* Philadelphia (Wm. Bradford), 1685. *Reprinted (Gowans), New York, 1865 ; Cleveland, 1902.

BULLOCK, CHARLES J. *Essays on the Monetary History of the United States.* New York, 1900.

CANNAN, EDWIN. " Early History of the Term Capital." *Quarterly Journal of Economics*, Vol. XXXV.

CARLEIL, CHRISTOPHER. A Briefe and Summary Discourse upon the Intended Voyage to the Hithermost Parts of America. 1583. Reprinted, *Hakluyt's Voyages*, Vol. VIII., pp. 134–150.

CHILD, SIR JOSIAH. *A New Discourse of Trade.* London, 1690. *5th Edit., Glasgow, 1751.

CLARKSON, THOMAS. *A Portraiture of Quakerism.* New York, 1806.

Connecticut, The Public Records of the Colony of, 1636–1776. Hartford, 1850–90.

COTTON, JOHN. (1) An Abstract of the Laws of New England, as they are now Established. London, 1641. Edition of William Aspinwall, 1655. *I. *Mass. Hist. Soc. Coll.*, V., pp. 173–192.
(2) *God's Promise to His Plantation.* London, 1630.

CROSBY, SYLVESTER S. *The Early Coins of America.* Boston, 1875.

CULPEPPER, SIR THOMAS. A Tract Against Usurie. London, 1621.

DAVIS, ANDREW McFARLAND. (1) *Colonial Currency Reprints.* Prince Society. 4 Vols. Boston, 1910–11.
(2) *Currency and Banking in the Province of the Massachusetts Bay.* New York, 1901. 2 Vols.

DEL MAR, ALEXANDER. *The History of Money in America.* New York, 1899.

DEWEY, DAVIS R. *Financial History of the United States.* New York, 1902. *8th Edit. 1922.

DONCK, ADRIAN VAN DER. (1) Description of the New Netherlands. Amsterdam, 1655. *Reprinted, Boston, *Old South Leaflets, General Series,* No. 69.
(2) *The Representation of New Netherlands.* The Hague, 1650. *Reprinted, New York, 1849.

DOUGLASS, C. H. J. *Financial History of Massachusetts.* New York, 1892.

Essay on the Laying Out of Towns, &c. Winthrop Papers, Vol. III., p. 474. V. *Mass. Hist. Soc. Coll.,* I.

FELT, JOSEPH B. *An Historical Account of Massachusetts Currency.* Boston, 1839.

FRAME, RICHARD. *A Short Description of Pennsylvania.* Philadelphia, 1692. *Reprinted, 1867.

GILBERT, SIR HUMPHREY. A Discourse to prove a passage by the Northwest, 1576. *Reprinted, *Hakluyt's Voyages,* Vol. VII., pp. 158–190.

GRAY, ROBERT. *A Good Speed to Virginia.* London, 1609. *Reprinted, J. P. Collier, Ed., London, 1864.

GROTIUS, HUGO. *De Iure Belli ac Pacis.* Amsterdam, 1632.

HAKLUYT, RICHARD. (1) Discourse on Western Planting, 1584. Printed, *Coll. Maine Hist. Soc.* 2nd Series, Vol. II. Cambridge, 1877.
(2) Notes given to certaine Gentlemen that went with M. Frobisher in his north-west discoverie. 1578. Reprinted *Hakluyt's Voyages,* Vol. VII., pp. 244–250.

HALES, JOHN. *A Discourse of the Common Weal of this Realme of England.* Edited by Elizabeth Lamond. Cambridge, 1893.

HAMMOND, JOHN. Leah and Rachel or the Two Fruitful Sisters, Virginia and Maryland. London, 1656. *Reprinted, *Peter Force Hist. Tracts,* Vol. III. Washington, 1844.

HAMOR, RALPHE. *A True Discourse of the Present Estate of Virginia.* London, 1615. *Reprinted, Albany, 1860.

HARTWELL, HENRY; BLAIR, JAMES; CHILTON, EDW. An Account of the Present State and Government of Virginia. Written, 1696–1698. Printed, London, 1727. *Reprinted, I. *Mass. Hist. Soc. Coll.,* V., pp. 124–166.

HIGGINSON, REV. FRANCIS. *New England's Plantation.* London, 1630. *Fac-Simile Edit. Salem, 1908.

HOBBES, THOMAS. *Leviathan.* London, 1651. *Dutton Reprint. New York.

HUBBARD, JOSEPH. *Economic Thought in Patristic Literature.* Harvard University Thesis. Cambridge, 1923.

HUBBARD, WILLIAM. *A General History of New England from the Discoverie to* 1680. Boston, 1815. *Reprinted, Boston, 1848.

HUGHES, WILLIAM. *The American Physician.* London, 1672.

HULL, JOHN. Diary. *Trans. & Coll. American Antiquarian Society,* Vol. III. Boston, 1857.

JENKINS, HOWARD M. *Pennsylvania, Colonial and Federal.* Philadelphia, 1903.

JOHNSON, E. A. J. (1) " Some Evidence of Mercantilism in the Massachusetts Bay." *New England Quarterly,* Vol. I, No. 3, pp. 371–395.
(2) " Economic Ideas of John Winthrop." *New England Quarterly,* Vol. II., No. 2, pp. 235–250.
(3) " The Mercantilist Concept of ' Art ' and ' Ingenious Labor '." *Economic History,* Vol. II., No. 6, pp. 234–253.

JOHNSON, EDWARD. Wonder Working Providence of Sions Saviour in New England. London, 1653. *Original Narrative Series.* New York, 1910.

JOHNSON, ROBERT. (1) The New Life of Virginia. London, 1612. *Reprinted, II. *Mass. Hist. Soc. Coll.,* VIII., pp. 199–223.
(2) Nova Britannia. London, 1609. *Reprinted, *Peter Force Hist. Tracts,* Vol. I., Washington, 1836.

LATIMER, HUGH. *Works.* Edited for the Parker Society by G. E. Corrie. Cambridge, 1844–45.

MALYNES, GERARD. *Consuetudo : vel Lex Mercatoria.* London, 1622.

MASSACHUSETTS. *The Acts and Resolves, Public and Private of the Province of Massachusetts Bay.* Boston, 1869.

MASSACHUSETTS. *Records of the Governor and Company of the Massachusetts Bay in New England.* Edited by Nathaniel Shurtleff. 5 vols. Boston, 1853–54.

MATHER, COTTON. (1) *Bonifacius, An Essay upon the Good.* Boston, 1710.
(2) The Bostonian Ebenezer. Lecture delivered April 7th, 1698. Reprinted, *Magnalia Christi Americana.* London, 1702. *Old South Leaflets,* No. 67.
(3) *The Christian Philosopher.* London, 1721.
(4) Some Considerations on the Bills of Credit now passing in New-England. Boston, 1691. *Reprinted, Prince Society, *Colonial Currency Reprints,* Vol. I., pp. 189–196. Boston, 1910.
(5) *Durable Riches.* Boston, 1695.
(6) *Fair Dealing between Debtor and Creditor.* Boston, 1716.

(7) *Magnalia Christi Americana.* London, 1702. *Reprinted, Hartford, 1853. 2 vols.

MATHER, INCREASE. (1) A Brief Relation of the State of New England. London, 1689. * Reprinted, *Peter Force Hist. Tracts,* Vol. IV. Washington, 1838.
(2) *Diary.* Printed by Mass. Hist. Soc. Boston, 1900.
(3) *The Excellency of a Public Spirit.* Boston, 1702.
(4) *Necessity of Reformation with the Expedients subservient thereunto : Agreed upon by the Elders and Messengers of the Churches assembled in the Synod at Boston.* Boston, 1679.
(5) New England Vindicated from the Unjust Aspersions. London, 1688. *Reprinted Prince Society, *Andros Tracts,* Vol. II., pp. 111–124. Boston, 1869.

MILLER, JOHN. *New York Considered and Improved.* 1695. Published from MSS. Cleveland, 1903.

MISSELDEN. *The Circle of Commerce.* London, 1623.

MITCHELL, JONATHAN. *Nehemiah on the wall in troublesome times, or a serious and seasonable improvement of that great example of magistratical piety and prudence.* (A Sermon preached at Boston, May 15th, 1667.)

A Model for erecting a Bank of Credit. London, 1688. Reprinted, Prince Society, *Colonial Currency Reprints,* Vol. I. Boston, 1910.

MORISON, SAMUEL ELIOT. *Builders of the Bay Colony.* Boston, 1930.

MORTON, THOMAS. *New English Canaan.* Amsterdam, 1637.

MOURT, G. *A Relation or Journal of the Beginnings and Proceedings of the English Plantation settled at Plymouth.* London, 1622. *Dexter Edit. Boston, 1865.

MYERS, ALBERT COOK (Editor). *Narratives of Early Pennsylvania, West New Jersey and Delaware,* 1630–1707. New York, 1912.

NEILL, EDWARD D. *History of the Virginia Company of London.* Albany, 1869.

New England's First Fruits. London, 1643. Reprinted, *Old South Leaflets.* No. 51. Boston.

The New Life of Virginia. London, 1612. *Reprinted, II. *Mass. Hist. Soc. Coll.,* VIII., pp. 199–223.

OSGOOD, HERBERT L. *The American Colonies in the Seventeenth Century.* New York, 1904. 3 vols.

Pastorius' Bee Hive. Edited by M. D. Learned. *Americana Germanica,* Vol. I., No. 4, 1897.

PASTORIUS, FRANCIS. A Particular Geographical Description of the Lately Discovered Province of Pennsylvania. Frankfort, 1700. *Reprinted, *Old South Leaflets, General Series*, No. 95. Boston.

PECKHAM, SIR GEORGE. A True Report of the late discoveries, and possessions taken in the right of the Crowne of England and of the New found Lands. 1583. *Reprinted, *Hakluyt's Vogayes*, Vol. VIII., pp. 89–131.

PENN, WILLIAM. Correspondence between William Penn and James Logan. Philadelphia, 1870. *Publications of the Historical Society of Pennsylvania*. Vols. IX. and X.

PETTY, SIR WILLIAM. *The Economic Writings of.* Edited by C. H. Hull. Cambridge, 1899.

Plymouth. *Records of the Colony of New Plymouth.* Edited by Nathaniel B. Shurtleff. 12 vols. Boston, 1855.

Publicans of New England, The Humble Address of the. London, 1691. *Reprinted, Prince Society, *Andros Tracts*, Vol. II., pp. 231–270. Boston, 1869.

RIPLEY, WILLIAM ZEBINA. *The Financial History of Virginia,* 1609–1776. New York, 1893.

SCHMOLLER, GUSTAVE. *The Mercantile System and its Historical Significance.* *Ashley Edition. New York, 1897.

SCOT, GEORGE. The Model of the Government of the Province of East New Jersey. Edinburgh, 1685. *Reprinted, *Coll. N. J. Hist. Soc.*, Vol. I., pp. 229–333 (1846).

SEWALL, SAMUEL. (1) Computation that the Importation of Negroes is not so profitable as that of White Servants. Attributed to Samuel Sewall. Boston, 1706. *Reprinted, *Historical Magazine*, June, 1864.

(2) The Selling of Joseph. Boston, 1700. *Reprinted, *Historical Magazine*, June, 1864.

SHAW, WILLIAM ARTHUR. *Select Tracts and Documents Illustrative of English Monetary History,* 1626–1730. London, 1896.

SHORTT, ADAM. *Documents Relating to Canadian Currency, Exchange and Finance during the French Period.* Edited by Adam Shortt. Ottawa, 1926–27.

SMITH, ADAM. *An Inquiry into the Nature and Causes of the Wealth of Nations.* Edited by Edwin Cannan. London, 1904.

SMITH, JOHN. (1) *Advertisements for the unexperienced Planters of New England, or Anywhere : or The Pathway to Erect a Plantation.* London, 1631. *Reprinted by William Veazie. Boston, 1865.

(2) A Description of New England. London, 1616. *Reprinted, *Travels and Works of Captain John Smith.* (Edward Arber Edit.) Edinburgh, 1910.

(3) The Generall Historie of Virginia, New England & the Summer Isles. London, 1624. *Reprinted, *Travels and Works of Captain John Smith.* (Edward Arber Edit.) Edinburgh, 1910.

(4) A Map of Virginia. Oxford, 1612. *Reprinted, *Travels and Works of Captain John Smith.* (Edward Arber Edit.) Edinburgh, 1910.

STRACHEY, WILLIAM. *The Historie of Travaile into Virginia Britannia.* Printed by Hakluyt Society. London, 1849.

SUMNER, WILLIAM G. " The Coin Shilling of Massachusetts Bay." *Yale Review,* November, 1898.

Thirty Important Cases, resolved with Evidence of Scripture and Reason. By Several Pastors of Adjacent Churches meeting in Cambridge, New England. (Published by Cotton Mather.) Boston, 1699.

THOMAS AQUINAS. *Summa Theologica.* Literally translated by Fathers of the English Dominican Province. New York, 1918.

THOMAS, GABRIEL. An Historical and Geographical Account of Pennsilvania and of West New Jersey. London, 1698. *Reprinted, *Narratives of Early Pennsylvania West New Jersey and Delaware.* New York, 1912. Pp. 307–353.

TIENHOVEN, CORNELIUS VAN. Brief Answer to " Representation of New Netherlands." MSS. The Hague, 1650. Printed as appendix to Van der Donck's *Representation of New Netherlands.* New York, 1849.

TYLER, MOSES COIT. *A History of American Literature during the Colonial Time.* New York, 1878. *2nd Edit. 1897.

USHER, ROLAND G. *The Pilgrims and their History.* New York. 1918.

VINCENT, P. A True Relation of the late Battel fought in New England. London, 1638. *Reprinted 3 *Mass. Hist. Soc. Coll.* VI., pp. 29–43.

Virginia State Papers, Calendar of. Edited by Wm. P. Palmer. Richmond, 1875.

Virginia, Extract from a Manuscript Collection of Annals Relative to. *Peter Force Tracts,* Vol. II. Washington, 1838.

A Perfect Description of Virginia. London, 1649. *Reprinted, *Peter Force Hist. Tracts,* Vol. II., Washington, 1837.

Reasons for Raising a fund for the support of a Colony at Virginia. 1607. Printed in Brown, *Genesis of the U. S.,* pp. 36–42. Boston, 1891.

A True and Sincere declaration of the purposes and ends of the

Plantation begun in Virginia. London, 1610. *Reprinted, Brown, *Genesis of the U. S.* Boston, 1891. Pp. 338–353.

WAGNER, ADOLPH. *Lehr und Handbuch der Politischen Oekonomie.* Leipzig, 1892.

WEEDEN, WILLIAM B. *Economic and Social History of New England.* Boston, 1890.

WHITE, JOHN. The Planters Plea, or the grounds of Plantations Examined. London, 1630. *Reprinted, *Peter Force Hist. Tracts*, Vol. II. Washington, 1838.

WILLIAMS, EDWARD. Virginia, More especially the South part thereof, Richly and truly valued. London, 1650. *Reprinted, *Peter Force Hist. Tracts*, Vol. II. Washington, 1844.

WILLIAMS, ROGER. (1) The Bloody Tenant of Persecution, 1644. *Reprinted, *Publications of the Narragansett Club*, Vol. III. Providence, 1867.

(2) The Bloody Tenant Yet More Bloody. London, 1652. *Reprinted, *Publications of the Narragansett Club*, Vol. IV. Providence, 1870.

(3) *Experiments of Spiritual Life and Health.* London, 1652. *Reprinted, Providence, 1862.

(4) The Letters of Roger Williams. *Publications of the Narragansett Club*, Vol. VI. Providence, 1874.

WINTHROP, JOHN. (1) Conclusions for the Plantation in New England. 1629. *Reprinted, *Pro. Mass. Hist. Soc.*, 1865. *Old South Leaflets*, No. 50. General Series, 1894.

(2) *The History of New England from 1630–1649.* Hartford, 1790. *Savage Edition. Boston, 1825.

(3) A Modell of Christian Charity. 1630. *Reprinted, 3 *Mass. Hist. Soc. Coll.*, VII., pp. 30–48.

WISE, JOHN. *A Vindication of the Government of New England Churches.* Boston, 1717.

WOOD WILLIAM. *New England's Prospect.* London, 1634. Reprinted, Boston, 1764. *Reprinted, Boynton Edit., 1898.

WOODBRIDGE, JOHN. Severals relating to the Fund. Boston, 1682. * Reprinted, Prince Society, *Colonial Currency Reprints*, Vol. I., pp. 109–119. Boston, 1910.

YARRANTON, ANDREW. *England's Improvement by Sea and Land.* London, 1677.

YOUNG, ALEXANDER. *Chronicles of the Pilgrim Fathers of the Colony of Plymouth*, 1602–1625. Boston, 1841.

SUBJECT INDEX

INDEX OF NAMES